Healing the Man Within

Healing the Man Within

A Guide to Healing from the Pain of Sexual Abuse

Randy Boyd

Courageous Healers Publishing
La Quinta, California

Copyright © 2015 by Randy Boyd.

All rights reserved. No part of this publication may be reproduced, distributed, or transmitted in any form or by any means, including photocopying, recording, or other electronic or mechanical methods, without the prior written permission of the publisher, except in the case of brief quotations embodied in critical reviews and certain other noncommercial uses permitted by copyright law. For permission requests, write to the publisher, addressed "Attention: Permissions Coordinator," at the address below:

Courageous Healers Publishing
P.O. Box 6506
La Quinta, CA
www.courageoushealers.com

Ordering Information:
Quantity sales: Special discounts are available on quantity purchases by corporations, associations, and others. For details, contact the "Special Sales Department" at the address above.

Healing the Man Within / Randy Boyd. —1st edition
ISBN 978-0-9863987-4-2 (hard cover)
ISBN 978-0-9863987-0-4 (soft cover)
ISBN 978-0-9863987-5-9 (e-book)

Spellbinding! The book spoke to me very deeply as both a man in recovery, who has dealt with several of his own personal traumas, and as a clinical psychologist, who works with traumatized men in his private practice. Randy's gut-wrenching honesty and his own personal journey and courage are inspiring and informative. He inspires me because his recovery shows us that there is a solution: we don't have to be victims, we can be survivors who are thriving. It was informative because he also integrates much of what we know about men and abuse and their recovery, and explains it in a very down-to-earth manner.

This book is a must read for anyone who is struggling with feeling like a victim or for clinicians who are working with men. My only regret is that Randy published this book after my second book was published. Had I known about Randy's book back then, reading it would have been included as one of the 12 Smart Things to Do When the Booze and Drugs are Gone.

—Allen Berger, Ph.D., Clinical Psychologist and author of *12 Stupid Things that Mess Up Recovery*, *12 Smart Things to Do When the Booze and Drugs are Gone*, and *12 Hidden Rewards of Making Amends*.

Randy Boyd has taken pieces of his heart and soul and put them into his book, Healing the Man Within, *to courageously and vulnerably share his experience as a man recovering from the trauma of childhood sexual abuse. Randy defiantly breaks the silence about male sexual trauma and offers a powerful example of what a man in recovery looks like. He surrounds his story with: the voices of other men who are also healing from various forms of sexual trauma; accessible academic concepts regarding trauma and the therapeutic process of healing; and very practical tips to help men take immediate steps toward their own healing. I have no doubt that this book will prove to be an essential resource for years to come in helping men to heal from trauma.*

—Dan Griffin, author of *A Man's Way Through Relationships: Learning to Love and Be Loved*

Healing the Man Within *is real, raw, but most importantly, inspiring. Randy opens his heart and exposes his wounds to offer hope that empowers others to overcome and live out a victorious life. Often life brings setbacks, hurts, and pains, but the prescription that Randy offers is faith for today and hope for tomorrow. This inspiring story is a must read for those who want to dream again and turn their pain into a life full of purpose.*

—Obed Martinez, Senior Pastor, Destiny Church, Founder of PassionatePastors.com

Randy Boyd has written a book that is gripping, affecting, and achingly honest, as well as being instructive with a strong sense of purpose. I strongly recommend that all clinicians read this book. It gives voice to a rarely heard population.

—Chris Jones-Cage, Ph.D.

Randy Boyd is a "Courageous Healer." There are few accounts of men's stories about sexual abuse and the healing process, and I am sure this one will become a tool that will help many survivors. Male survivors will learn that they are not alone, their feelings and thoughts are valid and are shared by other men who have been abused.

> —Carol Teitelbaum, LMFT, Founder of "It Happens to Boys" and Creative Change Conferences

Groundbreaking. Courageous. Engaging. Randy's book ends the silence and gives a voice to men who suffered from childhood sexual molestation. Randy helps us all to learn how a male survivor can return to himself and rekindle and rebuild his spirit.... This book will help us to progress in our awareness and understanding of childhood male sexual abuse, as much as Dave Peltzer's A Child Called It *did for childhood physical and emotional abuse.*

> —Kelly Lewallen, MFT, M.A.

Randy Boyd's life is a testament that it is possible to pass through fire and come out stronger on the other side—but this is so much more than his story. Healing the Man Within *is a relevant, inspiring, and helpful guide for those seeking understanding, healing, and inner balance. A must read for survivors and those who love them.*

> —Linda Emerson, Professor of Psychology, College of the Desert, Co-Advisor on Human Services, Alcohol and Drug Studies

Dedication

To the young boys and men whose voices remain hidden behind the dark walls of shame, may this book give you the courage and strength to begin your own healing journey.

To my wife, Cathy, who has shown me the true meaning of unconditional love, I truly believe if it were not for you, I would not be here to write this book.

To my children, who have endured the years of my fighting to become free of the darkness within me and continue to support me with unconditional love on my journey.

To my father, who, even though he is no longer with us, I know would be proud of the man I have become.

To my God, who has given me the strength, wisdom, and courage to walk through the relentless pain and shame I have endured on this journey.

In a futile attempt to erase our past, we deprive the community of our healing gift. If we conceal our wounds out of fear and shame, our inner darkness can neither be illuminated nor become a light for others.
—Brennan Manning

Contents

Foreword xiii
Preface xiv
Acknowledgments xvii
Chapter 1:   Getting Started 1
Chapter 2:   Reparenting 35
Chapter 3:   Trauma Triggers 61
Chapter 4:   Coping Mechanisms 77
Chapter 5:   Spiritual Abuse 107
Chapter 6:   The G–d Word 117
Chapter 7:   Hitting Bottom 131
Chapter 8:   Getting Clean 145
Chapter 9:   Secrets and Silence 163
Chapter 10: Confronting the Perpetrator 189
Chapter 11: Blame and Shame 211
Chapter 12: Forgiveness 231
Chapter 13: Finding Your Authentic Self 247
Relevant Websites 271
References 273

Foreword

I am very pleased to be writing the Foreword to this important contribution to the annals of addiction and recovery literature. This book is particularly relevant to anyone who has been or has known a victim of child abuse, because it is written from the standpoint of a person who has walked the road and survived, who can now offer a thorough and heartfelt account of his journey from wounded man to wounded warrior.

The subject of male sexual abuse has made headlines in recent years and is making slow progress into being accepted as an underreported but common injury. There are relatively few books on the subject written by survivors.

Unlike the authors of many survivor books, Randy has made the effort to research time-tested ways of dealing with deep pain that lead to the discovery of a life of freedom and happiness. He doesn't merely tell his story; he offers easy-to-understand exercises at the back of the book, which allow the reader to process the insights gained from reading the text.

This is also an important book for therapists to read and recommend to their clients, because it is highly accessible, in part by referring to the experts in the field of addiction recovery without being heavy-handed or overly scholarly.

In my experience as a psychotherapist, it is a common complaint for clients to say that many books make them more depressed or anxious by focusing too much on the problem and too little on the solution.

Although *Healing the Man Within* tells a painful story, it is written with the confidence and wisdom of someone who is continuing his own program of recovery, focused on a positive, upward movement toward happiness and well-being. Personally, I have had the pleasure of watching Randy transform from a survivor who was crippled by shame and addiction into a community leader who humbly offers his experiences to help others.

—Deborah Meints-Pierson, LMFT
October 2015

Preface

This is a book for men who have experienced childhood sexual abuse. I am not a psychotherapist or a psychologist; I am a survivor. This isn't a book about theories or philosophies or about defining the problem. Rather, it is about a journey out of pain and shame into wholeness and happiness. Every tool or suggestion in this book has been road-tested in the trenches of everyday life.

For many years, I was a drug addict and alcoholic, but finally got sober through Alcoholics Anonymous. I'm not sure that I would have made it without the support of my sponsor and the honesty of other people struggling with the same problems. A.A. helped me to overcome my addiction, but I was still living with the anger and shame from the abuse that had driven me to abuse alcohol and drugs in the first place.

There wasn't a Male Sexual Abuse Survivors Anonymous group that I could join. There wasn't a sponsor to whom I could turn for trusted advice. And there weren't meetings where other survivors were speaking frankly about their struggles and victories in overcoming the pain of their abuse. Thankfully, there are some great books about male sexual abuse written by knowledgeable and compassionate experts. But what I wanted to do was to talk to other survivors. I needed to know that I wasn't alone, I wasn't crazy, I was going to get better—and I needed to hear that from other men who had been there.

I wrote this book to help *you*—yes, *you*, reader and fellow survivor—to step into that void. I can't be your literal sponsor on this journey, but I can share my story, my struggles, my failures and victories to support you and stand in for that support group, sponsor, and guide while you journey through the peaks and valleys of the healing process. The journey to happiness and wholeness does not have an "end" point, but life gets increasingly better, and recovery is possible. The peaks and valleys eventually become rolling hills, and raw emotional wounds turn into faded scars.

I am not a typical author, and this is not a typical start-at-page-one-and-read-to-the-end book. In fact, I specifically recommend that you *not* do that. This book is medicine. It is great in the right dose, but not so good when you take too much at one time. Bite off only the information that

PREFACE

you are comfortable chewing, and take your time digesting the ideas and information. Also, if you become shaky at all, don't feel that you have to take the journey alone. In fact, it's best if you start this journey with the support of your partner, friends, or therapist.

I have chosen to use the word *survivor* instead of *victim* or any other word because I believe that we should all be proud that we have survived. Some experts see *survivor* as a derogatory term, but I disagree. As children, we found ways to adapt by making intolerable situations tolerable. We did what we needed to do to save our own lives. That is admirable.

We were and are resilient. We are here today because we fought through those dark times and chose to keep showing up, even when we felt that we were clinging to a painful life by our teeth and toenails. Although we might not have always chosen the best coping skills or the most enlightened paths, we have all done the best we could, given our knowledge at the time. I am proud of myself, of you, and of all our fellow survivors who have made it through to today. That you are here, reading these pages, proves your strength, your courage, and your ability to change and adapt. Now we are going to put those qualities to work by turning surviving into thriving.

Speaking of agreeing and disagreeing with experts, this book is not intended to be a scholarly work. Some footnotes just give me a chance to include information that I found valuable as a survivor or to expand on a particular topic without taking the chapter off on a tangent. There are website resources in the back of the book that I have found in the course of my journey. Also, all ideas and thoughts are only my opinions based on my own experiences, unless I specifically state that they come from other authors, survivors, or experts I have met along the way. Incidentally, I have changed a few of the names of individuals in this book to protect their confidentiality. Such names initially appear in quotations.

As with any other self-help book, take what you like from it, use what works for you, digest the ideas that stretch you, and leave the rest alone. This is a collection of years of personal development, sifted through my own experience as a survivor. Some of it will work for you, some won't, and that's fine. Some things will speak to you at different phases of your recovery, and that's good, too.

I've found that an honest voice, which doesn't try to fix you or change you, can be a shelter in the wilderness that gives you comfort even through the darkest times. By sharing experiences, that honest voice can put words to the emotional storms raging inside you.

Reading this book can be an intense journey. There are incredible highs and painful lows. But it's been my experience that the lows, even the worst of them, will not be as painful as you have feared they might be. Running from the fear of the pain of facing the past is worse than actually facing it.

More than anything else, though, I wrote this book to tell you that if I can make it, you can, too—one step, one page, one day at a time.

—Randy Boyd, Sexual Abuse Survivor and Counselor
October 2015

Acknowledgments

First and foremost, this book would not even have been possible if it were not for the grace of my loving God. He has always been by my side, protecting me even in my darkest moments in life, and for that I am and always will be eternally grateful. God has set me free from the bondage of my abusers, and my life is now better than I ever imagined it could be.

Cathy, my ever faithful wife, who has walked side by side with me through my lowest lows and highest highs, has been encouraging, kind, loving, and patient. She has never quit believing in me, and continues to inspire me to be the man of God I am intended to be. Thank you for your unconditional and undying love.

There are so many others: Deborah Meints-Pierson, my therapist, patiently and diligently helped me to overcome so many of the issues I had stemming from my abuse. My sponsors, Way Spiritual Dave and Roy, taught me what it is to be a real man, husband, father, friend, and contributing member of society. My buddy Duke pushed me and watched over me early in my recovery. Carol Tietelbaum, LMFT, Pastor Obed Martinez, and so many others believed in me and poured wisdom into me over the years. Thank you all.

And, of course, this discourse would not be the book it is, were it not for my editor, Paul Weisser. Thank you, Paul, for your friendship and all that you have taught me along this journey. My writing will never be the same.

Healing the Man Within

Chapter 1: Getting Started

I learned that courage was not the absence of fear, but the triumph over it. The brave man is not he who does not feel afraid, but he who conquers that fear.

—Nelson Mandela[1]

As the car wheels crunched against the rocks and twigs littering the driveway in front of the little mountain cabin, I heard my sons' voices arguing good-naturedly about the radio station. New Age music was vibrating in the cold, clear air as the headlights swung around, lighting the path my sons would take on the two-hour journey back down to the city. As the white Tacoma pickup truck disappeared around the bend, the silence grew so loud that my ears rang.

As darkness closed in around me, I slid to the ground, my hands falling to the rough dirt, my back bowed under the weight of the emotions I had been holding at bay through the small talk over dinner.

Look at what you've done to your family, I thought. *You're sick! You ruin everything you touch. They'd all be better off without you.*

I clapped my hands to my ears, but the voices inside my head only became louder.

You're throwing away your family.... And for what? Some woman you barely know? You make me sick! Do you feel like a big man now?

I stumbled to my feet and felt in my pocket for my keys. As I rocketed through the dangerous mountain curves, it was just starting to rain. Twenty minutes later, I ground to a stop in the poorly lighted parking lot of a run-down liquor store. Leaving my door open and the engine running, I ran in, grabbed a bottle of rum, threw some bills at the cashier (too ashamed to meet his eyes), and ran back to my truck.

---

[1] Quoted here from https://www. biographyonline.net/politicians/nelson-mandela.html/.

HEALING THE MAN WITHIN

I threw back the first swallows as if I were aiming cannon fire at the voices in my head. As the fiery liquid burned its way down my throat and into my stomach, I felt the voices growing weaker. I threw down round after round, so that by the time I headed back to my cabin, there wasn't much ammunition left. But the voices were still there—distorted now, as if they were coming from a long way off.

Twenty minutes later, as I pulled into the driveway of the log cabin I had built with my wife, the memories flared into sudden, agonizing intensity. I had just made it up the steps and opened the door when they hit with full force.

There was Jack, his thinning yellow hair damp with sweat and his sour-sweet whiskey breath on my neck as he bent over my bed. In a moment, his hands would be pulling back my baseball-themed sheets, reaching for the drawstring on my pajama bottoms. I shut my fourteen-year-old eyes tighter as his breath came faster against my skin.

I flinched as if I'd been shot. Throwing open the door and stumbling inside, I tipped the empty rum bottle into my mouth.

My mother's brown eyes narrowed into slits of rage, as if to say, "You've brought this on yourself, Randy. You've always been a bad boy."

As she turned away, Jack pulled out his leather belt, making a hiss.

I threw the useless bottle against the wall. It shattered into the darkness as I stumbled across the kitchen tiles, throwing open cupboards, hands groping for what I knew wasn't there.

Suddenly, the pastor from our church appeared, his greying hair looming out of the darkness in the 1970 blue Maverick that passed as his traveling counseling office. His dark eyes blinked behind thick glasses as he twisted around from the driver's seat to tell me that what was going on between me and Jack was just a normal part of growing up, and didn't mean that I was a homosexual.

Jack, sitting in the passenger seat, grinned at me from the rearview mirror.

Tidal waves of rage and shame crashed over my sixteen-year-old and my forty-seven-year-old selves at the same time. I fell to my knees, sick, clutching my head.

As my mother reached across the Impala's bench seat, her head disappeared into Jack's lap. I could hear the sound of a zipper and the whisper of fabric on skin. Jack's hands clenched the steering wheel as his

GETTING STARTED

blue eyes in the rearview mirror locked on mine. I squirmed in the back seat.

With my knuckles bloody from smashing my fist into the wooden planks on the floor, I lay there moaning.

You're broken, Randy, face it. Everyone would be better off without you. Your own mother wishes you'd never been born.

My teeth gritted against the maelstrom of pain. I curled in on myself and rocked, fighting against the desire to pull my old hunting rifle out of the safe and silence the voices in my head. The only thing keeping my hands from entering the combination was the sure knowledge that, if I did, it would mean Jack would have won. My hands shook so badly that I could barely hold the phone as I dialed the one person I had the least right to call....

*

I was forty-seven years old when I made that call and my wife talked me out of the darkness in my mind. I had lived with the pain and shame from childhood abuse for nearly four decades before I admitted I needed help.

I was sexually, spiritually, physically, and emotionally abused as a child.

I was a full-blown alcoholic from eighteen to forty-nine. Just about the only thing you could count on me for was being drunk and high.

I physically hurt my wife.

I said horrible, unforgivable things to my children.

I made and lost fortunes.

And I was about to leave my wife of thirty-plus years for a woman I barely knew. Why? Because the excitement of a new fling covered up the shame I felt, day in and day out. I used drugs and alcohol to quell the emotional storm for decades, and I was terrified when I started to realize that, no matter how much I drank or used, I still felt dirty. I still hurt.

I grabbed at any straw that promised an escape from the pain, no matter how temporary. But on that night at the cabin, I came face to face with the reality of what my reckless need for escape was about to cost the people I loved. And I truly understood that no affair, no drink, no amount of money would be able to fix what was broken inside me. I would have to face those demons head-on.

Untreated, the wounds left from childhood abuse spread like gangrene into all the cracks in our psyches. They rot out our self-esteem, damage our ability to love and be loved, and send the poisonous message that we are damaged and broken.

Many of us spend a lifetime running from this emotional pain as if it were some giant, slavering beast always at our heels, ready to tear us to pieces if we so much as stumble in our headlong flight through whatever escape route is closest. For me, the exit sign was clearly marked, glowing at the bottom of a bottle of Jack Daniel's.

Taking that first step to turn around and face your demons might be the hardest thing you ever do. (It certainly was for me.) But once you do, you will find that no matter how fearsome and hideous, those beasts are made of shadows and can only thrive in the darkness of avoidance and repression. It is only when you are held prisoner by fear that the beasts have the power to convince you of the lie that they are stronger than you are.

In this book, you will find the tools that I used to confront the monster that had chased me since I was twelve years old. The tools helped me to eventually shrink the beast down to its rightful size, which is now just a small part of a full and happy life.

These tools will hopefully help you to treat the emotional gangrene from the abuse of your own childhood and let the original pain finally close over and heal. Childhood sexual abuse does not have to be a life sentence of pain and shame. There is a way out, which begins with facing and naming that beast at our heels.

When we heal from pain, we become better. We have to. Easy answers and the plausible deniability that passes for good mental health for "normal" people just doesn't cut it for the industrial-strength pain that comes from childhood sexual abuse. We have to do the hard emotional and spiritual work that most people will never go near.

Because of the abuse I suffered, I grew up wounded. But in healing myself, I have become more compassionate, more loving, stronger and wiser than I ever would have been if I had been able to take my emotional health for granted. I am not, of course, advocating abuse or pain in any way.

We can't go back in time. All we have is forward. And what I discovered is that there is a powerful silver lining to this storm—one that we can all find if we are willing to keep moving until we reach it. All we have to do is get a little better every day. It takes courage, but I know you have guts because you have already picked up this book and started reading.

Myths and Realities About Sexual Abuse

It is unknown how many men have been sexually abused. Most will never talk about it. Instead, they will struggle with the emotional repercussions of abuse, never knowing the cause of their depression, anger, and pain.

I contend that any experience that makes a child feel isolated, ashamed, violated, or frightened due to sexual content is sexual abuse.

Sadly, although the issue of male childhood sexual abuse has become more visible over the past several years, our society still only accepts the severest forms of sexual abuse as valid evidence that a boy has actually been sexually victimized. Society as a whole remains reluctant to think that women can be sexual predators, but in fact a third of the sexual abuse of boys is committed by women.[2]

Societal myths about gender roles and molestation still make it difficult for others to understand that abuse is abuse, regardless of gender. Violent penetration of a helpless boy by an adult male is still the only form of sexual abuse that receives total support from society for the victim.

I'm not talking about how experts or psychologists understand male sexual abuse. I'm talking about the mainstream news-watching, TV-dinner-eating average Joe or Jane. That is who men must contend with when they face the difficult process of healing and asking for support from society.

It would be wonderful if all male survivors of sexual abuse had enlightened spiritual teachers in their families, but they don't.

This book is not about sterile academic studies or theories. It is about real life and what it takes for men to heal from sexual abuse in Western cultures.

Unfortunately, most of us have family trees filled with "normal" people rather than enlightened experts. And "normal" people still don't like to deal with the idea of male sexual abuse. That can leave male survivors with very limited options when it comes to getting help.

Men are therefore more likely to self-medicate with drugs or alcohol, gambling or sex addictions, control addictions, violence and rage, or

---

[2]David Lisak, Jim Hopper, J., & Pat Song, "Factors in the Cycle of Violence: Gender Rigidity and Emotional Constriction," *Journal of Traumatic Stress*, 9 (1996): 721–743.

depression than they are to reach out for help. In fact, the stigma of sexual abuse is so strong in our society that many male victims talk themselves out of the facts of their own traumas.

Defining sexual abuse is difficult because sexual practices vary greatly among different cultures. What Western cultures term sexual abuse is sometimes considered a "rite of passage" in less developed societies.

These discrepancies, however, do not make sexual abuse right, even where it is considered culturally normal. In most Western cultures, sexual abuse is seen as a perversion of human sexuality, but it comes with an intense stigma, not only for the abusers, but also for the victims. That can make us feel that we are wrong, bad, and dirty because we were abused. That is not fair or right.

Survivors Speak Out

S: I had to make sense out of what was going on. And the sense I made out of this was that I'm not really a good person. There's something different about me and something wrong.

S: I feel totally unacceptable. There's nothing about me that anybody else could possibly enjoy or accept.

S: That's at the core of all this, is that I feel inadequate and terribly less than, and I'm never going to be good enough.[3]

This is not a book about assigning blame. The intent here is not to indict society. Rather, this is a book about healing. But in order to heal, we need to stop stigmatizing the victims.

I am not out to make Western cultures wrong. I am here to discuss what it means to be a survivor of sexual abuse. The shame you feel, the isolation and the sense of being broken or bad, are not your fault, just as the abuse itself was not your fault.

---

[3]From David Lisak, "The Psychological Impact of Sexual Abuse: Content Analysis of Interviews with Male Survivors," *Journal of Traumatic Stress*, 7: 4 (1994), 541. In all the quotations from Lisak that appear in this book, each *S* stands for a different survivor of sexual abuse.

GETTING STARTED

The Many Faces of Sexual Abuse

Sexual abuse is a hard subject to deal with, and there are a great many misconceptions about it. For example, most people assume that incest refers to any sexual contact between two people who are related by blood, but that definition has been expanded. Incest also includes sexual contact between a child and an adult in a position of trust or power.

Although sexual abuse of any kind is traumatic, incest is particularly insidious. Children are resilient. Surrounded by a loving, supportive family system, they can heal from even the most terrible traumas. If a child is violently accosted by a stranger, but can return to a loving home to heal, that child has a good chance to recover at a young age.

But what happens to children who are hurt by the very people who are supposed to be caring for them? Those children have nowhere to go, and often will have to normalize their abuse in order to preserve their fantasy that their home is safe and their caregivers are loving.

The majority of childhood sexual abuse is committed by persons known to the victim. In fact, more than a third of those perpetrators are relatives. Delaplane and Delaplane define sexual abuse as: "Contacts or interactions between a child and an adult when the child is being used for sexual stimulation of the perpetrator or another person when the perpetrator or another person is in a position of power or control over the victim."[4]

Child sexual abuse comes in many forms. Some of the more obvious ones include:

- Having intercourse with a child.

- Having a child perform any sexual act on an adult or older child.

- Having oral sex with a child.

- Having a child perform oral sex on an adult or older child.

- Having a child touch an older person's genitals or any part of the body for the purposes of sexual arousal.

---

[4]D. Delaplane and A. Delaplane, *Victims of Child Abuse, Domestic Violence, Elder Abuse, Rape, Robbery, Assault, and Violent Death: A Manual for Clergy and Congregations. Special Edition for Military Chaplains* (Rockville, MD: National Criminal Justice Reference Service, 2001).

- Masturbation in front of a child, or having a child masturbate in front of an adult or older child.

What many people don't clearly understand is that sexual abuse does not have to include actual physical contact between the perpetrator and the victim. Less commonly understood forms of sexual abuse include:

- Exhibitionism, including deliberately having sex in front of a child, so that the child sees and/or hears the behavior.

- Fondling a child's genitals or touching the child anywhere for the purposes of sexually arousing the adult.

- Intentionally exposing a child to pornography via magazines, movies, or the internet.

One definition of sexual abuse that I often use is from Judith Lewis Herman. It is simple, direct, and covers all bases: "Any touch or other behavior between the child and the adult that must be kept a secret will be considered abuse."[5] We will go into more depth about secrets later in this book, but for now it is enough to know that abuse is anything that happened to you as a child at the hands of another person that you felt you had to hide.

Some of us have had very clear experiences of sexual abuse; there is no question that we have been molested, raped, or forced to perform sexual acts on one or more adults. But for survivors for whom the line is less clearly drawn, the next few pages are intended to give some clarification about what sexual abuse really is.

This is important to understand because many male survivors, in particular, do not understand that their emotional pain is linked to sexual abuse in their childhood.

They try treatments for other issues—anger, intimacy problems, drug or alcohol abuse—but they never truly heal because they aren't able to address the root cause of their pain.

Just as cancer cannot be effectively treated if it has been misdiagnosed as diabetes, the treatment for the unique mental traumas from sexual abuse is different from treatments for other emotional traumas.

---

[5]Judith Lewis Herman, *Father-Daughter Incest* (Cambridge: Harvard University Press, 1981), p. 70.

GETTING STARTED

The last thing I want to do is be a Chicken Little alarmist who runs around saying that everyone who has ever made a sexual joke around a child is a sexual predator. That's not the point of this book.

The point is to help men who have experienced sexual abuse to name it and therefore finally be able to treat it and actually get some relief from the mental torment it can cause.

The U.S. Department of Justice defines sexual assault as:

> Any type of sexual contact or behavior that occurs without the explicit consent of the recipient. Falling under the definition of sexual assault are such sexual activities as forced sexual intercourse, forcible sodomy, child molestation, incest, fondling, and attempted rape.[6]

Any type of sexual contact or behavior includes a wide array of conditions that American men (and women, also) are not conditioned to think of as "abuse." It helped me immensely when I learned all of the things that are considered sexual abuse. To begin with, it helped me to reconcile the emotional pain and confusion I had felt as a child when I experienced these situations that were presented to me as "normal" behavior.

It was a big part of my recovery process when I learned that I wasn't crazy or broken for being ashamed, confused, and unhappy. The fault lay with my abusers.

Sexual abuse includes any form of touching for a sexual purpose. I have heard stories from men who have suffered all of their lives with classic symptoms of being sexual abuse survivors who swore they had never been abused. In therapy, it would often come out that their mothers, fathers, older siblings, or coaches had given them backrubs, massages, or long baths, insisted on rigorous cleaning habits, or walked around naked or in provocative clothing. The men never realized that what they had experienced was a form of sexual abuse. They remembered feeling uncomfortable, dirty, or ashamed about their experiences, but because what had happened did not fall into the very narrow category of what they considered sexual abuse, they assumed they were wrong or bad.

Let me be completely clear. Any act that arouses the abuser and makes the victim uncomfortable is sexual abuse.

---

[6]Office on Violence Against Women, U.S. Department of Justice, *Sexual Assault* (2015), retrieved from http://www.justice.gov/ovw/sexual-assault/.

Again, we don't want to be Chicken Little by assuming that abuse is everywhere. Children and teenagers have their own, naturally occurring, perfectly healthy sexual fantasies and thoughts. That is not what we are talking about here. Healthy curiosity and sexuality are not a problem and do not create emotional scars that cripple us as adults. It is the unhealthy, abuse-related sexual thoughts that are harmful.

There is a big difference between bad boundaries and sexual abuse. Parents who make jokes about their sons' genitals, sexual prowess, masturbation, or anything related to sexual activity might not be consciously abusing their children. The line becomes clearer when the abuser is sexually aroused or feels empowered by inappropriate sexual behavior with a child.

Sometimes it is obvious that an abuser is connecting with a child out of sexual desire. Sometimes it is not so obvious.

Sometimes adults are not even conscious of their motivations and do not realize that they are being abusive.

Whether the behavior is conscious or not is irrelevant; the effects of child abuse, subtle or overt, are the same.

I know one man whose mother insisted on watching him take a bath until he was late in his teens. She didn't touch him in the bath, but he was miserably uncomfortable that she insisted on observing him.

We know deep down when a behavior is "off" or "wrong" in some way. Sometimes, it is the subtler forms of abuse that are the most destructive, because the victim does not recognize the behavior as abuse.

There are many instances of subtle forms of sexual abuse.

A survivor I know told me that his father made him look at pornographic magazines while his mother was in the room. His parents would then verbally and physically abuse him for getting an erection in front of his mother. After this, the parents would have sex in the next room with the door open.

Until being referred to a therapist, he had never guessed that he had experienced sexual abuse. For his entire adult life, he had been plagued by the classic symptoms of abuse, but he had never found a treatment that had worked for him. When he realized that his issues stemmed from his sexual abuse as a child, he was finally able to address the real pain he felt. After some inner-child work and targeted therapy, he experienced a dramatic improvement in his self-worth, his relationship with his wife and children, and the management of his anger and depression.

GETTING STARTED

Another survivor told me about a soccer coach who insisted on giving him massages as a "reward" for his playing. The coach never touched his penis, but the massages just felt wrong, so he tried whenever possible to find ways to never be alone with the coach. This survivor had wondered about the coach, but, like most children, had assumed that he was himself to blame for anything, and not the adult. He wondered for years if he were gay and went through two failed marriages because of his intimacy issues and crippling self-doubts.

The subtler forms of sexual abuse create a nasty mental trap for the victim. Because the sexual nature of the abuse is hidden, the child assumes that any sexual thoughts that arise are his. For example, the soccer victim clearly felt sexually aroused by the long massages, but because the coach never touched his genitals or was obviously aroused, the child assumed that he was the only one having thoughts or feelings of a sexual nature. He then blamed himself for being perverted or thinking of his coach in a sexual context. It wasn't until he was an adult that he realized that any sexual thoughts or feelings he had during the experience were not the result of any deficiencies in himself.

It's also important to state out loud and on the record that all children are under the age of consent. Even if they "agree" to the abuse—even if they seek out the abuse because it is the only way they receive approval and attention—all children are under the age of consent.

Children are completely dependent on the adults around them for their very survival. Even children who may have thought they were tough, strong, or smart were still only children, and therefore unable to truly give their consent. If they "consented" to the abuse, it was because they saw it as the best possible option among the available choices. If a safer, kinder, non-abusive choice had been available to them, they would have taken it. I hated myself for decades because I thought I had been complicit in my own abuse. It took years in therapy to realize that I was only choosing the option that was the least painful and least damaging, because I didn't have any better choices.

In many abuse cases, the perpetrators are highly aware of children's tendency to self-blame and will even prey on that tendency. It is common to hear stories about perpetrators intentionally causing sexual thoughts or arousal in a boy and then punishing him for having those thoughts. That shifts the blame from where it rightfully belongs—on the adult perpetrator—to the child's shoulders and causes more torment for the victim.

When an adult uses any form of coercion or abuses his or her power as an adult to create a situation in which a child feels trapped or forced into accepting unwanted physical or emotional intimacy, that is a form of sexual abuse. Even when the perpetrator warps the facts and makes the victim feel that he is himself to blame for the abuse, it is still never the child's fault.

Not ever.

Dealing with Male Sexual Abuse in Western Cultures

I was scared out of my mind when I committed myself to dealing with the issues related to my childhood sexual abuse. Any sane man raised in Western civilization would be crazy *not* to be scared. The wounds from childhood sexual abuse, especially for men in Western cultures, are pervasive and insidious.[7] Western cultures give men a clear picture of what is and is not acceptable behavior. It is one thing to share the struggle of getting over an addiction, since contemporary society has accepted the therapeutic process of A.A., and it's "okay" to talk about it. But in most circles, it is not okay to talk about being sexually abused.

The goal of this book and others like it is to overcome the stigma of sexual abuse and start a dialogue about the issue. It is easy to feel that the cards are stacked against you, and if you've felt that way, you're not alone.

That is the reality for most men who have been sexually abused as children.

Modern Western men are not supposed to be crippled by post-traumatic-stress-induced rage and shame. They are not supposed to cry. In fact, except for pride at a job well done and joy when their team wins a sporting event, they aren't supposed to feel anything much at all.

They are supposed to open jam jars, build woodsheds, take out the

---

[7]Denise A. Donnelly and Stacy Kenyon, "'Honey, We Don't Do Men'": Gender Stereotypes and the Provision of Services to Sexually Assaulted Males," *Journal of Interpersonal Violence*, 11:3 (September 1996), 441–448. These two researchers, who examined the effect of gender role stereotypes on the provision of services for men and women who had been sexually assaulted, conclude that "although official reports of male sexual assault victims are relatively uncommon, our research confirms that male victims do exist, and that they are more numerous than official statistics indicate. Moreover, our findings suggest that traditional gender role stereotypes, lack of responsiveness to male victims, and gaps in service provision prevent sexually assaulted men from getting the help they need" (p. 448).

garbage, and bring home a paycheck.

They are supposed to be ruggedly independent, self-made men who go ice-fishing in the morning, broker a few deals on the golf course in the afternoon, and take their women out dancing, Fred Astaire style, at night.

They might "know" that these ridiculous stereotypes are absurd fantasies, but the deepest part of their psyche is deeply committed to these primal archetypes. And, sadly, these cultural stereotypes keep most male survivors from ever seeking help.

Because of the stigmas around male sexual abuse in our society, male survivors rarely get the help they need. The effects of sexual abuse on a child's psyche are the same for boys and girls, but society's judgments about male sexual abuse often make the experience more devastating for boys.

Sexual abuse sends conflicting messages about intimacy and physical boundaries to children. At the deepest level, abused children believe that they must subjugate their emotional and physical sense of well-being and safety in order to gratify someone else's desires. They accept that their wants and needs are not as important as other people's.

They learn to live out of a place where they find safety, approval, and affection when they allow others to harm them. For instance, male survivors who were abused by women often report that they have a hard time establishing boundaries with women or maintaining healthy sexual relationships with them.

Survivors Speak Out

S: The defeat that I felt with my mother comes back often. I find it in my sexual relationships. A lot of times, I'll allow people to be invasive because I'm used to it. And I've had a hard time setting up boundaries. I've had a hard time believing that my boundaries were worthwhile, that they were worth keeping. I guess I often felt like I was the property of somebody else. And that anybody could just do whatever they wanted. And that I didn't have a right to have feelings about it. All the scenes in college where the girls would seduce me, and I'd just kind of let them do whatever they wanted to do. Or I would do for them whatever they wanted me to do. And then just get out.

> *S:* I just had to put up with it. That's the way she was. . . . They were her rules. If she said I have to kiss her, I have to kiss her. If she says I have to hug her, I have to hug her. It was like I kept trying to fill her cup, and it just kept running out. And she's standing there screaming, "Fill it, fill it, fill it!"[8]

This is the legacy of sexual abuse. If we don't get help, we can live in a state of trauma for the rest of our lives.

Psychologists call this a loss of the sense of agency. It is a profound helplessness that is directly related to the most basic sense of self. It comes from having been the helpless object of someone else's sexual gratification. All survivors must deal with this. However, men have an additional hurdle to overcome in this area.

Being a helpless victim violates Western society's gender norms for men. To compensate for this, male survivors generally take one of two self-destructive paths:

- They can become extra-masculine, conforming to the most "macho" stereotypes, often downplaying or completely denying the facts of their abuse.

- Or they cannot get away from the "unmasculine" feelings they experience after their abuse, so they feel deeply inferior because they have emotions that men are not "supposed to have."

I myself went through both of these paths. I am naturally "outdoorsy," taking up the most manly careers and hobbies possible. I hunt, I drive a big truck, and I am extremely competitive. I went through periods of dark and desperate depression, but I only showed the world my anger.

It is acceptable for men to express anger, but not sadness. In my case, I suffered not only from sadness, but also from the self-hatred for being sad at all.

---

[8]Lisak, "Psychological Impact," 534.

GETTING STARTED

Survivors Speak Out

S: I think what was harmful about the abuse was a number of things. One was that, first of all, I was like a tough from the projects. You got to be a man, you got to like football, and yet I had no control.

S: Well, I decided to go in because the Marine Corps has a reputation as being the toughest. And, of course, I could never picture myself being in anything except the Marine Corps.[9]

Male survivors not only face an internal battle for self-acceptance, but an external one as well. Society understands that an abused girl will have behavioral problems, intimacy and sexual issues, and a damaged sense of self-worth. In general, however, society does not give men the same understanding, even though men experience the same effects.

In the early 1990s, Dr. David Lisak, a sexual abuse survivor himself and a founding member of One-in-Six, a national nonprofit organization dedicated to helping men recover from childhood sexual abuse, set out to discover just what the effects of childhood sexual abuse on men were.[10]

Lisak found that men who were sexually abused as children experience the following issues:

- Anger
- Anxiety
- Depression
- Disassociation
- Dysfunctions or compulsions
- Fear
- Gender confusion and struggles
- Guilt and self-blame
- Homophobia and confusion about sexual orientation
- Hostility
- Impaired relationships
- Low self-esteem and negative self-images
- Obsessive-compulsiveness
- Post-Traumatic Stress Disorder (PTSD)
- Problems with intimacy

---

[9]Lisak, "Psychological Impact," 538.
[10]Lisak, "Psychological Impact."

Sexual problems
Shame
Sleep disturbances
Substance abuse
Suicide attempts
Tendencies to delegitimize the traumatic experience

In Lisak's study, 81% of the survivors had a history of substance abuse, 50% had thought about suicide, 23% had attempted suicide, and 31% had victimized others (children, women, or other men). Perhaps saddest of all is the fact that Lisak found that, of all these emotional wounds, the most pervasive was fear, including the fear of being "found out" and exposed as a sexual abuse survivor. In my opinion, this sense that there is something wrong with the victim is the single most painful effect of sexual abuse for men in Western cultures.

There is less of a stigma for women who have been sexually abused than there is for men. Also, to help women overcome the damaging effects of abuse, there are more resources, including books, workshops, programs, and support groups. Therefore, women are more likely than men to reach out for and receive help, which ideally should include compassion and understanding for depression, anger, and intimacy issues to help them find a way out of the pain of their own thoughts.

If a female survivor is having trouble connecting with a sexual partner, she is far more likely to understand that her issues are related to her abuse. This reduces the shame associated with the abuse. She can come to understand that she herself is not broken, she is just reacting the way other abused women often do. It is easier (although not easy) for women to understand that the abuse was harmful and wrong, but that she herself is not broken.

However, men in our society are often unable to make this crucial distinction. Society says that male sexual abuse either proves a boy's frailty or his homosexuality. When a man has trouble connecting with his partner, he doesn't think that it might be because of his childhood sexual abuse; instead, he automatically believes that something must be wrong with him. After all, "everyone knows" that male sexual abuse almost never happens—except to Catholic altar boys.

In our society, men are not seen as victims, so how can they feel that they deserve to get help and have their experience legitimized?

> **Survivors Speak Out**
>
> S: For women, you just call your local 800 rape line, and you've got everything from a place to stay, to food and money. They take care of your bills and your kids and everything else. I can call up and plead all I want, but I can't get a cup of coffee. And that is like one of the biggest, most frustrating things in the world for me.
>
> S: It's like, men aren't abused? You know, whoever heard of that? Who talks about that? If men aren't abused, how could *I* have been abused?
>
> S: But as a man, in that same respect I feel like this is typical of my life. There are all these women's organizations that are starting, they're becoming very conscious of not treating women as victims, not having violence towards women. But women have been victims, and now they're reasserting themselves, and women are physically different from guys. So they can see themselves as victims. Maybe they can see for themselves that victims are okay, they're good somehow, they martyred themselves. So why, if you can have a black and white, good or evil, women were good and men were bad, well, I'm the victim and I'm a guy but guys are bad. So I can't even be a victim, right?[11]

An extremely damaging myth about male sexual abuse is that unless a boy is violently penetrated by an adult male, it's not really sexual abuse.

This myth is compounded by others, such as, "It's easier for a boy to be sexually aroused than a girl," and "If a boy gets an erection, he enjoyed the experience, so it can't be rape or abuse."

And that's dead wrong.

Just as females can be aroused during sexual abuse, males can experience arousal without ever wanting the attention in the first place.

Even in modern-day America, the overarching cultural message is that sexual intercourse between a boy and a younger girl is rape, whereas

---

[11]Lisak, "Psychological Impact," 531.

sexual intercourse between a boy and an older girl is just that "lucky" boy's passage into manhood. Furthermore, if a woman or older girl abuses a boy, the abuse is often treated by the boy's peers as an achievement for the boy. His buddies and perhaps even his father will give him a big high-five for losing his virginity at a young age. He is the stud of the block, yet on the inside he feels confused and, most likely, ashamed.

Because young boys showing vulnerability in our society are usually given macho advice such as "Suck it up," "Be a man," or "Get over it," it is highly likely that an abused boy will stuff his feelings and act as though nothing is wrong. According to the rules of our society, if he admitted to feeling ashamed or upset, he would be deemed less of a man.

Cultural myths still keep our society from accepting that women can and do sexually abuse children. In fact, in David Lisak's study, 42.3% of the cases involved female perpetrators, with an additional 11.5% involving male and female perpetrators.[12] The following statement by John Lee, author of sixteen books, including *The Anger Solution*,[13] sheds some light on the insidious and often overlooked form of abuse called emotional incest:

An Expert Speaks Out:
John Lee on Emotional Incest

Over twenty-five years ago, I attended my first ACOA (Adult Children of Alcoholics) meeting. Every time someone had the courage to speak their pain about being molested or incested, it would make my skin crawl and make me want to head for Austin's beautiful Hill Country.

I would relate so much to what they were saying that it was quite disturbing. Finally, I called my mother and asked her, point-blank. She promised to God no such thing occurred to me.

A few years ago, I was in Clearwater, Florida, at a conference for Adult Children of Alcoholics. My mother,

---

[12]Jacquie Heatherton, "The Idealization of Women: Its Role in the Minimization of Child Sexual Abuse by Females," *Journal of Child Abuse and Neglect*, 23: 2 (March 1999), 161–174.

[13]John Lee, *The Anger Solution: The Proven Method for Achieving Calm and Developing Healthy, Long-lasting Relationships* (Philadelphia: Da Capo Press, 2009).

who lived only a few miles away, decided to attend the conference. A friend drove us all to the site. I had been on the road for several weeks in a row, lecturing and doing workshops, and was near to exhaustion. I was talking about how tired I felt when all of a sudden my mother started massaging my shoulders. I wept gentle tears as I realized I had no memory of my mother ever comforting me this way before.

Here I was, at the time a grown man, unable to remember a time in my childhood when I did anything but rub her shoulders and soothe her brow. I kept hearing her words: "Come give me a neck rub. Bring me a wet rag to put on my head." The unspoken message was: "Dance for me, my darling. Mama needs you to be her little man."

At the end of a lecture I gave in Vancouver, a woman said, "I heard you talk about how to love appropriately and how to connect with your children. Sometimes I feel so lonely. My husband and I have been divorced for five years, and I just haven't been able to find anyone that I really am attracted to. When I'm feeling really lonely, I call my six-year-old son over and ask him to give me a hug. And he does, and I feel better, but should I be worried that I'm doing something really wrong and harmful to him?"

I replied that a six-year-old's body and soul are not equipped to meet the psychosexual needs of a mother who longs for adult companionship. Nor would it be appropriate for a son, of any age, to give such companionship to his mother. It is the mother's responsibility to create a network of supportive friends and family who can meet those needs.

Her natural longing for touch should be met by people who are equipped to deal with the mutual outflow and inflow of energy that comes between two adults during closeness and intimacy. This will give her a full reservoir of energy, so that when her son needs a hug she has plenty to give, rather than bringing her own neediness to him. Otherwise her loneliness will pull at the boy's body, draining it, making it difficult for him later on to enter adult relationships based on an equal flow of giving and receiving.

This awkward, unhealthy exchange of energy will teach him to find lovers who'll take from him the way his mother did. Or he will look to his children to fill his longing. He'll remain unsure about when to stay, when to leave, or whether he'll ever be able to live according to his own internal rhythms of closeness and distance. It wasn't the answer the woman wanted, but she appeared to hear it just the same.

This kind of love is what Dr. Patricia Love calls "emotional incest," in her book, *The Emotional Incest Syndrome*, because a child is not emotionally equipped to support an adult's emotional and psychological needs. This may contribute to or cause a man to look at a woman and see her body but not her soul. If he is driven from the breast at too early an age, but is later called on to soothe his mother's body, then women become mere bodies. If women—mothers and mates—carry the man's feminine soul, he will be unable to live in his own body and will seldom feel like he owns his soul. So the adult son stores in his body his feelings of resentment. He tries to snatch the woman's soul in myriad ways, tries to cram it into his own body to complete himself. All the while, somehow he knows it's not her soul he wants, but his own that he has lost in an unspoken agreement with his mother.

Anaclitic depression is a kind of depression that borders on despair at a lack of non-sexual, energetic love, usually given from the mother (but sometimes from the father). It is a very little known, even less discussed type of depression that both men and women can experience, but is very likely to be present in men who were enmeshed with their mothers. This very serious form of depression is caused by and is due to a child who did not receive non-libidinous love, who as an adult still yearns and longs for it, even if he's never heard of it or had it diagnosed by a clinician. My own therapist, Dr. James Maynard, for many years introduced the concept and the constraints this form of depression can create. This type of depression can come from the act and fact that the mother, for whatever reasons, tends to depend on her son, sometimes in an emotional/sexual manner rather than in a clean, clear, and consistent, non-usurping way.

Consequently, the son comes to be super dependent on his mother as an alpha and omega of his existence. This is especially true if the boy's father is absent emotionally or physically or both. The mother turns to the son for comfort, and the son says, does, or tries to become whatever his mother seemingly needs him to be—because in his mind, if he loses her like he lost his father, he would truly be abandoned and die. This son becomes the beginning and end to his mother, a dynamic that can go on for decades, creating a level of depression no one seems to talk about.

Some examples of emotional incest involving an adult son follow: Charles went out to dinner with his mother, and they ran into a couple of her friends. She introduced Charles to them, saying, "Isn't my son handsome? The only way that I could get someone this handsome to go out with me was to make him myself."

Another man, Ronald, brought his twenty-year-old daughter to a workshop I was teaching in New York. He said, "She's my date; I take her everywhere I want to go and leave her mother at home." In both these instances, the parent may have thought they were complimenting their child, making him or her feel special, rather than putting that child into an inappropriate role. With no malice intended, we were taught to believe a lot of things that simply are not true, and this is one of them.

Emotional incest appears when the mother tries to live vicariously through her son, and it is the unconscious act of draining the boy's energy to make her feel better, less tired, less lonely, and more fulfilled. It is characterized by mothers or fathers giving their sons or daughters age-inappropriate information; using them as surrogate counselors or confidants to talk about a parent or grandparent or sibling, and looking to them to figure out what to do; talking about a child's body, genitalia, or commenting on his weight; or, as in the last two examples, having a son or daughter stand in where an adult partner would. Emotional incest is the fertile ground from which most co-dependency stems.[14]

---

[14]John Lee, *Breaking the Mother-Son Dynamic: Resetting the Parents of a*

Sexual Abuse and Sexual Orientation

If a man or older boy abuses a younger boy, the victim becomes associated with the stigmas attached to homosexuality that still run rampant in this country. Even today, usually among the least educated, lowest socio-economic classes or among the fanatically religious, homosexuality is considered deviant behavior, perhaps even more so than child abuse.

One survivor remembers going to his mother for protection, "and her response to me when I told her that he [a perpetrator] used to make me suck his cock was, 'How dare you make up something so horrible about another human being? How dare you!'" The stigmas associated with homosexuality when coupled with the pain and stigmas of sexual abuse can cripple a child. This boy was not only left unprotected from abuse, but he was also unfairly forced into the role of abuser, as if he had harmed the perpetrator! The long-term ramifications of sexual abuse can erode the very foundations of one's identity. Some survivors of male-on-male sexual abuse wonder about their own sexual orientation.

A Survivor Speaks Out
S: And it's like, am I gay? And then the homophobia comes in, being afraid of gay people. And I'm like paranoid to death because maybe inside I am.[15]

Depending on the survivor's own beliefs about homosexuality, this can lead to internalized or externalized hatred.

A Survivor Speaks Out
S: If I get in a crowd, and I think a person is of questionable character towards the offensive-gay type, ah, that I will defend myself and ah, I would not think twice about doing violence to that person or anyone else associated with him that tried to do the same thing to me again.[16]

I sometimes wonder if the overwhelming prejudice against homosexual men in our culture doesn't stem from unrecognized male sexual abuse. If a boy experiences sexual abuse from a man, the boy might mistakenly correlate the normal reactions of anger and fear with homophobia. As

---

Man's Life and Loves (Deerfield, FL: HCI Books, 2015), pp. 42–46.

[15] Lisak, "Psychological Impact," 532.

[16] Lisak, "Psychological Impact," 534.

it turns out, homosexuality and child sexual abuse are *not* related. Most men who abuse children, male or female, are heterosexual. *Pediatrics* (the *Official Journal of the American Academy of Pediatrics*) reports that the rate of child abusers appears to be constant across sexual orientations. In other words, if x percent of men are child abusers, that percentage will apply to all men, both heterosexual and homosexual.[17]

People who sexually abuse children often molest both boys and girls. It is not the gender of the child that arouses a pedophile, but the domination of the child. On the other hand, a child who is sexually abused may be aroused, or even reach orgasm. I did several times over the five-year span of my abuse. This can make abused children question their sexuality, and if they were raised in a "Christian" household, being gay was the same as being evil.

We will talk more about spiritual abuse later, but I understand the fear and pain of questioning one's sexual orientation in a fear-based environment. I now know how complex human sexuality is.

Our bodies are designed to experience pleasure and pain, based on the type of stimulation we receive. Just as girls can be sexually aroused during sexual abuse, boys can, too. Sexual arousal is a biological function, like digesting food or experiencing cold.

Sexual abuse cannot affect sexual orientation one way or the other. But it can royally screw with our heads around the issue. I know gay men who spent years of their lives believing that they were gay because they were abused. They linked their sexual orientation to their abuse, and went through one abusive relationship after another.

I know other gay men who believe that their being homosexual is some kind of punishment for being abused when they were young boys. And I know a lot of heterosexual men who are terrified to get help for sexual abuse because their family, pastor, rabbi, imam, or social circle would find out that they had been sexual with someone of the same gender.

Survivors Speak Out
S: I didn't have anybody to talk to. There was nobody
I could confide in. Or nobody I thought I could confide in.
Nobody I thought would be able to understand or do any

---

[17]Carole Jenny, Thomas A. Roesler, and Kimberley L. Poyer, "Are Children at Risk for Sexual Abuse by Homosexuals?" *Pediatrics*, 94: 1 (1994), 41–44. Of 269 cases, two offenders were identified as gay or lesbian; 82% of the perpetrators were heterosexual adults; and the rest were other children or teenagers.

good. And I thought just to reveal this secret to anybody would just kill me.

S: Sometimes I wonder because of it, until I really got into therapy and things, if, you know, if it was me. Maybe I was bisexual or things like that.

S: I didn't feel like everyone else. I felt different. I was different. I was different because I had done this weird thing with this man, and I don't know what that's about, but I did it. And definitely no ordinary person would do that.[18]

The stigma of homosexuality affects gay and straight men alike, leading to isolation and alienation regardless of one's sexual orientation. The stigma keeps people from getting help, keeps them living in fear of being "found out," and perpetuates the idea that they were somehow complicit in their own abuse. It is truly sad that dangerous myths like these are allowed to fester and grow. Left unchecked, these myths turn into "rules" about what a man should and should not be or do.

Man Rules

These societal "rules" for men can make the pain of sexual abuse even harder to bear. During my own recovery, I was lucky enough to come across the writings of Dan Griffin, whose work on cultural male stereotypes should be a vital component in any male survivor's recovery toolbox.

An Expert Speaks Out:
Dan Griffin on Gender Roles

Has it ever felt like you were following some set of unwritten rules on how to be a man? Men can do this, but can't do that. These are the Man Rules I referred to in the Introduction. They are unwritten yet very real, and they guide our lives from an early age, telling us how to be boys and men. We follow these Rules to let the world know that we are real boys and men. When we don't follow them, we run the risk of being viewed by others and viewing ourselves as being less than real boys or men. Where did these rules come from? The answer is that

---

[18]Lisak, "Psychological Impact," 535.

they come from many different sources, some personal and some societal. The rules come from both of our parents and other caregivers, from other family members, coaches, and teachers, from the kids on the playground, and from the media based on the images of "real" men presented on television and movies, and in print and broadcast advertising. Adolescence can be a particularly brutal period of indoctrination to the Man Rules.

Think about your day-to-day experiences and look at how many Man Rules you follow. Think about how you may judge yourself as less than manly if you don't follow them. There is the Rule that men do not ask for help. This rule contributes to many men remaining lost for much longer than necessary, among other problems. You may be pretty good at asking for help, but how do you feel when you do it? It's still hard for me to ask for help, and when I do, it is frequently accompanied by some sort of self-criticism. If you are anything like me, every time you ask for help it is a struggle just to get to that point, and once there you probably have at least a twinge of shame around feeling or appearing weak or incompetent or stupid. But with time and practice, it gets better. Luke spoke for a lot of the men in recovery whom I know: "I had a huge amount of self-hatred before recovery, due to the nature of my acting out and hiding my true self from others. I had issues and doubts of myself about even being a man. Since recovery, the self-hatred has been greatly reduced, and I'm more confident in my masculinity and how I express it out in the world."

Some of the most common Man Rules I hear about from men and women are:

- Don't be weak.
- Don't show emotion.
- Don't ask for help.
- Don't cry.
- Don't care about relationships.

Do these sound familiar?

Into Action

Take some time right now to write as many Rules about being a man as you can think of. Think about the Rules you learned from your parents/caregivers, school, neighborhood/community, the media, and workplace. If you are having trouble, think of them in the following areas: Self, Relationships, Activities, Power, Sexuality, and Spirituality.

Think of rules that reinforce a healthier idea of masculinity. While the majority of the Rules are neither inherently bad nor good, how they tend to be enforced can be rigid and restricting. However, there are Man Rules like integrity and self-discipline that seem to be inherently healthy traits.

What does your list of Man Rules look like? My guess is (if your experience is anything like mine and most survivors I work with), you have not spent a lot of time consciously thinking about and attempting to identify these Rules. [19]

For many of us, adhering to some of these unspoken rules saved us from more pain and humiliation in the short run. We learned not to show any sign of weakness—physical or emotional—because we'd get teased. In my boyhood, the nicest thing that sensitive boys were called was "pansy," "sissy," "pussy," or "weakling." Generally, other boys or family members, to help "toughen him up," would beat up the "whiner." If we grew up in America in the last fifty years, unless we were brain-dead, we figured out that adhering to the rules would keep us from getting black eyes and being shunned. But for those of us who were unable to put on that front, we just felt isolated and alone.

Survivors Speak Out

S: Feeling like a man, an adult, that passage of

---

[19] Dan Griffin, *A Man's Way Through Relationships: Learning to Love and Be Loved* (Las Vegas: Central Recovery Press, 2014), 1–3. Reproduced here by permission of the publisher.

adulthood and feeling significant and important, it was just not attainable for me.

S: I never hung out with the guys. I didn't have a girlfriend that often. I didn't get to do things a lot of the other guys did.... When you're the brunt of people's jokes, people make fun of you, you're not as tough as the other guys are.... I always backed down.[20]

Survivors like me already felt broken and "less than," and most of us made a conscious choice to follow the rules to the letter and to act as though nothing bothered us. *Ever*. No matter what it cost us, we appeared strong and stoic on the outside, even though we might have been terrified and heartbroken on the inside. The rules state that showing emotion and crying are not manly. In reality, it is not only natural for boys and men to be able to express emotion, it is necessary for healthy psychological development. Apparently, though, when I was growing up, no one I knew got that memo.

I vividly remember every time I cried as I endured either a physical or emotional beating, always accompanied by the famous words, "Stop crying or I'll give you something to really cry about." And then the beating would get worse.

Survivors Speak Out

S: It embarrasses me to see somebody sad. If I had to guess, it probably has to do with male programming. That you're not supposed to be sad, and you're not supposed to cry.

S: I hate violence. I was always the wimp or pussy to back down in school. I always shied away from violence. I even get nervous if people are yelling. Like somebody being mad at me for whatever reason. It's all interrelated.[21]

Even when I was an adult, the rule that men must not show emotion was reinforced for me. During my first marriage, I remember looking at pictures of my father and being moved to tears. My wife at the time approached me to ask why I was crying. When I told her that I missed him, she snapped, "Get over it! Your father has been dead for ten years now."

---

[20]Lisak, "Psychological Impact," 538.
[21]Lisak, "Psychological Impact," 538.

I don't blame her for that—she was just repeating the rules that she had been taught about men.

These rules are frustrating for both men and women. In movies and TV shows, it's often funny to see a man trying to deal with a crying woman. The man is usually portrayed as overwhelmed and comically startled. The message is clear: men don't know how to handle emotional women.

But it has been my experience that women are just as freaked out when men show emotions. They think that they want men to be more emotional and vulnerable, but, more often than not, when we do open up, we are violating society's unspoken rules about how men are supposed to behave, and women don't know how to handle that.

Another rule states that men should be self-sufficient and independent. Needing help is verboten, and asking for help is out of the question. When I was a boy and asked adults for help, the nicest thing I was told was to "figure it out for yourself." The more abusive adults in my life used those occasions as opportunities to criticize me for being incompetent and stupid. Yet, I would see the same adults responding differently to girls who asked for help. That was deeply confusing to me.

Don't get me wrong. Women in our society have just as hard a time with their Woman Rules. It's not fair on either side of the fence. This is not a diatribe on how unfair society's rules can be. This book is about the male journey to emotional wholeness. Exposing the rules and judging them for ourselves is a necessary first step on that journey.

The danger of letting unexamined rules continue to run us is that they reinforce negative self-talk. We already have enough negative self-talk in our heads: we don't need additional sources of confirmation that we are bad, worthless, or wrong, especially when those sources are as absurd and unfounded as society's Man Rules.

As we noted earlier, one of the most painful rules for survivors of sexual abuse is that men "can't" be sexually abused. The societal myth that supports this rule is that males get erections and therefore enjoy all forms of sex. In other words, if a male has been sexually abused, it probably means that he enjoyed it and encouraged it.

More destructive self-blame comes from the confusion felt by men who experience arousal as a natural part of sexual touching. Even if an abuse victim is aroused by the abuse—even if he or she in any way *enjoyed* the abuse—that does not mean he or she *wanted* the abuse. This is one of the most difficult aspects of dealing with the repercussions of sexual abuse on survivors.

This "rule" that men cannot be sexually abused is responsible for the secrecy that ruins so many lives. Because of this rule, boys or men are afraid to tell anyone about their abuse, or they downplay it. This often leads them to suffer from the effects of being abused without being able to get help for the original wounds. As boys become adults and see the negative repercussions for men who dare to admit being abused, it becomes even harder for them to ask for help. Over and over again, survivors report that they are afraid to say anything, for fear of looking less "manly."

When men reach out for help, most of them are told to "get over it, just move on with your life, it happened years ago." They feel shut down and invalidated, often in an even worse emotional state than they were in before they reached out for help.

The website of the Rape, Abuse, and Incest National Network, or RAINN, states that, "Psychological outcomes can be severe for men because men are socialized to believe that they are immune to sexual assault, and because societal reactions to these assaults can be more isolating."[22] Men are not immune to sexual assault, but our society's overwhelming message to them is that if they get an erection, they must be enjoying the experience. That is patently untrue.

When I started my own recovery, I decided that society's Man Rules stank. Those rules had hurt me deeply. I had been suicidal many times because those rules told me that I was wrong for having feelings, wrong for wanting to be loved, wrong for hurting. Those rules left me no way out. They taught me that it was better to kill myself than admit that I needed help.

When I realized that I was living by some ridiculous, made-up, unfair rules, and that I could change them, my whole life turned around. I came up with my own rules—rules that made sense to me, rules that were compassionate and that made me a better, stronger, more loving man.

My rules today state that:

- It's not merely *acceptable* to feel weak and vulnerable, it is *essential*—because that's how I grow and become better and stronger.

- Reaching out for help not only saves me time and money,

---

[22]*Sexual Assault of Men and Boys* (2009), retrieved from https://www.rainn.org/get-information/types-of-sexual-assault/male-sexual-assault/.

it saves the people around me, too.

- Any child, male or female, can be sexually abused and needs special help to heal from that trauma.

- Sexual abuse is *not* the child's fault, *ever*.

- Just because men have an erection doesn't mean that they want to be touched or violated.

Suggested Exercise

- What are some of the rules that have governed your life?

- Do they seem fair?

- Have they had an overall positive or negative impact on your life?

- What would you change about those rules?

- If you could write your own set of rules for yourself and your children, what would they be?

Psychologically, it is the breaking of cultural norms and the shame from hiding the abuse that cause the most severe and long-term emotional pain and damage to a child. Thus, the effects of abuse are most severe in societies that fully accept and enforce the Man Rules.

If every child in a society undergoes an overt cultural practice, even one that we would consider abusive, the children are not forced into a life of secrets and shame. To the contrary, even the most violent and disturbing societal rites of passage bring acceptance and inclusion rather than shame and degradation in the eyes of that society.

What we in America deem to be sexual abuse may be an acceptable rite of passage in some faraway Third World culture. For instance, in New Guinea and adjacent islands, the Semen Warriors practice a bizarre homosexual rite of passage whereby young boys must "accumulate" semen for several years, either by regularly receiving anal penetration or by swallowing the ejaculations of older males they fellate. This ancient custom springs from a religious belief system that regards sperm as the essential conduit of masculine energy. Puny boys, it is believed, are only transformed into virile warriors if they ingest large quantities of sperm. This rite of passage by the Semen Warriors would be deemed an extreme case of sexual abuse in our society; yet in New Guinea, it is a simple and mandatory ritual that must be performed to pass into manhood.[23]

What Sexual Abuse Is Not

It is important to talk about what sexual abuse is not. If a parent or older sibling or friend cracks a sexual joke about a child, and that child feels momentarily uncomfortable, but the feeling passes because the child has a home with healthy boundaries, feels safe expressing his emotions, and is capable of isolating the incident, sexual abuse is probably not involved.

It really is not possible to turn this grey area into perfectly delineated patches of black and white. For the purposes of your own healing, that is not necessary. This book is not about blaming others or tallying up the counts of abuse; it is about your recovery.

Whether or not an action is intended as sexual abuse can only be known in the mind of the perpetrator. But even if the perpetrator did not intend the action to be abusive, if a child experiences it negatively, it is highly likely that that child will live out the patterns of an abused child. You are probably living out the experience of a sexually abused child if: (1) you feel afraid of an adult or older child touching you, talking to you, or exposing himself or herself to you; (2) you feel coerced into staying silent about sexual contact of any kind; or (3) you feel dirty or ashamed of what other people did to you as a child.

Some people may tell you, "Move on with your life," or, "Why are you still crying over things that happened thirty years ago?" The fact is that you have a right to your feelings. When I was writing this book, I initially hesitated to list all the characteristics of sexual abuse because of the tendency of many male survivors to deny that they were ever sexually abused. But the truth is that any form of contact that made you uncomfortable as a child can cause you to feel ashamed, less than, and dirty.

You picked up this book for a reason. Trust yourself, and know

---

[23]For example, see Hank Hyena, *Semen Warriors of New Guinea* (September 16, 1999), retrieved from http://www.islandmix.com/backchat/f6/semen-warriors-new-guinea-80304/.

that you have a right to heal from whatever is hurting you. If you were subjected to the worst possible torture at the hands of your abuser, or you felt uncomfortable because older women were seductive around you, you have a right to hurt and you have a right to heal.

I also hesitated to draw this line in the sand because it could lead to a process of keeping score. This is detrimental on two counts:

> 1. There is no degree of pain that has any meaning when it comes to the recovery process. Pain is pain. If you're hurting, you need to address the hurt and heal it. The cause of the pain is less important than the process of recovery.

> 2. It is tempting to fall into the trap of assigning blame rather than getting on with the recovery process. Assigning blame is not necessary to your healing process, and in many cases can be highly detrimental.

It is important to label abuses as physical, sexual, emotional, or spiritual, because each type of abuse leaves specific wound patterns, and some treatments are more effective for certain kinds of abuse. But obsessing over assigning and proving blame only keeps you stuck in the position of an abused child. You feel helpless to change the past (because no one can change the past), and you will slowly be poisoned by your own rage and bitterness.

Feeling and expressing anger are a critical part of the healing process, but you don't want to get stuck there. That won't change the past or hurt your abuser, but it will keep you reliving the worst moments of your abuse—like a horror-movie version of *Groundhog Day*.

I'm speaking here from very personal experience. For years, I raged inside against my mother and my stepfather, Jack, both of whom abused me. Jack abused me sexually, but my mother's abuse was just as damaging in her complicit acceptance of Jack's behavior. Playing the events over and over again in my head only kept me stuck in a self-destructive loop.

The sexual abuse started when I was twelve and stopped when I was seventeen. During those five years, I experienced perhaps three or four dozen sessions of abuse. But after I left home, I kept abusing myself, tormenting myself by replaying those old memories in my head. For thirty-plus years, I tormented myself while my mother and Jack were out and about enjoying their lives. My reliving of those memories did not hurt them one bit, but just about killed me.

Once again, this book is not about reliving past traumas or assigning blame. I've come to understand that whether or not the perpetrator even intended to hurt the victim, the damage is the same. Our healing journey has nothing to do with our abusers. They have had enough of our lives. It's time to start living the life *we* choose.

Chapter 2: Reparenting

It's never too late to have a happy childhood.

—Tom Robbins[24]

Have you ever wondered how your life would be different if you hadn't been abused? God certainly knows *I* have. I pestered Him about it for decades, obsessed with the idea that I had been cheated out of something precious that I could never get back. This chapter is about learning how to give ourselves the childhood we wanted, starting *right now*. We can't change the past, but there is a very hurt child living inside you who deserves a chance to be loved, protected, and encouraged.

As an adult, I was so full of anger and bitterness that I relived my painful childhood on a daily (and sometimes even hourly) basis, letting my mother and Jack live "rent-free" in my head. I was depriving myself of any chance to be happy.

The journey to my own recovery has been a process of consciously learning how to reparent myself. As I started to discover who I was without the filter of drugs and alcohol, I began to realize that there was a twelve-year-old boy inside me who was hurting very badly.

He was still screaming for love and attention.

He still wanted to feel safe and cared for.

He still needed loving parents.

I cannot literally replace the lost years of my childhood, but I can become the parent I wish I had had to the boy I still am inside.

In this chapter, we will examine the lives and needs of our abused inner children in order to discover some different ways to reparent our way back to wholeness.

---

[24]Tom Robbins, *Still Life with Woodpecker* (New York: Bantam Books, 1980); quoted here from http://www.ahaparenting.com/blog/its-never-too-late-to-have-a-happy-childhood/.

There is a myth circulating out in the world that childhood is supposed to be one continuous joy ride, filled with nothing but happiness, sunshine, and ponies. Sitcoms, cartoons, and fairy tale movies support this fantasy. Dad is supportive and wise, Mom is loving and gentle, and no problem is so big that it cannot be solved within a half-hour programming slot. From these fantasy images, we build up idealized "family values," believing that we know what a family "should" be. The trouble starts when we compare our families with these fantasy ideals.

Since you've picked up this book, the chances are that you didn't have a perfect nuclear family, which the media would have you believe is the norm. At best, you may remember absent or unavailable parents who were unable to protect you because they were lost themselves. At worst, your home life was filled with rage and terror, and you remember cowering in your room, hiding from physical, mental, and/or sexual abuse.

Maybe you don't remember much from your childhood at all. Or maybe you idealized your family, pretending to yourself that everything was "fine," because the alternatives were far too scary.

Childhood is rough. Even with a happy, stable home, children must navigate the turbulent waters of growing up. Few of us make it out of childhood without a few scars. For survivors, however, the list of emotional wounds can be overwhelming.

For a time, many of us manage to get by using various coping mechanisms to numb out and escape from the pain of our pasts. But there comes a time when we face a crisis in our adult lives and are no longer able to stay in denial about being "just fine." For some of us, this crisis can come in a relationship with our partner or children; others may face it in their careers; some will hit bottom in their addictions; and others (like me) may be so stubborn that we have to be hit on every one of these levels at the same time.

In our society, this kind of crisis tends to come later for abused men than it does for abused women. Both by biology and sociology, women have greater access to their inner worlds than men do. By their late teens and early twenties, many young women have hit their existential bottom. The good news for them is that they tend to get treatment early.

Men, on the other hand, tend to carry those wounds for another two or three decades before they reach a place that is so painful that they are finally willing to reach out for help.

But when they do, if they stick with a recovery program, it turns out that the light at the end of the tunnel is pretty bright. I know that the past thirty-plus years, painful as they were, have shaped the man I am now. I'm not a pop psychology guru, spouting feel-good psychobabble at you. I've walked through hell to get here, and some days I find myself back there, hanging out in the muck and bad feelings. More often than not, however, I live in the productive world of recovery, which is better than I ever could have imagined.

No matter how wonderful or terrible our formative years may have been, we all long for the idealized version of home and family that we've seen on TV and in movies. For those of us who had abusive childhoods, this longing is intensified. Left untended, it may grow into a cancer that can choke the joy and happiness out of our adult lives.

Some of us who long for a loving home build walls against love because we fear being hurt again. Others of us may become addicted to being loved, even at the cost of our own self-esteem.

At the core of this maelstrom of longing and pain is a traumatized child—one who desperately needs safety, love, boundaries, attention, and approval.

Although we may be chronological adults, there is a part of our psyche that has not aged. We are stuck, usually at the age the trauma began, unable to heal, still desperately seeking acceptance.

It's Alive!

Clinical and forensic psychologist and author Dr. Stephen Diamond has observed that "the inner child is real! Not literally, not physically, but figuratively, metaphorically real."[25] At the best, our inner child contributes to our creativity, spontaneity, and joy and delight in the little things in life. At the worst, a wounded child fears the world, wants what it wants when it wants it, and will act out in the worst ways when confronted with frightening experiences or strong emotions.

Think of the conscious process of living your everyday life as being similar to driving a car. No big deal. Nothing you can't handle. You know how to drive. But for those of you with wounded inner children, your life can go from "just fine" to "out of control" in the blink of an eye.

Survivors tend to be hair-triggered. Because we are dealing with so many unresolved emotional wounds, we are highly sensitive. We drink or

---

[25]Stephen Diamond, Ph.D., *Essential Secrets of Psychotherapy: The Inner Child* (June 7, 2008), retrieved from https://www.psychologytoday.com/blog/evil-deeds/200806/essential-secrets-psychotherapy-the-inner-child/.

drug or engage in other compulsive behaviors to blunt that sensitivity, but that's not always practical. If someone cuts us off on the freeway, or if our partner says something that we take the wrong way, we may go from being able to handle our emotions to being out of control far more quickly than unwounded people do.

Picture an actual child throwing the worst tantrum you have ever seen. Now give that child your credit cards, your phone, and your keys. When you lose your tenuous grip on your emotional state, your adult self becomes a passenger, and your inner child self takes the wheel.

Have you ever noticed that small rational voice in the back of your mind that you can hear even when you're in the middle of a fit of rage with someone? You don't mean the things you're saying, but you still can't stop yourself from saying them. All the logic and reason in the world can't get out in front of an inner child with his hands on the wheel.

Your inner child is not trying to ruin your marriage or get you fired or thrown into jail. That frightened, hurting little boy inside of you is handling the overwhelming emotions the only way a child can—by throwing a fit. Children don't have an internal censor that regulates the expression of their emotions. Adults celebrate this lack of filter on shows like *Kids Say the Darndest Things*, and think it's hilarious on sitcoms and in movies. But when you have an angry child experiencing full-powered adult emotions, it's like putting a rocket on a roller coaster—a lot more fun to watch than to experience.

It is helpful to keep in mind that you, the adult, are doing great; you are logical, strong, and resourceful and have accumulated a lifetime of wisdom and know-how. The problem is that you may have a little saboteur who is keeping you from always being able to apply those skills to your life. The good news is that by addressing the root issues, you will be able to get back into the driver's seat and work with your inner child, instead of fighting him for control.

A big part of the trouble is that, since you didn't know about him, you have been a very permissive parent to yourself. Without realizing it, you have given in to most of your inner child's demands. All those times when you knew better than to do something but did it anyway—that was most likely the behavior of your wounded inner child. Those times in your life when emotion has overwhelmed reason, logic, and higher thinking—that was probably him, too.

An Expert Speaks Out: John Bradshaw

> At first, it may seem preposterous that a little child can continue to live in an adult body. But that is exactly what I am suggesting. I believe that this neglected, wounded inner child of the past is the major source of human misery.[26]

It sounds nuts to talk about an inner child. I might be from California, but I'm not a vegan, and I don't go around hugging trees. However, the truth remains that I've got this deeply wounded inner child.

In fact, everyone has an inner child. Even the most rational, well-adjusted, emotionally healthy people have one. For most people, the extent of their inner child's control over their lives is the occasional midnight ice-cream run. But the inner children of survivors of sexual abuse tend to be deeply wounded and often very angry.

The following pages present examples of the types of behaviors that abused children exhibit at various life stages, depending on when their inner child was wounded: Group 1 for the preschool age; Group 2 for the grade-school age; and Group 3 for the adolescent age.[27]

You may find that you relate to a combination of behaviors, or that your typical tantrums are different from the ones below. This is not a comprehensive guide by any means; it is only intended to give you a starting place to get a picture of the possible areas of your life that are being hijacked by your traumatized inner child.

---

[26]John Bradshaw, *Homecoming: Reclaiming and Healing Your Inner Child* (New York: Bantam, 1990), p. 7.

[27]See, for example, National Child Traumatic Stress Network (NCTSN), *Understanding Child Traumatic Stress* (2015), retrieved from http://www.nctsn.org/resources/audiences/parents-caregivers/understanding-child-traumatic-stress/; South Eastern CASA (Centre Against Sexual Assault), *Trauma Responses in Children* (September 3, 2012), retrieved from http://www.secasa.com.au/pages/trauma-responses-in-children/; and YWCA of Greater Flint [Michigan], *Sexually Abused Child Trauma Response by Age Group* (March 30, 2011), retrieved from https://volunteermanual.wordpress.com/2011/03/30/sexually-abused-child-trauma-response-by-age-group/.

Group 1: Signs of Trauma Responses

- You become anxious and clingy, fearing separation from loved ones. You often crave attention, and have a chronic fear of abandonment.

- You have trouble falling and staying asleep.

- You become overly competitive, even extremely aggressive, when you play with friends or loved ones.

- You set up a rigid routine that, if altered, makes you feel unsafe.

- You do the same thing over and over again to regain emotional control.

- You have "magical thinking" about your life (for example, "Bad things will happen if I am too happy").

- You are often told that you look "mean" or "angry" or "intense" when you don't feel that way.

Group 2: Signs of Trauma Responses

- You obsess over your influence on the people around you, both in terms of how they react to you as well as how you impact their lives (e.g., thinking that someone is mad at you for a minor infraction, or wondering if you make others unhappy by having angry thoughts or feelings about them).

- You compensate for feelings of helplessness by being highly controlling.

- You feel that your future is unsure, which causes you to engage in reckless behavior.

- You become angry and feel betrayed when you follow the rules and other people don't, or when things don't turn out the way you thought they would.

- You have a hard time maintaining close friendships because you often feel let down by others.

Group 3: Signs of Trauma Responses

- You suffer from the crushing effects of feeling that no one can truly understand you.

- You turn to drugs, alcohol, risky sex, or compulsive spending to escape from or manage feelings of anxiety or helplessness.

- You have a hard time with finances because you feel that the future is limited or uncertain, and therefore that planning extensively for the future is pointless.

- You are highly critical of yourself because your self-image is extremely low. You find it difficult to celebrate any victories, since nothing is ever good enough.

- You often engage in revenge fantasies against a person who hurt you in some way, but then feel guilty about those vengeful feelings.

- You isolate yourself and have a tendency toward depression and suicidal ideation.

Inner children are all different. Some are spoiled and angry, some are shy and anxious, and some are fearful and self-harming. But regardless of their personality, the good news is that, like flesh-and-bone kids, inner children respond quickly and well to even the smallest interventions.

When you reparent your inner child, providing a safe, loving environment in which he can heal from the trauma, you finally stop the doomed attempts to fix your pain externally (such as with a career, a mate, drugs, alcohol, status, or money) and start really healing from the inside.

Reparenting is about giving yourself the love, support, guidance, and boundaries that you didn't receive as a child. It's about taking the time to stop and notice that a part of you is still stuck, usually at the age that the abuse began. It's about caring for that part of you that has been hurting for years, perhaps even decades.

Your reparenting doesn't have to be dramatic. No one else even has to know you are doing it. The reparenting involves a mental shift from being critical to being compassionate toward yourself, which comes when you realize that you're dealing with a traumatized child.

How Working with the Inner Child Can Be Successful

Your inner child is a very real part of your psyche. Although, as an adult, you are chronologically past childhood, your inner child still influences how you respond emotionally to what people around you say and do. But you may not be aware of what your inner child is doing because it behaves at an unconscious level. Stephen Diamond puts it this way:

> True adulthood hinges on acknowledging, accepting, and taking responsibility for loving and parenting one's own inner child. For most adults, this never happens. Instead, their inner child has been denied, neglected, disparaged, abandoned, or rejected. We are told by society to "grow up," putting childish things aside. To become adults, we've been taught that our inner child—representing our childlike capacity for innocence, wonder, awe, joy, sensitivity, and playfulness—must be stifled, quarantined, or even killed. In fact, these so-called grown-ups or adults are unwittingly being constantly influenced or covertly controlled by this unconscious inner child. For many, it is not an adult self-directing their lives, but rather an emotionally wounded inner child inhabiting an adult body.[28]

---

[28]Stephen Diamond, Ph.D., *Essential Secrets of Psychotherapy: The Inner Child*, retrieved from https://www.psychologytoday.com/blog/evil-deeds/200806/essential-secrets-psychotherapy-the-inner-child/.

REPARENTING

We are taught how to grow up, get a job, and be a good provider, but we are never taught how to deal with our inner child. We don't understand that impulses that feel like self-sabotage are usually the mischief of our own neglected and hurt inner child.

The following list presents some of the most common reasons that your inner child needs active, loving reparenting from you as an adult:

- You suffered from chronic parental neglect or abandonment.

- You suffered from physical, spiritual, mental, sexual, or emotional abuse.

- You had highly critical or domineering caregivers.

- You had caregivers who were addicted to drugs or alcohol.

- You had caregivers who suffered from mental illness.

- You experienced the death of a primary caregiver while you were young.

When we were six or seven, we didn't think to ourselves, "Well, Mom's a drunk, and Dad's violent abuse is just him acting out his unhealed childhood traumas. That's why it feels so rotten at home." Instead, we did what kids do—we internalized the pain of our primary caregivers in order to keep our world, if not ideal, at least operational.

According to John Bradshaw, a child has two ways of expressing his most basic needs: "My parents are okay" and "I matter."[29] When these needs are not met, a child will adapt to survive. However, most of these adaptations will be maladaptive. In the terrifying face of a world where primary caregivers are mentally unhealthy, a child will do whatever he has to do in order to twist the facts to suit the outcome he needs.

"My Parents Are Okay"

If we could slow down the mind to actually see the mental gymnastics necessary to make this work, it might look something like this: *I need my*

---

[29]John Bradshaw, *Homecoming: Reclaiming and Healing Your Inner Child* (New York: Bantam, 1992), p. 21.

parents to be okay. If they are not, my world is fundamentally unsafe. If they are okay, it must be me who is not.

From this premise, an abused child begins the cycle of self-blame and recrimination that leads to low self-esteem.

"I Matter"

The violation of the most basic personal boundaries makes it almost impossible for a child to feel that he truly matters. But incest often has an additional emotional component. The child is made to feel *special* because of the abuse. This sends a conflicting message to the child that is potentially even more damaging than the abuse itself. Because survivors often feel that for them to matter they must place their basic needs below other people's desires, normal social interaction becomes very difficult for them.

People can get stuck in destructive behavior patterns because they are seeking the validation that they didn't receive when they were young. This desire to matter and be loved by others is a normal human impulse. However, any form of child abuse can warp this basic need into a constant torment in which the need for external validation of our "okayness" is all-consuming.

The first building block of self-esteem is the sense that we have a place in the universe, that we matter. At first, we learn that we matter to our mother and father. From that basic position, we learn that we matter to ourselves. We learn to identify our wants and needs, and, since we believe that we matter, our needs and wants matter, too. From there, we engage in increasingly complex interactions to fulfill increasingly complex desires.

If this process is interrupted at the first stage and we don't feel that we truly matter to our parents, we are then unable to take the next step, which is to learn that we matter to ourselves. We are stuck in an endless loop, desperately seeking validation from people around us that we matter. It is an instinctive response. But ultimately, it is doomed to fail.

Adults cannot easily replace the primary bonding that is meant to occur in early childhood. First of all, it isn't practical. It isn't even ultimately desirable for a friend or mate to step into a parenting role, especially if the parenting role that is needed is based on unmet needs from early childhood.

Babies and toddlers need their parents all the time. Unless they are asleep, babies are always right next to their primary caretakers; and toddlers may stray a few feet away, but rarely let their parents get out of sight. Trying to replicate this in adulthood with another adult is a foolproof recipe for a failed relationship, an addiction, or both.

Whether we are still seeking approval from our invalidating parent, or we are looking for approval in a romantic relationship, or we even seek it out from our own children, we cannot replace the internal need for validation through external sources.

But hope is not lost.

When adults feel emotionally empty and instinctively try to fill that void with the love of another person, they will ultimately be unfulfilled. But when they recognize that feeling of emptiness for what it is—the need to know that they matter in the universe—they can fill that basic need for themselves consciously and systematically.

Conscious reparenting is the deliberate act of telling your inner self, through words and actions, that you matter and that you are loved. You do this the same way you would parent an actual child who has been severely traumatized—namely, with compassion and patience.

An Expert Speaks Out:
Jerry Moe, M.A.

> In working with children challenged by alcoholism and other drug addiction in their families, I have found there are many essential ingredients that can make a difference in their lives. Structure, consistency, understanding, kindness, and caring are all critical. Creating a safe place and listening with heart empowers children to find their own voice. Spending quality time and providing opportunities for fun, laughter, and play create a sense of connection, belonging, and hope. The inner child needs all of these nutrients as well.[30]

Reparenting and Therapy

Ultimately, the reparenting process is an internal one. But it is possible to get help along the way. It can be helpful to find temporary positive reparenting experiences with other people, such as therapists or spiritual mentors. But unless the other person knows what is going on and how to direct the process, these relationships can end up as unhealthy dependencies for the survivor.

---

[30]Personal communication. Jerry Moe is the National Director of Children's Programs for the Betty Ford Center, in Rancho Mirage, California.

Feeling heard, being truly validated by another person, can show us what it feels like to matter in this fundamental way. But if we anchor that feeling to a person, when that individual separates from us in any way, it can feel like abandonment, which just makes us feel worse. We have to learn validation from others, but then anchor it within ourselves.

For many of us, therapy is our first experience with structured, positive reparenting. Therapy offers a safe, professional connection with another person who is truly validating and supportive. For survivors of sexual abuse, the therapeutic reparenting aspect is one of the unique and most effective benefits of going to therapy.

When we are truly validated by another, that person can show us how to validate ourselves. Many of us have spent so many years putting ourselves down, or last, or in destructive situations that we have no idea how to validate ourselves.

Once we have been validated externally, we can start the process of creating internal validation. We may have wonderful partners, children, and friends, but the therapeutic relationship is unique, in that it requires nothing from us except participation. Good therapists do not require their clients to be anything other than what they are. For some of us, this healthy unconditional acceptance offers the first experience of being fine just as we are.

I remember experiencing this with my therapist, Deborah Meints-Pierson. It was such a relief when I realized that I didn't have to *do* or *be* anything. I could be late, stubborn, sad, or even angry, and she would still care for me and be there for me. It finally began to dawn on me that I was free to be honest with myself in the presence of another person.

Many survivors learn to be chameleons from a young age. They twist and contort themselves into whatever they think will please the people around them in order to minimize the abuse. While all human beings are people-pleasers to some extent, survivors make a career out of keeping others happy. They can easily lose track of who they truly are and what they really want because they are so busy guessing what they think everyone else wants from them.

This makes personal relationships very complicated. It is also why therapy can be so effective in showing clients how to reparent themselves. This is not to say that all therapists are good. You can expect to go through some intense emotions in therapy, but if you consistently leave the office feeling bad and confused, and without learning positive coping skills to use on your own, then you might want to consider finding a different therapist.

REPARENTING

What Story Have You Been Telling Yourself?

For many years, I told myself a story about myself that was not true. The "facts" of the story were based on false beliefs that I had allowed into my life for the previous thirty-plus years. Dysfunctional parents had driven those beliefs into me, and so I believed a story that could not be further from the truth.

Words and actions that I accepted as a child as absolute truths turned out to be warped representations of reality that I attempted to untwist into some semblance of "normal" in order to feel safe. I truly believed that the abuse I suffered was my own fault, that I was a bad child, maybe even evil. I believed that, since my mother did not love me, I must be unlovable. I believed that, since the pastor of my church told me when I was fourteen that my stepfather's sexual abuse of me was a "normal" part of my growing up, and that I would not turn out gay, there must be something wrong with *me* because I was so sick about it. I believed that I didn't deserve to be happy. I believed that in order to be loved, I had to subjugate my needs to someone else's abusive desires.

I held on to those false story lines well into my adult years. Eventually, the twisted reality that I created to serve my needs as a child turned into a personal belief system that served no purpose in my life other than to destroy me as an adult. By using the tool of reparenting my inner child, I have been able to solve the deeper issues that many of us face in recovery, yet can never seem to heal. It is difficult for us to identify these issues because they have become so much a part of our fundamental belief system by the time we become adults.

After I worked the twelve steps in A.A. and in Co-dependents Anonymous (CoDA), I felt that there was still something missing. Although I was much better, I continued to have a lot of self-doubt and low self-esteem issues. In addition, I wanted a life of freedom, which for me meant not being married to A.A. for the rest of my life. Don't get me wrong. A.A. saved my life. And for many other survivors, A.A. is the only thing that makes them feel complete. But I noticed that the constant turning to my sponsor was keeping me stuck in my victim role, looking for someone else to solve my problems and make me better.

I didn't want to keep sticking a bandage over my wounded self-esteem; I wanted to be full of deep and abiding self-confidence. I didn't want to talk about my problems every week; I wanted to replace my problems with a life of purpose and victories. For me, that meant searching for additional tools to use in my recovery—tools that I could use to do some emotional surgery on myself and to treat the deeper causes of my pain.

There are many survivors who feel the same way. A.A. is designed to help people stop abusing alcohol. However, it is not designed to address the specific needs of sexual abuse survivors. I would encourage any sexual abuse survivor to seek out all available tools, try them, and then decide which are the best fit.

At this point in my own recovery, I have a toolbox that is overflowing with recovery tools that I use all the time. But the best tool for me has been reparenting. I realize that this might be hard for some fellow survivors to hear. Inner-child work can be seen as a challenge to masculinity.

Chapter 1 addresses many of the issues that come up with regard to the roles of men in Western cultures, but I think one of the saddest effects of these gender values is that men are afraid to get in touch with their own sore hearts. We are supposed to be emotionless, muscle-bound desperados. We aren't supposed to process feelings or be sensitive. We definitely aren't supposed to have an inner child.

But according to those same societal rules, children aren't supposed to be sexually abused. Yet, they are—and as a result, men have abused inner children. We have to stop accepting other people's broken stories as our truth. It's not true that I was a bad kid. I didn't deserve to be abused. And society is wrong, too. Boys are abused every day—and it is okay for us to heal from that, which involves being strong enough to deal with our past. If being manly is about being brave, strong, and courageous, then survivors who work to heal their past traumatic wounds are the manliest guys on Earth.

For me, even though the journey to wholeness started with A.A., it wasn't until I started doing inner-child work that I went from crawling to sprinting toward recovery.

It's Never Too Late to Have a Happy Childhood

For years, I "did everything wrong." I sought validation through sex, money, approval, and obsession. When those failed me, I turned to alcohol and drugs. It wasn't until I became consciously aware of what that emptiness was really stemming from that I was able to truly address it. I needed to reparent myself. No other human being would be able to give me the time, attention, or understanding that a functioning parent would have. But I could give those to myself. I couldn't go back in time, but I could give my inner child a better, happier life, starting now.

I first saw a therapist about my abuse in 1988. It's not a new story. From the outside, my life was amazing: a beautiful and loving wife, great kids, a big house, two cars, a successful career, and everything else that society said would make me happy. Yet, I was spiraling into an increasingly hopeless depression. I felt like a ticking time bomb.

Grief and shame had a chokehold on my heart that was so intense that I could literally feel it. When I started to seriously plan how to take my own life, I decided to see a therapist as one final hopeless Hail Mary.

As it turned out, my therapist was pretty great. He put me on Prozac, which reduced the suicidal ideation, and he talked me through many a depressing moment. The trouble was that I was not a great client at that time. I chased the medication with a shot or two of whiskey and a line or three of cocaine. Sometimes I even went to a session drunk or high. I managed to limp through two years of therapy-lite, but it relieved enough of my built-up pressure that I was able to function.

Nevertheless, true to form, I decided that I was fixed as soon as I had the tiniest bit of relief. I discontinued the meds, left the therapist, quit my excellent job, packed up my family, and moved to the California desert to start my own company. In fact, I quit just about everything except drinking and drugging.

Death and taxes might be certain—but Benjamin Franklin forgot to mention one other crucial thing that is also quite permanent in your life: You.

All those love songs have it wrong. Instead of "I've got *you*, babe," we should be singing, "I've got *me*, babe." Wherever I go, there I am. In my mad dash to the Coachella Valley, I did my level best to escape my own demons, but I soon found that I couldn't run fast or far enough to leave myself behind.

I couldn't even ditch the parts I didn't really like. Alcohol and drugs followed me everywhere like a shadow. I had thought that moving to a new area, away from all my childhood pains, would somehow make everything better. However, all I accomplished was to enjoy a few weeks of vacation time. It was not long before all my self-doubt, low self-esteem, depression, and despair showed up at my door.

This time, I didn't hesitate to get help. But like addicts the world over, I didn't really *want* help, I just wanted a shortcut. Again, I saw a therapist, but quit seeing him in record time, telling myself that he was a jerk. The reality is that he was just doing his job. I was the one who was being a jerk. A surefire way to make therapy a total waste of time is to lie to your therapist, especially about cocaine and alcohol addiction.

It took another four years for my tolerance of pain and self-destruction to give out again. (For all the details, see Chapter 7, below, "Hitting Bottom.") In 2005, desperate to save my marriage, I started to see my third therapist, Deborah Meints-Pierson. I felt comfortable and safe with Deborah, so eventually I starting talking about the sexual abuse, but at first only in relation to the affair I had recently had. For the first few months, I went alone. Then Deborah suggested that she see Cathy and me as a couple, so for the next year, Cathy and I worked on our relationship together.

Every time the topic of drugs or alcohol abuse arose, I turned into a denial machine. The drinking and drugging kept me in the victim role. It was my way of anesthetizing my pain and shame. My inability to be honest about my substance abuse made it impossible to do the deeper work that would be necessary to heal from sexual abuse. I had to find out for myself that no amount of alcohol or drugs (prescription or street) would ever permanently take away the pain and shame. I was going to have to do the work to heal myself. There would be no shortcuts.

Once I got alcohol and drugs out of my life (a long story that I will tell later), I was able to start working on my abuse-related issues. Some experts say that a person must have at least a year of sobriety before starting this work. However, I agree with the experts who believe we must begin our healing journey the moment we can. It is a long road, and the journey is not harmed by a slow and gentle start.

After a year of doing a lot of intense work with Deborah, I found it relatively easy to make the transition from working on my "everyday issues" to delving into the much deeper wounds associated with my sexual abuse. To recover, I was finally willing to do whatever it would take.

I had heard the term *inner child* mentioned in the past, but, quite frankly, I thought it was nuts. The first time Deborah brought it up in session, I had to do a great deal of self-reminding that "Randy 2.0" was open-minded. But I am eternally grateful to Deborah for not giving up on me out of sheer frustration. I am also grateful to myself for taking that first step toward healing my inner child, a part of me that had been hurting for virtually my entire life.

I will never forget the first time I saw my broken inner child. I was sitting quietly on the couch in Deborah's office, in a meditative state with my eyes closed. I don't remember her exact words, but I vividly recall my inner child coming out from the shadows. I felt that a door had inched open, and from behind it a sad-faced and scared kid cautiously peeked his head out. He was so little and so hurt. It broke my heart to see the expression on his face and know exactly what he was feeling: too terrified to trust anyone, but desperate to be loved.

The whole time, Deborah was letting me and my inner child know that we were in a safe space. I remember Little Randy asking me if I was sure that Deborah could be trusted. I *felt* more than I heard the words when he asked, "Are you sure it's okay to come out?" He was so scared and untrusting, so broken and hurt, so unsure.

Most of that hour was spent just helping him to feel safe enough not to bolt back into the shadows. Hell, he really didn't even trust *me*. I just remember seeing him look at me, asking over and over again if it were safe. "Remember," he would say, "we have trusted others before, who have failed and hurt us. Are you sure it's okay to trust Deborah? Am I going to be able to trust you? Are you really going to protect me?"

Seeing this part of me that was so frightened was devastating. I suddenly understood that all those years of self-condemnation and self-criticism had come down on a twelve-year-old boy. I had hurt myself for too long. All I could do now was assure my inner child that I was going to be there for him and protect him. I would have to save him from myself.

I don't know how many times I had sponsors, therapists, or friends tell me, with total, moist-eyed sincerity, "Randy, you need to learn how to love yourself." I choked down those words like syrupy-sweet cold medicine: quickly and with a self-congratulatory pat on the back. I loved myself, thank you very much. And if I thought about it during the dark days and darker nights, it was only with fist-to-the-wall frustration.

How was a person who didn't love himself supposed to go about doing it? I was learning that it was not only ineffective but unfair to foist that burden onto my wife. But how was I supposed to just start loving myself? After decades of needing a line of coke just to look myself in the mirror, that seemed impossible.

It wasn't until that session when I saw the small, bruised, and terrified face of the boy I had once been that I understood that loving ourselves isn't something we learn how to do. Rather, it's something we learn how *not* to do.

Although I would have walked on hot coals before admitting it to anyone, even Deborah, the protective walls I had built to keep myself from loving myself came crashing down that day.

As I held the little boy in my arms, he and I wept together. I can't describe how relieved I was that I was finally there for him—forty years late, but I was there.

Reparenting Through Journaling

Reparenting didn't come naturally to me. My default settings were always on self-condemnation, so I didn't know how to stop being hateful to myself. That first experience of "seeing" my inner child and realizing how small and vulnerable he was went a long way toward curbing my self-abuse. But I still had to learn how to effectively communicate with him on a regular basis, or I was just going to fall back into my old patterns.

The most direct and effective communication process I used then (and still do) was journaling. When I sat down to write, I would invite both God and my inner child to journal with me. Sometimes, if no words came to me right away, I would start by drawing a small picture of how God looked to me on that day. Then I would draw a stick figure image of my inner child that showed how *he* was feeling that day. God would be at the top left of my journal entry, and Little Randy at the top right.

Mind you, I am no artist. What was important was that those little scrawls meant something to me. I was just starting to get used to the idea that my life belonged to *me*—that I didn't have to spend every minute of every day figuring out what the people around me wanted from me, and then twisting myself into a pretzel to give it to them. I was starting to live as if *I* were the person who mattered most to me. The concept of "good selfishness," which comes so easily to people with healthy self-esteem and good boundaries, was finally starting to get through to me. People had told me for years that I needed to take better care of myself, but I had no idea how to do that.

Getting to know my inner child was a big part of that new understanding. Although I was scared to start the dialogue, fearing that I would be overwhelmed by painful memories and emotions, I found that, instead of being overwhelmed, I was actually able to be gentle with and compassionate toward my own story for the first time.

I reacted to my inner child much as I would have to a real child who was in my care and hurting. I even found that I was able to listen to his feelings and memories with a very small but profound distance. Instead of crying for myself as a victim, I was able to cry for the boy who had been victimized.

This was not a little thing for me, since I had spent decades feeling victimized by my past, feeling that I was subjected every day to the anger and shame of the abuse. Through this healing process, however, I was beginning to understand that I had been hurt as a boy, but in the decades since then, there had been no abuse except for that I had inflicted on myself.

I began to feel the difference between letting the past truly be the past and holding on to it so closely that my whole identity was shaped by the worst moments in my life. I still had to deal with the psychological wounds and traumas of my past, but I was starting to see how they didn't have to define me.

These profound revelations did not just drop out of my head and into my journal, like manna from heaven. Rather, I just described the most boring details of my day-to-day life and how I felt about them. As I sat at my desk, Little Randy would be sitting contentedly, resting his chin in his hands, watching me write. Soon, I invited him to be a part of my life through journaling, but at first he preferred to just sit quietly with me.

Those were good times, and they also helped me to remember the good times I had had as a child. I could remember the real Little Randy sitting with chin in hand, watching fat bumblebees do their slow, lazy dance through the summer grass at my grandparents' house. In those days, I felt as safe and happy as any boy in the world. When old memories like that had surfaced before, I had been filled with bitterness and anger that my happy past had been stolen from me, along with my innocence and sense of self-worth.

But seeing that bumblebee memory through my eyes as a boy gave me so much pleasure. I understood that stealing my inner peace by covering up all my happy memories with anger and pain meant stealing the joy from the little boy inside me. And I was no longer willing to do that. By learning how to protect him and helping him to feel safe, I was also letting myself be happy. By loving him, I was loving myself. I needed that bridge to take "loving myself" from a frustrating mental exercise to a positive experiential process. After that, my recovery progressed much more quickly.

Non-dominant Handwriting (aka Journaling on Steroids)

My experience with journaling became more profound after I was introduced to non-dominant handwriting by John Bradshaw. According to him, writing with your non-dominant hand (your left hand if you are right-handed; your right hand if you are left-handed) calls on the non-dominant side of your brain, bypassing the more controlling side. That makes it easier to get in touch with the feelings of your inner child.

When Deborah, my therapist, first introduced me to this method, I thought it sounded ridiculous. I didn't tell her, but I actually thought she should ask for a refund for all those years she had spent in graduate school. But I had told her that I would be open-minded, so I was willing to do an inner-child meditation, and it paid off some amazing dividends.

At first, still thinking the whole method was hogwash, I grudgingly agreed to complete an assignment written only with my non-dominant left hand. Then I heard my therapist's voice in my head: "Randy, just put the pencil on the paper and start writing. Don't edit, don't second-guess what's being written, just let it flow."

I started writing about how stupid I thought the exercise was and what a waste of time it was. But then the strangest thing happened. Once I started focusing on writing instead of fighting it, my inner child came out. Right off the bat, he told me how scared he was and how he didn't trust me, and how hurt he was because I had quit surfing and playing the guitar. But he was glad, he said, that I was allowing him to have his voice, the voice he had not had for some forty years, and he said he was hopeful that we could start healing together. But then, as quickly as he had emerged, he slipped back into the shadows of my heart.

As I put down my pencil, I sat back in my chair, flooded with thoughts and feelings. I certainly couldn't call the process hogwash anymore. It was powerful and real, and committed me to taking better care of myself than I had in years. I felt that I had been confronted by a beloved child whom I had inadvertently hurt. That deeply saddened me about what I had done, but I also felt protective of Little Randy. I knew I had abandoned my dreams and some of the things I loved to do, but I had no idea of the extent to which that had harmed me.

Finding my inner child gave me the bridge I needed to make self-care a real practice. It makes sense that inner-child work would be so powerful for survivors of sexual abuse: it is our inner child, after all, that was abused. At some level, we stopped growing and became "stuck" at the time the trauma took place. For years we have had an inner child running the show because we didn't have the tools to reach or heal him.

To use this handwriting method, find a quiet place to sit where you can close the door and shut out any distractions. Put on some relaxing music if you like. When you're ready, start writing with your non-dominant hand. You put a pencil to paper and let what happens happen. It is important that you not edit or second-guess what you write. You want to let your inner child speak freely.

Right about now you may be thinking, *Randy, you have truly plunged into the deep end of the crazy pool!*

But I couldn't argue with what was happening. I really was getting in touch with some deep, stuffed-away part of myself, and that part had a lot to tell me.

There was one session I remember really well, when Little Randy was trying to tell me a story, and I became impatient with how long it was taking him. Suddenly, he said, loud and clear: "Look how impatient you are with me! You never let me have any fun! You have to rush everything I want to do, and be so perfect. I'm tired of it! I quit! I'm trying to tell you how I feel, and you're in a big hurry to do something else. You never give me a chance!"

After I got over the shock of listening to me literally telling myself off, I took in how true those words were. They gave me a perspective that I had never had before. I had always known that I was impatient with myself, but I hadn't understood that my impatience caused my inner child to get stubborn and shut down. He is highly sensitive to being rushed, especially by someone who doesn't have time for him. The triggers for each inner child may be different, but what will be the same is how the inner child will take over control when he is triggered.

For years I had believed that my impatience was a character flaw. Whenever I felt rushed, I turned into a tantrum-throwing child. When I wanted something, I wanted it *now*, and if I couldn't get it now, then to hell with it, I would figure out something else. I had messed up jobs, relationships, and even my own personal goals because of this tendency to shut down whenever I didn't immediately get what I wanted. I blamed this on my impatience, but it wasn't that at all. My inner child was getting triggered by my own impatience and shutting me down.

I had often wished that someone would just tell me what I had to do to stop hurting so much. And here was the answer: a prescription for happiness—*for* me and *from* me. Written on the page, right there: "Take time for yourself. Give yourself space to think and feel. Slow down and listen to your inner self."

That session helped me to understand how important it is to learn these lessons myself. I couldn't have gotten this kind of insight if I had googled a few articles and taken advice from other people's experiences. My inner child wasn't looking for lollipops or toys. He wanted me to chill the heck out. He wanted an extra five minutes of my time for him to gather his thoughts and tell me his stories. I can't tell you what a difference five minutes have made in my life. My triggers are unique to me, just as yours are unique to you, but it's worth the time to find out for yourself what they are. And it's important that you honor whatever your inner child wants to write. Do not fight it or hurry him. His voice desperately needs to be heard.

Other Ways to Engage with Your Inner Child

Through those journaling sessions with Deborah, I learned that there were other simple ways that I could help my inner child to feel safe and loved. Just making him a part of an afternoon as we played fetch with my dog could make my whole being calm down—as if a tense muscle that I hadn't even known I possessed suddenly relaxed after forty years. Simply including my inner child in the game was enough to release that long-held tension.

Sometimes I go for a walk, consciously bringing my inner child along with me. Or, when I'm out riding my bike, I may act like a kid, weaving in out of the lines on the street like a slalom racer (but only when it's safe to do so). Or, while I'm walking near the ocean surf with my wife, I may let my inner child play a little by splashing Cathy as the waves crash on the beach. Sometimes I may dash through puddles in the rain, not caring if I get dirty or look "cool." I knew all of this as a child, and now Little Randy is helping me to learn it again. There are countless ways you can get in touch with your inner child; you just have to be willing to have fun and not care what anyone else thinks. Your innocence may have been stolen years ago, but there is no reason you have to keep stealing it from yourself now.

The best and fastest way that I have found to reparent my inner child is to systematically, moment-by-moment and day-by-day, write in my journal with my non-dominant hand. Whenever I have trouble figuring out why I am in a funk or beating myself up, journaling in this way lets my inner child talk to me to reveal the real problem. If I ever start to get the feeling that I am on the verge of spiraling down into negative self-talk, I realize that I am starting to push my inner child too hard, and I take a break. I can play with my Labradoodle or go for a walk to get out of my adult role and let my inner child have a reward. When I come back, I am refreshed and ready to focus. I don't have to worry about the little saboteur inside me.

Whenever my emotions start to overpower me because I feel neglected or like a failure, I simply talk with Little Randy, reminding him that he is not a failure, but a lovable human being. Simply devoting a few minutes to journaling about my lovable attributes and the victories in my life can make all the difference in the world.

Before I learned this journaling technique, I would just argue with myself and find ways to undercut my positive character traits and past accomplishments. When it came to my self-image, I was an expert at snatching defeat from the jaws of victory. But when I discovered my inner child, my instinct was to protect rather than to criticize the sad and scared twelve-year-old child in front of me. I can't emphasize enough how healing these journaling exercises can be.

The Reparenting Journey

Children, inner or real, don't hold grudges. They are eager to be loved, to have fun, and to be soothed. Reparenting takes some time, requiring (1) a commitment to trust the process, and (2) the willingness to offer yourself the loving, safe space that you wished you had been given as a child. In return, you get to soothe your own soul and find your own unique prescription for a happy, healthy life.

There will be times when you fall short. You may forget to keep an appointment with your inner child. You may be overwhelmed by emotions and shut down. You may brush your inner child aside when he is asking for attention. All of those things are okay. They will happen. But now you get to be the parent that you wish you had had.

If you had a critical parent, it's highly likely that you will be critical of your inner child's process at some point. Instead of ignoring that, or justifying the criticism, tell yourself what you most wanted to hear from your critical parent. Your amends might sound like, "Hey, I'm sorry about that. I'm learning every day how to be a better parent for you, and I made a mistake. I just want you to know that *you're* not the mistake. I love you. I get that I was critical, and I hurt your feelings. In the future, I will work on pointing out the things I love about you. There are so many. You're an amazing kid. For example, I love that you are creative" (or athletic, kind, smart, funny, or whatever).

If you had a distant or abandoning parent, you will probably be distant with your inner child at some point, or abandon him by failing to make time for him. In this case, your amends might sound like, "Hey, I'm really sorry I went away without telling you. I didn't realize I was doing that. I'm working to be more present with you. I love spending time with you. You're my favorite kid in the whole world. What can I do to make it right with you?"

Perfection is not important in this process—being consistently loving is and having the willingness to try again. Practice observing your inner child's behavior. You may want to experiment with letting him tell his abusive parent how he feels. Give him a safe place to express his emotions. The goal is to heal the wounded places inside yourself and to give yourself the loving parenting that you didn't get as a child.

Setting Boundaries

Almost as important as creating a safe, loving place for your inner child is creating healthy boundaries for your adult self and sticking to them. Remember, the chances are pretty good that your inner child is spoiled and is used to throwing a tantrum to get his way. All of your emotional triggers are not going to disappear the day after you start working with your inner child. You will still get triggered sometimes, and your inner child will still throw fits. Your old patterns may be to overeat, to have compulsive sex, to spend money, or to get into fights. It's important to start setting boundaries with your inner child so that *you* get back into the driver's seat.

Instead of waiting until you are in the middle of a triggered emotional response to your inner child, take the time to set and maintain healthy boundaries with him as a day-to-day practice. When you ask him what he wants or needs at various times during the day, and he says, "a box of candy," or "a new toy" or "a day at the park," you can set loving boundaries in a gentle way. Instead of a whole box of candy, let him have one piece after dinner. Instead of a new toy, have him make something with you, or tell him he will have to wait for a birthday or special event. Instead of spending a day at the park, devote an hour to running around the block or playing with a pet. Just the way you would handle an actual child, you can set boundaries with your inner child.

What is truly fascinating about this reparenting process is that survivors who spend time setting and keeping boundaries wake up a few months down the road, discovering that they are suddenly able to stick to that diet or exercise program. They are more productive at work and less forgetful. They have more money because they are no longer compulsively overspending. And all of these benefits come naturally from learning to set and keep healthy boundaries with your inner child. So go on: lose that extra twenty pounds, pay down that debt, and start that project you have been putting off.

You are your own best guide on this journey. You know what good, loving, healthy parenting looks like—and now is your chance to have that perfect father figure that you longed for when you were growing up. It is never too late to have a happy childhood. Just because someone robbed you of it once doesn't mean that you have to let him or her rob you for the rest of your life. So, have a happy childhood, starting today! You've earned it. And the little child inside you certainly deserves it.

Chapter 3:
Trauma Triggers

After a traumatic experience, the human system of self-preservation seems to go onto permanent alert, as if the danger might return at any moment.

—Judith Lewis Herman[31]

In order to successfully reparent your inner child, you must be able to identify your psychological triggers. A psychological (or "trauma") trigger is any current experience that sets off a distressing memory of a painful past experience. The trigger can be an image, a sound, a smell, or a combination of two or more stimuli.

Although our emotional responses when we are triggered can appear to be inappropriate to the circumstances, the abused child within us is expressing emotions that he has repressed for months or years, perhaps even for decades. As we reparent ourselves into wholeness, we have to make space for our inner child to acknowledge his feelings instead of repressing them. This involves a difficult balance because we want to be able to express our emotional responses without creating more problems for ourselves in the present.

We can be triggered by a food that has a certain texture, by a pair of shoes positioned in just the wrong way, or, as was the case for me recently, by words innocently spoken to me by my wife. Although the trigger itself is not necessarily frightening, the experience it provokes in us is not based on the present reality, but on our past trauma. And that can be devastating.

When triggers hit, they often feel overwhelming. By their nature, triggers take us by surprise. A romantic partner coming on to you by touching you in the same place your abuser did can instantly send you into a traumatic trance. You spiral down into shame and go "passive," or you

---

[31]Judith Lewis Herman, *Trauma and Recovery: The Aftermath of Violence—From Domestic Abuse to Political Terror* (New York: Basic Books, 1992), p. 35. Judith Lewis Herman, M.D., is an Associate Clinical Professor of Psychiatry at Harvard Medical School.

push your partner away emotionally, physically, or both.

If you walk into a room that smells like the one where you were most often abused, you go into hyperdrive. Your entire body tenses, you are "on alert" for danger, and even an unintended sarcastic comment can send you into a past memory of an emotionally abusive situation from your childhood. You might laugh on the outside, but on the inside you just want to disappear.

The following list provides a few examples of triggers and the conditioned responses they can set off. Your list will be unique, but the triggers below are often mentioned by survivors of sexual abuse:

> *Smells:* alcohol, perfume, cigarettes, cigars, lotions, candles, burning wood, charcoal, incense.
>
> *Sights:* wallpaper patterns, shoes, clothing, pictures.
>
> *Sounds:* car engines, car exhausts, car horns, train whistles, music, TV programs.
>
> *Anniversaries:* birthdays, holidays.

It's important to be sensitive to our own triggers and to treat ourselves with compassion when we are triggered. Being triggered can be like experiencing the trauma or abuse all over again. Some triggers can be so intense that they actually set off a post-traumatic stress disorder (PTSD) flashback to a specific abusive incident. A PTSD flashback is a mental reexperiencing of the traumatic event. PTSD flashbacks can be indistinguishable from present reality. Triggers can feel as traumatic as the original injury.

An Expert Speaks Out:
Aphrodite T. Matsakis, Ph.D.

> Having triggers, or reacting to them, does not mean you are crazy or defective. However, when you are blind to what you are feeling and why you are feeling it, you may be driven to act in ways that do not serve you well.[32]

---

[32] Aphrodite T. Matsakis, *I Can't Get Over It: A Handbook for Trauma Survivors*, 2nd ed. (Oakland, CA: New Harbinger, 1996), pp. 113–114.

TRAUMA TRIGGERS

While the abuse was happening to us, we often suppressed the natural feelings of rage, fear, and shame. If we didn't deal with those feelings at the time, they can come out years later during moments when we are triggered, which feels terrible. The triggered emotions can be sadness, irritability, shame, hopelessness, or rage. After the trigger has passed, we may judge ourselves very harshly. From an outsider's perspective, we may be overreacting, but from the inside, our emotional response feels entirely appropriate.

Communication with our loved ones is the key to success in emotional growth. If we are able to clearly and lovingly state our needs to our loved ones *before* we are triggered, when we do react to unintentional triggers, our loved ones are more likely to be understanding and less likely to take our overreaction personally.

Communication with loved ones is especially important in the early stages of the recovery process, when these triggers can occur frequently, and we are less aware that we are reacting to past traumas rather than to present circumstances. As we start to deal with our abuse and its effects on us, we become less numbed and repressed. But when we begin to feel our emotions, we can become hypersensitive to experiences that remind us of the abuse.

This is particularly true for those of us who (like me) started recovery for substance abuse around the same time that we started dealing with childhood traumas. Before that, I had been using drugs and alcohol to stay numb and shut down my feelings. When I stopped that, I didn't at first have any good coping skills to replace the bad coping skills of substance abuse. I was just one walking emotional wound, feeling hurt by anything and everything that touched me. For the first time since I started drinking and drugging at fifteen, I was actually feeling my emotions without the filter of a chemical anesthesia.

Whenever I walked into a coffee shop that brewed the same kind of coffee that my mother used to make, I would be filled with overwhelming feelings of grief and anxiety. If a stranger cut me off on the freeway, I would react with the most powerful feelings of rage I had ever experienced. It wasn't the rudeness of the driver that I was reacting to in the present moment; it was the feeling of being out of control of my own experience. Being cut off by another driver triggered feelings of helplessness, which in turn started a cascade of related emotions that led from rage to depression.

If it hadn't been for my sponsor, my therapist, and all the supportive people who had already been through those first painful steps in the healing process in their own lives, I'm not sure I would have made it past those first terrible months.

One of the most important skills that I learned from all those people was how to ask for support around my triggers. By reaching out when I *wasn't* triggered, I was able to ask for help in a clear, calm manner. In the early stage of my recovery, I let my wife and close friends know that I sometimes become angry when my inner child is triggered, but they should not take that anger personally. In most cases, when I got triggered, they were highly supportive. In fact, they often recognized before I did that I was being triggered, and they helped me to recognize the triggers that set me off. Today, I still get triggered, sometimes on a daily basis. But I am starting to recognize how the triggered emotions differ from my normal responses.

Whenever I feel sad, anxious, or angry, it is almost always due to a past trigger and not the current situation. The very depth and force of the feelings let me know that I am in a triggered response. Triggers are not limited to the obvious ones, which usually occur right after the trauma. Triggers can last for years, but generally diminish in strength and duration over time. Subtle triggers, on the other hand, grow in intensity and frequency over the years—but we are often unaware of them. Subtle triggers may start with an innocuous experience, but then set off a cascade of stressful thoughts that can lead to a spiral of negativity.

Just the other day, I was deeply triggered by my beautiful wife, Cathy. Although I have not earned a paycheck since I closed my business in March 2011, I am the one who pays all the bills in our house every month. It's not that I don't work. I do. But it is all volunteer work for the Courageous Healers Foundation. I am also a full-time student, working to earn a master's degree in order to become a Licensed Marriage and Family Therapist (LMFT). Cathy makes more than enough money to support us, but it is still hard on my pride as a man to accept that she is the breadwinner.

When I sit down to pay the bills and get them all sorted out, I will call Cathy into the office to go over them with her. On this particular day, I was feeling some stress over the bills, since we were a bit tight financially. When I expressed my concerns to her, Cathy looked at me and said, "We're going to be okay. It will all work out." That is her usual response to life's problems—and, as usual, she was right. But because my ego was feeling bruised that day, I dismissed her words, although I said nothing.

After she left, I sat in the office, seething inside because I was frustrated by what I perceived as her lack of concern about something that had me worried. I had no idea how she could be so positive about what appeared in my eyes to be a dark hole. The truth was that I was already starting to be triggered by my feeling that I was worthless as a man, because I had been conditioned since childhood to believe that a man's worth lies primarily in his ability to protect and provide for his family. That self-criticism initiated a surge of trauma-based self-talk about how I was fundamentally damaged goods.

As I finished paying the bills, my feelings grew stronger and more painful. I didn't realize at that moment that I was falling into a trauma trance, but I recognized that I wanted Cathy to agree with me so that I could feel better. Now, as someone who has been in recovery for many years, I know just how insane that kind of thinking is. But when we are caught up in a trauma trigger, we don't have access to higher-order executive functions, and what we "know" doesn't always get downloaded into our conscious brain in time to keep us from engaging in destructive interactions.

My sane self would have chosen different coping skills. I could have journaled about my feelings, called my sponsor or therapist, meditated or prayed, or even just gone for a bike ride or sat down with my guitar to clear my mind, so that I could return to the situation with a fresh perspective.

But that wasn't where I was at that moment. Instead, I did what most of us do when we want to stop feeling terrible. We turn to the people around us to demand that they meet our needs. So, of course, after "rationally" deciding that I needed to talk further with Cathy about the situation then and there, I marched into our living room, where she was reading a book.

"I'm unhappy with the way our conversation just ended," I said. "I want to resolve the issue immediately."

She looked up at me in a calm and loving manner, and said, "Not now. I'm not in the mood to discuss it at this time. We'll discuss it later."

Now, I should mention that Cathy has done an enormous amount of work in Co-Dependents Anonymous around setting healthy boundaries. On that day, she was communicating her needs in a clear, loving way to set those boundaries. At that time, she wasn't ready to talk. In fact, she was not only protecting herself, but our relationship as well.

But that's not how I took it at the moment. I was already feeling less than good enough, so as soon as I heard the words *not now*, I went on the defensive. Feeling a warm, flushed feeling come over my body and a knot form in my stomach, I began shaking and literally went into a fit of rage. Unwilling to take no for an answer, I was going to argue until she saw things my way.

"I'm going for a drive," she said, and got up to leave.

I immediately blocked the door so she couldn't get out of the house. I was out of control emotionally, turning a minor situation into a major problem.

When I finally came to my senses, I asked myself what had happened, and why I had become so upset. She hadn't said we would *never* talk. All she had said was that we would talk *later*. The reality is, I was triggered. When she said, "Not now, later," I heard my mother telling me the same thing when I was a boy.

The difference between Cathy and my mother, however, is that *later* rarely, if ever, came with my mother. When she said we would talk about something later, it really meant that she had no interest in dealing with whatever it was that was bothering me. And since I had some major issues going on when I was a young boy, I was an emotional wreck and needed help. But my feelings were never a priority with my mother.

So when Cathy told me "not now," at a time when I was already feeling shame over my inability to provide financially for my family, I went right back to the times that I felt equally worthless when my mother said, "Not now."

There were hundreds of times that Cathy had told me, "Not now," and then kept her promise to talk about the issue later. But this time I was already in a triggered response. This kind of overreaction occurs over and over again with triggers. Something we do, say, see, or smell all the time without any negative effect can suddenly throw us into a shame spiral for no apparent reason. At least, the reason isn't immediately apparent to us. It takes self-reflection to discover why we had such a disproportionate response to a familiar scenario.

The good news is that, with time and practice, it gets easier to find the source of the trauma trigger. When we start to recognize the triggered behavior for what it really is, it becomes easier to calm down quickly and return to sanity with our loved ones.

What most survivors often do instead is blame the people around them for any of their own out-of-control emotions. We think, *If only other people changed, I would be okay.* We fight and rage and sulk and indulge in destructive patterns in an attempt to get other people to change. But the truth is, we need to look inside ourselves and start to become sensitive to our trauma triggers.

This is not to say that we need to shut down our emotional responses when we are triggered. For one thing, that's impossible. Triggers are aptly named. We can't stop a bullet after we pull the trigger on a gun; we have to let it run its course.

The same thing goes for our emotional triggers. When we're set off, our emotions are already in play and have to run themselves out. However, we can still become familiar with the physical sensations that are associated with a trauma trance, which will help us to realize more quickly when we are being triggered.

Because we all have memories, we all have triggers. Even people with happy, wonderful childhoods have triggers. It's just the nature of the human brain. By the way, we can also have positive triggers. Certain smells, sounds, or sights can put a smile on our face out of the blue.

But what we don't want is for our negative triggers to remain unconscious and rule our behavior. We don't want our triggers to set off the triggers of the people around us. That just turns us into trigger-happy people, going off on each other, never realizing that we aren't even really upset with each other. Becoming aware of what triggers us can help us to maintain loving relationships with other people in our lives, and help to keep our own emotions balanced.

Recognizing the Onset of Trauma Triggers

There is a great saying in A.A. that "awareness is often curative." When it comes to trauma trances, I have definitely found that to be true. The moment I realize that I have been triggered, I am usually able to see the present situation differently. I realize that my overpowering emotions are not caused by what is happening in the present moment, but are due to decades of repressed feelings and abuse.

Physical sensations are often the quickest tip that we are being triggered. When I am triggered, I feel the emotions start in my stomach. I get nauseous, my heartbeat speeds up, my face feels flushed, my armpits begin to sweat, and my arms become weak and shaky.

Your physical signs will most likely be different from mine. It is important for you to discover for yourself what they are.

Suggested Exercise

- Keep a journal for the next seven days. When you experience strong emotions of any kind, practice taking a moment to notice how your body is feeling. Take notes.

- When you are happy, how does your head feel? Is there a color associated with that feeling? For example, I notice that when I'm happy, my head feels light and open, and the color I associate with this feeling is yellow.

- Notice the little things. How do your legs feel? Your chest? Your stomach? Your hands and feet?

- Over time, make this practice more and more subtle. Try to distinguish the smallest things that change from emotion to emotion.

While awareness can be curative, it does not necessarily mean that your trauma trance will lift, the moment you become aware of it. The feelings still have to run their course, and you still have to do the work to unravel the trigger and deal with the repressed emotions. But with that awareness, you will be able to get a different perspective on your emotions. It's the difference between surfing a wave and being pummeled by it—between being reparented and being retraumatized.

With the awareness that you have been triggered comes compassion for yourself. In my own case, I am reminded that there is a twelve-year-old boy inside me who is still hurting very badly. And just as if I were confronted in person by an angry, crying twelve-year-old child, I have a natural reaction as a loving adult to help the child feel better. If you have raised a child, you know that sometimes kids have to cry themselves out before you can talk to them.

For me, the ideal scenario is not to put myself into a bubble world in which I try to protect myself from ever being triggered, but to have the awareness to respond to triggers with the same compassion for myself that I would have for an abused boy in my care.

A Note About Physical Signs of Trauma

The term *psychosomatic* has gotten a bad reputation. Most people think that someone who suffers from a psychosomatic condition must be a hypochondriac who imagines pain that isn't there. But *psychosomatic* does not mean that a malady exists only in your head; rather, that its symptoms are based on the mind-body connection—*psyche* meaning "soul" in Greek, and *soma* meaning "body." *All* trauma-induced disorders are psychosomatic. Trauma, which is an extremely distressing experience, often manifests itself as physical symptoms—from sleep disorders to teeth grinding, headaches, and stomachaches. We can use this mind-body connection as part of our recovery toolkit.

A common coping method for survivors is to emotionally distance themselves from their traumas. But blocking out thoughts and feelings can leave them numb and disconnected, which can make it difficult to identify their triggers, since they are disassociated from their own pain.

But even when our minds are too shut down to notice, our bodies will let us know that there is trouble. Chronic physical conditions that doctors cannot explain, and stray symptoms that appear isolated and random, can be signals that we are experiencing traumatic emotions that are manifesting as physical symptoms. (Needless to say, if you have any medical concerns, go to your doctor.)

When I was a boy, I suffered from violent stomachaches, which began about the same time that Jack started abusing me, but I didn't make the connection until many years later. The pain back then was so intense that I would be doubled up in agony for hours.

When I moved out at the age of eighteen, the stomachaches subsided and eventually went away completely. In fact, I had totally forgotten about them until, one day in my twenties, I woke up with violent stomach pains in the middle of the night. I was sweating so badly and convulsing with so much agony that my wife rushed me to the nearest emergency room. However, the doctors found nothing that could be causing such pain.

When I got home that night, I wondered what in my life had provoked the same physical reaction that I had had in my teens. Then I realized that my current boss reminded me of Jack. He had the same sarcastic, belittling tone and would fly into similar unpredictable rages.

I was so used to normalizing this kind of abuse that I had fallen back into the same pattern I had learned as a boy. That is, I took the abuse from my boss, swallowed my emotions, tried to be perfect, and berated *myself* whenever I fell short. My mind had gone straight into a trauma trance at my job, and I was becoming numb and dissociated. It took a stomachache to jolt me out of that painful but familiar behavior pattern. With that recognition, the stomachache gradually vanished and has not returned to this day.

If you ever have psychosomatic symptoms, it can be useful to sit down and listen to what your body is trying to tell you. Find a comfortable position in a quiet place where you won't be disturbed. Then locate the source of your discomfort by asking yourself, *If this feeling had words, what would it be saying to me?* You can even ask your body directly, *What would you like me to know about this sensation?* When it comes to your recovery, even a stomachache can give you priceless information to help you on your path.

Mindfulness: Becoming Less "Trigger-Happy"

Being human can be wonderful. It can also be hell. For evidence of this, look no further than your memories of falling in love—and your memories of your first broken heart. It is the power of the imagination that sets human beings apart from everything else. Our imagination has sent us to the moon, written mind-blowing poetry and novels, and built skyscrapers. Everything begins as a thought. Great things begin in the mind—but so do devastating ones.

The average person has 60,000 thoughts per day, 80% of which are negative.[33] As humans, we are conditioned to think negatively. That is because, at many points in human history, our survival has depended on our ability to foresee the worst possible outcomes and choose the best options to avoid or overcome them. If our minds are left to their own devices, they will unravel any situation into the worst-case scenario in a matter of seconds.

Mindfulness practices have helped me to tame my negative thoughts, allowing me to live more peacefully and be less reactionary when I am triggered. Sixty thousand thoughts per twenty-four-hour day amount to forty-two thoughts per minute, of which thirty-three are negative. That's a negative thought roughly every other second. And that's for the *average* person. For survivors, most of whom are already conditioned to see the world through a negative lens, it makes sense to assume that the number is even higher.

So what happens to all those thoughts? Why are some people happy, even though they have a negative thought every other second?

Have you ever had someone tell you that you should "just choose to be happy"? If so, that is the most insane piece of advice in the world—

---

[33] Anne Balaban, *Common Sense Is Uncommon: Helping You Live Up to Your Potential* (Bloomington, IN: iUniverse, 2011).

especially for anyone who is unhappy in that moment. If it were in our power, we would *all* choose to be happy. The problem is, for those of us who live from a reactionary state instead of a witnessing state, we don't feel that our happiness is in our control.

Why don't we latch onto those eight precious neutral or positive thoughts, instead of the thirty-four negative ones? Perhaps it's due to our conditioning, or maybe some biological imperative. A better question to ask is, How can we reduce our natural propensities to accept negative thoughts and reject positive ones?

One way to develop a practice of mindfulness is through meditation, by which we learn how to be present and aware, with no attachment or reaction to our thoughts. We can learn how to observe the thoughts flowing in and out of our minds like a river running at forty-two thoughts per minute. You learn to let the thoughts come and go, without spinning yourself off into stories about them. You practice being present and witnessing all of those negative thoughts—mental "grenades" if you will—exploding in your mind without having to do anything about any of them. In meditation, you learn to just notice the thoughts and let them flow in and out of your consciousness while returning your focus to your breath.

Mindfulness is becoming more and more popular these days in Western cultures. At one time solely a practice of religions in the Far East, meditation is catching on in the West because it *works*. In fact, modern science and medicine have proven that even the most minimal and basic forms of meditation reduce stress and increase well-being. Even on only a commonsense level, it is clearly beneficial to take a few moments out of our hectic, fast-paced lives to relax and be present.

What may be surprising to some people is just how beneficial meditation is. New research has found that meditation has a positive effect on the brain even when the individual is not actively meditating. And the area that is most affected is the amygdala, the part of the brain associated most strongly with emotions, memory, and trauma triggers.[34]

To clear up the most common misperception about meditation, it is definitely not a religion, although every major religion incorporates some form of meditation into its practices. Meditation is simply the practice of bringing your awareness out of the past (memory) or future (imagination)

---

[34]Sue McGreevey, "Meditation's Positive Residual Effects: Imaging Finds Different Forms of Meditation May Affect Brain Structure," *Harvard Gazette*, November 13, 2012), retrieved from http://news.harvard.edu/gazette/story/2012/11/meditations-positive-residual-effects/.

and into the present moment (reality). To meditate, you can be a devoutly religious person or a confirmed atheist. The nice thing about meditation is that, like exercise or healthy eating, you don't have to "believe" in anything to benefit from it. It works, regardless of what you think about it.

The most common form of meditation is the practice of mindful attention. This form of meditation does not refer to any concept of a deity, nor does it focus on anything remotely related to religious doctrine of any kind. Mindfulness practices usually involve simple attention to the breath, with the intention of bringing you into the present moment and training you to engage in the "witness" aspect of consciousness. This is crucial for anyone struggling with PTSD or past trauma. When you are hurt, you tend to become more and more reactive. Triggers are the outward manifestation of reactivity.

Being reactive is a horrible, painful, stressful way to live, which wears on our physical bodies as much as it does on our hearts and minds. Living from a witness perspective is the opposite of being reactive. When we are able to acquire even a little perspective, we can sit back (if only briefly) and decide how we are going to react in a positive instead of a negative manner.

In mindfulness exercises, we practice focusing on our breath and noticing our thoughts as they come into our minds. We usually attach our interpretations to these thoughts. For example, as our minds are being filled with a barrage of ideas, we might think to ourselves, *This is stupid.* Remember, the purpose of meditation is to observe your thoughts, and then return to focusing on your breath as it flows in and out. This is something that takes consistent practice to achieve.

In our non-meditative life, when a thought comes into our mind, we often spin out stories from it. Even innocuous thoughts can spiral out of control astonishingly fast. If a driver cuts you off at a light, you may think, *How rude!* Watch how natural it feels to go from that little thought to something like this: *Drivers shouldn't be so rude. It's unsafe! Where are the cops when you really need them? He could have totaled my car! Or killed me! People like that make me sick!*

If you're anything like me, being cut off by another driver may lead to violent rage or soul-shriveling depression. But it isn't the other driver who makes us feel angry or sad. It is our own human tendency to spin stories out of thin air, jumping from one thought to another, like a frog on a hot rock.

Now go back to the *This is stupid* thought that you might have had when you first sat down to meditate. If you had that thought in a non-meditative context, you might latch onto it, which can lead to having other thoughts, such as, *I should be working instead. No wonder I'm behind on my bills. I'm such a loser. I don't make enough money. I'm such an idiot!*

Keep in mind that sometimes you do not experience these thoughts as thoughts, but rather as emotions. This will often be the case until you learn to slow your mind down. You may not be able to track the mental process between *This is stupid* and *I am stupid*, instead experiencing a sudden feeling that can range from sadness to depression to anger. When you feel bad, it is because you have attached to a negative thought, even if your mind moves too fast for you to notice the individual ideas.

In meditation, you get to experience the insight that thoughts can be powerless. It is when you attach to them that you give them power, for good or for ill. Mindfulness shows you how to be less reactive by simply not accepting as the gospel truth everything that pops into your head. You learn that you don't have to react to every thought that comes to mind. In fact, life is a lot more peaceful when you choose to let the negative thoughts slide, while attaching to the productive, positive ones.

You may be thinking, *But I need those negative thoughts to motivate me, to whip myself into shape*. If that is where you are right now, I have some questions for you:

- How's that working out for you so far?
- How does it feel to badger and berate yourself?
- Does it feel familiar?
- Who did you learn that behavior from, and is that a person you really want to emulate?

Imagine talking to a little child the way you talk to yourself on a regular basis. How productive or effective would that child be if all he heard was the kind of fear-based pushing that you give yourself? How much more productive would that child be with encouragement and support?

I leave it up to you to try meditation for yourself. Your recovery is your own experiment. Try everything on for yourself to see how it fits. You already know the results of the way you've been going through life up till now. Take some new ideas, shake them up, and try them out. What do you have to lose?

Be kind to yourself. You didn't get a lot of security or kindness when you were growing up in abusive situations. Isn't it time you got a chance to be happy and safe? Instead of waiting for the world to be perfect in order for you to be happy, start with yourself. Make your own mind a safe place to be. And see what happens.

How to Meditate (the Short Version)

There are thousands of books on meditation, but I suggest that you explore this tool for yourself, searching for a type of meditation that brings you consistent relief. Meditation practices are easy to learn, require no prior knowledge, and can be done by anyone.

Meditation is about being in the present and quieting the mind. A simple way to start practicing is to find a comfortable place to sit where you won't be disturbed. Set a timer for five minutes and sit quietly, becoming fully aware of your surroundings without making any judgments. Observe the colors on the wall, the temperature of the room, and the sounds around you. If you find yourself making judgments of any kind, bring yourself back to your breath.

Practice being present by looking around you and giving everything you see what Byron Katie calls "first-generation names" (for example, "couch," "table," "clock," etc.).[35] If you start moving into what Katie calls "second-generation names" (for example, "comfortable couch," "old table," or "ticking clock"), just notice this and gently bring your mind back to the first-generation names.

Now close your eyes and begin to practice mindfulness with your inner world, the same way you did with your surroundings. Use your breath as an anchor to the present moment. Follow your breathing in and out.

In my own case, meditation helps me to cool down. By just noticing my thoughts instead of reacting to them, I become less intense. I can see, for example, that most of my *shame* comes from the times that I attach to a thought and use it to spin myself into a story about my past, whereas most of my *fear* comes from attaching to a thought and spinning myself off into a story about my future.

Taking a break from flip-flopping between past shame and future anxiety lets me rest in the present and see that I am okay right now. This a much better place from which to decide how to act. I make better decisions

---

[35]Byron Katie, *I Need Your Love—Is That True?* (New York: Three Rivers Press, 2005).

when I am not reacting to shame or anxiety. I am happier when I notice that my thoughts just come and go, like a river flowing at forty-two thoughts per second. In your mind, it's fine to step out of the river, sit on the bank, and enjoy the sun. Let the river of your thoughts run its course while you rest for a few precious minutes every day. Those few minutes will start to infuse the rest of your life with peaceful present calmness.

Chapter 4: Coping Mechanisms

One day I looked at something in myself that I had been avoiding because it was too painful. Yet once I did, I had an unexpected surprise. Rather than self-hatred, I was flooded with compassion for myself because I realized the pain necessary to develop that coping mechanism to begin with.

—Marianne Williamson[36]

We use dozens of coping mechanisms every day, consciously and subconsciously, to minimize stress and to solve our personal and interpersonal problems. Coping skills can be maladaptive or constructive, ranging from abusing alcohol, drugs, or sex to meditating, praying, or playing a musical instrument.

Coping skills fall into three main categories:

- *Appraisal-focused*, which are related to how we see a problem.

- *Problem-focused*, which remove the source of a problem by changing or eliminating the stressor behind it.

- *Emotion-focused*, which attempt to mitigate the stress by minimizing, reducing, avoiding, or preventing the unwanted emotional response.[37]

---

[36]Marianne Williamson, "Only Light Can Cast Out Darkness," in Deepak Chopra, Debbie Ford, and Marianne Williamson, *The Shadow Effect: Illuminating the Hidden Power of Your True Self* (New York: HarperCollins, 2010), retrieved from http://www.theshadoweffect.com/custom/book.php/.

[37]See Wayne Weiten, Margaret A. Lloyd, Dana S. Dunn, and Elizabeth Yost Hammer, *Psychology Applied to Modern Life: Adjustment in the 21st Century*, 11th ed. (Belmont, CA: Wadsworth, 2012), p. 114.

Coping mechanisms can also be categorized by the result they bring:

- *Adaptive mechanisms* provide positive support.

- *Attack mechanisms* transfer pain onto another person or object.

- *Avoidance mechanisms* provide some kind of escape from a problem.

- *Behavioral mechanisms* change one's actions.

- *Cognitive mechanisms* change how one thinks.

- *Self-harming mechanisms* transfer emotional pain into physical pain.[38]

Defense mechanisms and maladaptive coping skills reduce unwanted symptoms in the short term, but only strengthen and intensify the underlying problem in the long run. Since many abuse victims come from dysfunctional homes, it is unlikely that they were taught many healthy coping skills as children. It's far more likely that they picked up maladaptive ones instead.

A coping skill is anything that gets you through the day. Some coping skills are healthier than others, but if they keep you alive, they are working. The goal is to learn healthier coping skills as your recovery progresses. However, it is important not to discount the skills that have brought you to your present state of mind.

Take a moment to appreciate yourself for staying alive and making it through the dark nights and tough times. Then take a look at the following list to create a personal inventory of some of your coping skills, good and bad. In recovery, it is helpful to get to know yourself better and better. When it comes to maladaptive coping skills, it's good to know what you want to change; and when it comes to positive coping skills, it's good to know which ones you want to keep.

Here is one attempt at a complete list of coping mechanisms:

---

[38]Weiten et al., *Psychology Applied to Modern Life*.

COPING MECHANISMS

Acting Out: not coping; giving in to the pressure to misbehave.

Adaptation: the human ability to change.

Aim Inhibition: the lowering of goals to what seems more achievable.

Altruism: unselfish concern for the welfare of others.

Attack: an offensive attempt to defeat a threat.

Avoidance: the act of mentally or physically staying away from something that causes distress.

Compartmentalization: the division of conflicting thoughts into distinct categories.

Compensation: something that makes up for a weakness in one area by gaining strength in another.

Conversion: subconscious alteration of stress into physical symptoms.

Crying: the release of tears to relieve stress.

Denial: refusal to acknowledge that an event has occurred.

Displacement: the act of shifting an intended action to a safer target.

Dissociation: the act of intentionally or unintentionally disconnecting from one's own conscious experience of reality, due to a perceived threat of danger or annihilation.

Distancing: the act of moving away.

Emotionality: outbursts of extreme feelings.

Escapism: the act of using fantasy or entertainment to forget about unpleasant realities.

Fantasy: the act of escaping reality into a world of possibility.

Idealization: the act of playing up a subject's good points and ignoring its limitations.

Identification: the act of copying others to take on their characteristics.

Intellectualization: the avoidance of emotion by focusing on facts and logic.

Introjection: the adoption of values or attitudes from the outer world to the inner world.

Passive Aggression: the indirect expression of hostility.

Performing Rituals: patterns that delay.

Post-Traumatic Growth: the act of using the energy of trauma for good.

Projection: the act of seeing one's own unwanted feelings in other people.

Provocation: the act of making others angry so one can retaliate.

Rationalization: the creation of logical reasons for bad behavior.

Reaction Formation: the avoidance of something by taking a polar opposite position.

Regression: return to a childish state to avoid problems.

Repression: the act of unconsciously hiding uncomfortable thoughts.

Self-Harm: the act of physically damaging the body.

Somatization: the act of turning psychological problems

into physical symptoms.

Sublimation: the channeling of psychic energy into acceptable activities.

Substitution: replacement of one thing with another.

Suppression: the conscious holding back of unwanted urges.

Symbolization: the transformation of unwanted thoughts into metaphoric symbols.

Trivialization: the act of making small what is really big.

Undoing: the psychological reversal of an action.[39]

Maladaptive Coping Mechanisms

Some coping mechanisms work especially poorly for survivors of sexual abuse. These include dissociation, avoidance, anxiety, and escapism, just to name some of the more prominent ones.

Dissociation

In my work with survivors of sexual abuse, I have found that dissociation is the most commonly relied on coping mechanism. We tend to distance ourselves from the world, almost as a habit. Because the world is often a painful and scary place for us as children, we learn early on to pull away from it. Dissociation can range from daydreaming to severe fugue states and depersonalization disorders.

As a short-term survival strategy, dissociation may be highly effective. But chronic dissociation can impair cognitive function and create a tendency to avoid (or even forget) unpleasant people, places, or experiences.

Alexandra Katehakis, the Clinical Director of the Center for Healthy Sex, in Los Angeles, has nicely stated both the diagnosis and the prognosis for dissociation:

The process of dissociation is an elegant mechanism built into the

---
[37]This list is adapted from Changing Works, *Coping Mechanisms*, retrieved from http:// changingminds.org/explanations/behaviors/coping/coping.htm/.

human psychological system as a form of escape from (sometimes literally) going crazy. The problem with checking out so thoroughly is that it can leave us feeling dead inside, with little or no ability to feel our feelings in our bodies. The process of repair demands a re-association with the body, a commitment to dive into the body and feel today what we couldn't feel yesterday because it was too dangerous.[40]

When I was twelve and thirteen, I was an unwilling witness to sexual acts between my mother and Jack. One time, as we traveled from California to Texas and back again, we stayed at various motels, always in one room with two adjacent beds. Many times, my mother's moaning, groaning, and screaming would wake me up in the middle of the night. I would lie awake, frozen and confused about what was happening, terrified of what would happen if they discovered I could hear them. My dissociation usually took the form of staring at the ceiling, imagining I was traveling through some distant galaxy.

Today, I strongly believe that my mother and Jack not only knew I was awake, but they intentionally set up scenarios in which I would be trapped in the same space with them as a way to satisfy their unhealthy sexual appetites. For example, my mother would masturbate Jack in the car as we were driving across the country. Back then, my only defense was to roll over on my side, hide my face, and pretend I was asleep. I had no way to escape or leave, so I took the best way out I could find. While I was lying there, I would imagine myself hunting or engaged in some other activity related to what I saw outside the windows.

In normal situations, we learn how to dissociate from unpleasant experiences by mentally removing ourselves from the immediacy of our surroundings. This can be a good thing. But when we learn to dissociate through abusive situations, we are using this coping skill to escape both external unpleasantness *and* internal pain. When situations are painful inside and outside the self, we start to disconnect from both our world and ourselves. If this becomes our habitual response to pain, we learn to run from *all* pain, thereby losing the ability to self-soothe. When all pain makes us want to run, we start to live half-lives, rarely being truly present. It is then difficult to engage with others, and difficult for us to feel loved.

---

[40]Alexandra Katehakis, *Mirror of Intimacy: Daily Reflections on Emotional and Erotic Intelligence* (Los Angeles: Center for Healthy Sex, 2014), p. 15.

Survivors Speaks Out

S: I was alone. I was drifting. I would go from one social group to another, and just never stay anywhere enough time to develop any kind of deep relationship with anyone. I felt very isolated and alone.

S: We had talked about intimacy and pain and how I equate intimacy with pain. The people that I was intimate with from childhood, I went through incredibly painful experiences. Who would want to get intimate with someone? Basically, if you get that intimate, someone could kill you if you make one false move.

S: Nobody cares, nobody loves me, and no matter how much people tried to care for and love me, I always said nobody did, because I couldn't feel.[41]

Avoidance

The coping strategy of avoidance is also pretty common in survivors. To some extent, avoidance is a normal coping mechanism, since it just involves staying away from unpleasant situations and people and is not detrimental in and of itself. For survivors, avoidance may start to become a problem when it is coupled with anxiety.

Anxiety

Anxiety makes problems and people seem more powerful and frightening than they actually are. When combined with avoidance, anxiety can become quite harmful. We all use avoidance to some extent, but some of us don't stop at assuming the worst of people and situations; instead, we let those assumptions cripple us in our day-to-day life.

We create huge stories in our minds, focusing on worst-case scenarios, and then we are filled with fear that we have generated precisely what we were trying to avoid. I know survivors who scare themselves into avoiding shopping at grocery stores, attending classes, or going out to eat.

This crippling pattern can quickly spell disaster in a survivor's life. I have a brilliant friend who recently returned to college, but instead of earning the 4.0 grade point average that he is more than capable of getting, he scrapes by with average grades. He has shared with me that he often

---

[41]From David Lisak, "The Psychological Impact of Sexual Abuse: Content Analysis of Interviews with Male Survivors," *Journal of Traumatic Stress*, 7: 4 (1994), 535–536.

gets all the way to the classroom door, and is then unable to enter, due to this crippling anxiety and avoidance pattern. Sometimes he doesn't even make it out of his car to the building.

This does not mean that he is choosing to be unhappy or to miss out on parts of his life. No one chooses to be unhappy, frightened, or sad. When I say that my friend scares himself, I am not being judgmental, only truthful. We can waste a lot of time justifying our behavior and blaming the world for our fears, but the vast majority of the time, it is the way we *choose* to see the world that frightens us. We can either be invested in remaining a victim of the world we imagine, or we can take responsibility for our part of it. The world is never as frightening as the terrifying stories we tell ourselves.

Survivors Speak Out

> S: It's like my reoccurring dreams, like I can't run. I always have dreams of the same thing. If I'm running, I can't move my legs and my arms. And somebody is coming down on top of me, and I can't get up.
> S: The world was evil, it's coming to get you, and you could do almost nothing to defend from it.
> S: My hands were sweating, my knees were shaking. I mean, I'm shaking now, just remembering how scared I was that night.[42]

Escapism

While it is good common sense to take the nearest exit when you're in an unpleasant situation, escapism is more about the chronic need to run away from everyday life. We tend to carry such a large load of pain that every little additional cut and scrape can seem unbearable. When the pain exceeds our ability to handle it, we bail out, even when the situation is not truly dangerous or upsetting. Some obvious and well-known examples of escapism include abusing drugs and alcohol, cutting, sexual addictions, and overeating.

✳

Besides just being painful ways to get through the day, these

---

[42]Lisak, "Psychological Impact," 532, 533.

maladaptive strategies reinforce the psychological trauma from childhood abuse. Well-meaning people try to give advice such as, "Make different choices," or "Stop self-sabotaging." The problem is that no one would choose painful, maladaptive mechanisms over positive, healthy strategies if they felt they had a choice.

Either we are in so much pain that we don't feel that we have the luxury of trying good coping skills, such as meditation, exercise, or journaling, or we reach for the industrial-strength painkillers like alcohol, drugs, cutting, and sex.

We all have our breaking points: moments when the pain we feel exceeds our skills and ability to cope. For many of us, at some point in our lives, the bottom line is that our pain exceeds our ability to handle it. The trouble is that using maladaptive coping mechanisms is like buying on credit: the mechanisms become less and less powerful over time, whereas positive ones become stronger over time. Using maladaptive coping skills becomes more and more emotionally costly over time. When we turn to drugs and alcohol, sooner or later we will need more and more to get the same effect. Eventually, we will either die of the addiction, or we will get sober and deal with the underlying cause of the pain.

Using positive coping skills is like investing in a savings account. The rewards may seem small at first, but they compound over time, and after a while, the rewards grow exponentially.

Recovering from sexual abuse will not eliminate all the pain we will ever feel. It just gives us a bigger toolbox, filled with better coping skills, which can help us to rise above the cycle of abuse, instead of continuing to perpetrate it on ourselves.

Self-Blame

Male survivors of sexual abuse often find it easier to blame themselves for it than to deal with the actual facts. Blaming ourselves for being abused is a way to regain control over situations that were originally out of our control. Those of us who self-blame either become obsessed with control or chronically feel victimized by the world.

Self-blame is a vicious cycle. We blame ourselves in order to normalize the abuse, but we set ourselves up to fail in everyday life by holding ourselves to impossible standards. Countless times I have heard men weep and rage at themselves for not "fighting back" against the perpetrator or speaking up to other people. I have felt that way myself. Then the shame of my memories doubled as I watched my child-self passively accept the abusive situations and try to make the best of them. I used to believe that I must have been complicit in my abuse because, after all, I didn't say anything, I didn't stop it. That shame can be crippling when combined with the shame and rage from the abuse itself.

Survivors Speak Out

> S: I used to blame myself for it..., so why didn't I get out of it? I blame myself. I don't blame him. I could have got out of it. I was plenty smart enough.
> S: I still blame myself for all that happened.... I feel I was real intelligent at that age, and I should have been able to get out of it.[43]

The truth is that we need to stop blaming ourselves, period. Self-blame can either become a shield that keeps us from engaging with the world, or it can lead to control disorders. A huge part of my own recovery has been looking back and understanding the world as I saw it—not from my perspective today as a man in my fifties, but as a frightened boy. I didn't realize how much self-blame was running my life. I was a control freak in my work, at home, and even on vacations. I always had to be the best. If the smallest detail didn't work out, it was always my fault.

Intertwined with self-blame is the tendency to blow things out of proportion. I couldn't ever just make a little mistake. Everything felt like it carried a life-or-death consequence, because everything was tied to my self-image. I had to be perfect in order to escape from my self-persecution. Of course, it was impossible to meet those standards. I was never good enough for myself.

One of the exercises I do when I visit recovery houses is have the men paint their childhood pain on a t-shirt I provide. The age at which most sexual abuse occurs is between six and twelve, so that is the range of shirt sizes I bring. It is a huge reality check to hold one of those tiny shirts in your adult hands. It really stops you in your tracks to make you remember how small you were as a child. Sometimes not fighting back was the best defense you had. Once you can internalize the fact that your abuse was not your fault, you can begin to heal.

That kid inside you is a survivor. It is important to honor the fact that

---

[43]Lisak, "Psychological Impact," 543.

the choices you made as a boy are part of what got you here today. You did whatever you had to do to be able to face the world every morning. You did the best you could with what you had, and you can't ask any more of yourself than that.

Denial and Minimizing

The coping skills of denial and minimizing can look a lot like self-blame. Rather than blaming yourself, however, you talk yourself into pretending that everything is fine. To make it through each day, children often need to believe that what is happening isn't "abuse" but just "part of growing up."

To cope with my own sexual abuse as a child, I had to believe that it was normal behavior between a father figure and a son. I told myself that it was no big deal. But deep in my gut, the wrenching feeling of wrongness persisted. It is frightening for children to blame parental figures for painful, violent, and abusive acts. Children are at their most vulnerable when they are utterly dependent on their caregivers for their emotional and physical well-being.

We cannot admit, even to ourselves, that there might be something wrong with our parents, because that can place our whole life in danger. To begin with, without parents, where would we get food and shelter? Thus, children internalize guilt and shame, blaming themselves for somehow "causing" the abuse. It is painful, but psychologically safer, for children to blame themselves instead of their parents.

Survivors Speak Out

> *S:* And when someone says that something's wrong, like it's pathetic, the first thing I think it's me, that I did something wrong.
>
> *S:* I felt ashamed, like I had done something really dirty, really bad.
>
> *S:* But it's so much easier to just take the blame for it. That there's something wrong with me. There was something defective from the beginning.[44]

As a teenager, I believed that the abuse in my childhood must have been normal—just a regular part of growing up. In fact, I *needed* it to be

---

[44]Lisak, "Psychological Impact," 543.

normal, but the hollow, gnawing ache in my gut would not go away. I dealt with it by telling myself that *I* was the one with the problem. I just had to learn to be comfortable with it.

But minimizing or normalizing abuse creates additional problems. Crafting elaborate justifications for abusive situations might make the victim feel better temporarily, but it doesn't heal the wounds that were caused by the abuse. Later on, as the survivor gets older, he will most likely still struggle with the unresolved pain from the abuse, but because he has normalized it, he denies himself the opportunity to get the help he needs to heal.

If a survivor of sexual abuse has convinced himself that he was never abused, or even that his childhood "was not that bad," he won't be able to seek out a therapist or support group, or even to read books that might help him to heal. In addition, denial and minimization can actually perpetuate the cycle of abuse. If a victim has made himself believe that sexual abuse is in any way "normal," he is far more likely to become one of the 30% of survivors who then become abusers themselves.

I want to reiterate that this book is not about assigning blame, dredging up old painful memories, or ranting about the devastation caused by sexual abuse. I don't want you to rip off whatever protective mechanism you have used in the past in order to cope with your abuse before you are ready. I do, however, want to make you aware of the possible repercussions of some of those coping mechanisms and to help support you in your healing process.

Seeking Approval

It is possible that seeking approval is the single most common, and by far the most painful, addiction ever created by mankind. More devastating than heroin, more addictive than cocaine, more ubiquitous than food, the desperate need for approval has done more harm than any substance ever could. If this sounds too dramatic, consider the following:

- More harm has been done in the name of love or wanting to be loved than has been done purely for the desire to be evil.

- Addictions, depressions, and desperate actions are often caused by wanting to end the feeling of not being loved or accepted by others.

- Reflecting on your own life, notice when you have said yes when you meant no, in order to earn the approval of someone else.

I should clarify that there is no reason for you to feel bad about seeking approval. Everyone does that. The degree to which approval-seeking is harmful, however, is directly proportionate to the extent to which you feel like you need someone else's love or approval in order to be okay. The more you feel that you need love and approval, the more harmful that approval-seeking can be for you.

Children raised in healthy, loving homes tend to have high self-esteem. In terms of seeking approval, this means that they are able to self-validate. They need the approval of others in order to feel good about themselves to a lesser degree than children do who have lower self-esteem.

Survivors of sexual abuse tend to have very low self-esteem, which can create a powerful addiction to the approval of other people. Since we can feel incapable of loving ourselves, we need other people to do it for us.

Because abused children lose their sense of self, they tend to seek external validation, and even become dependent on it as a surrogate sense of self. Seeking approval from others is incredibly painful. By needing other people to approve of you, you are sending yourself the message that your opinion of yourself is not good enough. Approval-seeking tells you that other people are more important than you are. It reinforces the horrible belief that often comes from incest that you need to suppress your own desires, personality, and needs in order to win approval from others.

Early in my teens, I began to seek the approval of others for assurance that my outside was not reflecting how dirty I felt on the inside. I remember walking to school, obsessing over my clothes. I was consumed with wearing the right pants, shirt, and shoes because I thought it was my façade that would make other people think my life was perfect, while on the inside I felt terrified, lonely, and dead.

Some boys act out and dress like gangsters to fit in, but any efforts to win attention from other people always come at the expense of our own sense of true self-worth.

At first, the youth group in my church gave me some solace. I played the guitar, used my humor to make people laugh, and had fun with the girls. I felt important, and pretty girls were giving me attention. However, the second I lost what I saw as the "top dog" position at church, I swung into total devastation.

Since my self-worth was entirely dependent on the approval of others, even the smallest slight or insult sent me crashing into a painful cycle of self-recrimination and anger.

I craved attention, which is a common coping behavior for children who have been abused, but that craving pushed people away. The need for approval is a deadly addictive drug.

We abrogate our responsibility to care for ourselves by insisting that others care for us. We only love ourselves if others see us as lovable, and ultimately we twist ourselves into tightly wound knots, trying to become what we think others want us to be. It is impossible not to lose ourselves when we fall into this kind of cycle.

Eventually, church, sports, clothes, and playing the guitar quit working—they all only made me feel worse. All of those activities depended on external approval. I felt that no one appreciated me for the things I did, especially for playing the guitar at church. I was no longer playing for myself or because I loved the music; rather, I was playing so that people would love me and think I was special.

I imagined slights everywhere, constantly assuming that people in church thought I wasn't good enough, or wanted someone else to play instead of me. Eventually, I became so tortured by the thoughts of rejection that I couldn't even look at my guitar. That left me with a devastating feeling of emptiness. In the end, I turned to drugs and alcohol to fill that void whenever I failed to win the approval of others.

Looking back now on that time, I realize that I never had any reason to believe that the other children and adults thought poorly of me, but I was like an addict. Every little drop of approval fed my desire for more. I never had enough.

It is frightening to step away from the temporary high that we get when other people approve of us, but the alternative is even scarier. Unless we detach from this cycle of approval, we can live and die without ever truly learning how to love ourselves.

Suggested Exercise

Notice where and from whom you seek approval in your life. What happens to your body when you get the approval you are seeking, or when you do *not* get it? What happens to your peace of mind? Now think of a time that you felt that you were completely true to yourself. How did that experience differ from the experience of getting or losing the approval of others?

Numbing Out with Drugs, Alcohol, and Food

Feeling that I had nowhere else to turn, I relied on drugs and alcohol. Although I knew deep inside that drugs and alcohol were not the answer, I had nothing left to lose. I knew that snorting cocaine and chasing it with rum was not going to fix my life, but it fed my approval addiction. I had found a group of kids who accepted me for what I was—so long as I was doing drugs and drinking with them.

In my junior and senior years of high school, drugs and alcohol became my two main coping mechanisms. For the first time, I found a way to take the edge off my mother's indifference and Jack's abuse. I was still scared to death of Jack, who had only become more violent with the passing years. Although the partying was extremely destructive, drugs and alcohol gave me the courage to finally tell Jack, when I was seventeen, how much I hated him. He punched me in the face, which hurt terribly, but it hurt far more to see my mother standing there, doing nothing to protect me. That time, however, the drugs and alcohol gave me a bit of a shield, a numbing that I desperately needed.

Because drugs and alcohol are more destructive than the trauma that led me to abuse them in the first place, I would never advocate their use. That said, the use of drugs and alcohol as well as other maladaptive coping mechanisms played a big role in helping me to deal with the onslaught of abuse I endured as a teenager. To a degree, knowing that gave me some relief from the overwhelming guilt and shame I was carrying. But while the drugs and alcohol helped me to escape from reality, they did nothing to fulfill me spiritually.

Food is an equally addictive substance. Arguably, it may be even more difficult to overcome than alcohol and drug addiction. Unlike alcohol and drugs, we need food to survive, and one of the most addictive foods is sugar, which is in everything. Sugar is added to almost all processed foods in addition to naturally occurring in fruits and vegetables. Imagine trying to overcome an addiction to alcohol if you needed to drink something three times a day that had alcohol in it.

The effects of overeating can alter the chemistry of the brain as much as cocaine or heroin do. In fact, too much food can alter the levels of dopamine in the brain, creating a literal addiction.[45] Rats addicted to the effects of overeating don't quit eating even when exposed to electrical shocks. Phil Werdell, the Director of the Food Addiction Institute, in Sarasota, Florida, notes the similarity between food addiction and dependence on alcohol and drugs:

> Food addicts frequently experience what is referred to as euphoric recall, remembering the good experiences of taste and the mitigation of pain, but forgetting the negative emotional and physical consequences. They also suffer obsessions of the mind, such as rationalizing the eating of addictive foods and/or bingeing based on irrational thoughts. Finally, they encounter what are often called mental blank spots, unexplained absences of any logical thinking that would serve to prevent one from engaging in behaviors known in the past to inflict pain.[46]

So why is this important for you as a survivor of sexual abuse?

In order to find the most effective treatment for addiction, it is important to understand what you are facing. Every day, more studies from major universities come out that link mood swings and disorders to addictions. Food addictions are particularly insidious because people often fail to make the connection between the candy they had before bed and the irritability, depression, or fatigue they experience the following day. That pattern is more obvious to individuals who are addicted to drugs or alcohol because they know what the actions of the previous day create in terms of consequences for their lives. Nevertheless, in order to curb the way they feel, they drink more alcohol or use more drugs, and the cycle keeps repeating itself.

The addictiveness of food is not nearly so clear-cut. Only in the past few years has hard science validated the effects of food addiction on the body and mind. If you think you may be addicted to food, Overeaters Anonymous has often been successful where "diet," "exercise," and "willpower" have not, because chronic overeating is much more likely to

---

[45]Katherine Harmon, "Addicted to Fat: Overeating May Alter the Brain as Much as Hard Drugs," *Scientific American*, March 28, 2010, retrieved from https://www.scientificamerican.com/article/addicted-to-fat-eating/.

[46]Phil Werdell, *Science of Food Addiction*, retrieved from http://foodaddiction.com/wp-content/uploads/acorn_brochure.pdf/.

be an addiction than a preference.

I also recommend www.foodaddiction.com as a resource to anyone struggling with this issue. Any addiction, whether it is to cocaine or carbohydrates, will only temporarily mask the pain you are feeling. Addictive substances grow increasingly less potent with time, requiring more and more of them for less and less of the relief. Addiction does not treat any type of trauma or heal you. In fact, in the long run, it will make the healing process more difficult.

There is not enough alcohol, drugs, or food to get rid of the excruciating emotional pain that survivors of sexual abuse live with. Substance-generated numbness is not the answer that you are looking for. But you probably already know that.

I can tell you from my own experience with addiction that although the healthy way looks harder from the bottom of the hill, it is actually much easier than addiction, and far more effective. All you have to do is keep taking small steps toward your own healing, one day at a time—occasionally one minute at a time.

Learning Positive Coping Skills

Fast-forward a few decades. The coping mechanisms and skills that I developed over a period of thirty-plus years were well engrained in the fiber of my being. I was an alcoholic egomaniac with an inferiority complex, a million-dollar business, and rage issues, but I felt that I was in control most of the time. Then the drugs and alcohol stopped working.

I had worked hard to become financially successful, but because my motivation was to prove that I wasn't a failure, no success was ever enough. I was trying to run away from a monster, but the monster was *me*. As a child, I was never good enough for Jack or my mother; but as an adult, I was never good enough for myself. No matter how much money I made, I still felt like a failure. Although it brought no real fulfillment, everything I did in life still had to be the best. I threw whatever morals and ethics I had out the window whenever it felt like my fragile ego was on the line. I did whatever I had to do to prove to others that I was the best.

Whatever *you* had, I was going to get something better and make sure you knew it. You may have thought you had the latest and greatest, but I was determined to make sure that your pride was short-lived. I not only had to keep up with the Joneses, I had to one-up them. I was losing business, my wife secretly despised me, and my closest friends thought I was a jerk. My old ways no longer worked, and something had to change. My coping mechanisms had become out-of-control monsters that were destroying my life.

I remember the day clearly when I decided I needed to get help. No one was nagging me, no nudge from a judge. It was February 1, 2006, and I was packing for a hunting trip. I had bought a half-gallon of Jack Daniel's to take with me, as part of my normal routine. As I was packing, I suddenly realized that I had consumed a quarter of the bottle in twenty minutes. At that moment, I recognized that I had a problem. I couldn't quit drinking and had already had several close calls with the law. In fact, after being involved in a pretty bad accident while driving intoxicated, I was told by the officers, "Have a nice night, Mr. Boyd, and drive home safely."

But as I looked at that bottle of Jack Daniel's, I heard a soft voice whispering in my ear, "Randy, you need help, and you need it today. Your 'Get Out of Jail Free' cards are all used up. You need to make a change."

I knew deep down that I had to quit drinking; and to do that, I had to stay out of slippery places. I walked away from friends and acquaintances, and in a short period of time, I learned who my true friends were. I had to start from scratch and learn all new coping skills, but before I could learn the good ones, I had to admit to the destructive ones.

It was terrifying to give up my armor, my ego, and my temper, and to even imagine a world in which I didn't hide behind my money and success. I was afraid of being genuinely vulnerable with people. Those defective coping skills had served me—if not perfectly, then well enough. Or so I thought.

They had allowed me to become financially successful, and to travel to amazing and exotic places. They had allowed me to achieve and acquire everything I had set out to do, and then some. So I said to myself, "How can they be defects?" In order to get a true understanding of my defects, I had to do a searching and fearless moral inventory.

I have to emphasize how important it is to have support throughout this process. When we start looking at our past behavior, it is all too easy to fall into the familiar pattern of self-hatred and self-blame. There is a difference between owning up to past wrongs and over-owning-up. The idea is not to create more opportunities to stay in the cycle of shame-guilt-anger-rage-remorse-overcompensation and back to shame.

We must walk through the pain and shame of our past if we are to recover and have a better life. Finding the ways in which we are responsible for our bad choices restores our power. It is the only thing that can. If we are going to be happy, we have to stop being victims. Going through the healing process is not easy and definitely does not feel like it has much to do with happiness.

All I felt was guilt and shame. I had discovered all my destructive coping skills, but I still didn't know how to change and start using constructive ones. Thirty-plus years, with some good but mostly bad choices, made for some seriously entrenched bad habits. I started the healing process by becoming aware of my character defects. Only then could I start working on replacing those with character assets.

This chapter is about helping you to become aware of your own defects. But you want to be easy with yourself during this process. Most survivors of sexual abuse are highly talented self-blamers and self-haters. That is *not* what this chapter is about. This stage of recovery is about learning to look at our faults so that we can change them.

We want to be honest with ourselves, but that honesty must be tempered with compassion and kindness. We may have used "bad" coping skills in the past in order to make it to this point, but we *did* make it here, and now we have the priceless opportunity to acquire better skills.

Whatever you have used to make it through served a purpose. You did what you had to do out of a desire to stop the pain, and you did the best you could, given the circumstances and what you believed were your options at the time. Now you can learn about new and different options, so that the next time you're faced with a painful situation, you have more tools in a bigger, better toolbox from which to choose.

Sometimes we have coped by using outright aggression, rage, and anger. Sometimes we use passive aggression and become overly self-deprecating when we feel guilty, thereby manipulating others (whose anger we probably richly deserve) into taking care of us because we are hurting. Sometimes we use workaholism, alcoholism, or narcissism. You can pick your own out of a dozen "isms." Addictions to sex, gambling, money, food, and exercise are other examples of destructive coping mechanisms.

They are all obviously destructive, but they can also feel safe, and we can feel naked and vulnerable without them. Although it's like wearing porcupine skin with the spines turned inward, we feel safer with our defensive armor on.

As I went through each day, certain situations would arise. I would feel intimidated, challenged, or threatened by a client or my wife, and

I would start in with my old behavior patterns. But because I was now willing to see and change my character defects, I started to become aware that my old reactions of manipulation and intimidation were not working.

Bullying someone into believing how I believed or using my power over another only made the situation worse. My wife would only despise me more, and my client would likely call another contractor.

I had to learn to quit taking things personally, both at home and in business. On more than one occasion, I had to swallow my pride and make phone calls to apologize for my actions. Those phone calls, as hard as they were to make, returned huge dividends in the long run.

How to Replace Bad Skills with Better Ones

"Quit taking things personally" sounds easy. It's just four words, after all, but it's still not easy. What worked for me was realizing that I was more than my wounded self-image. As I started to believe in myself, in my healing, and in my inherent goodness, it became easier and easier to take things less personally.

I replaced the coping skill of rage with the time-tested "counting to ten," not only because I didn't want to damage my new relationships, but because I was starting to realize that I hated myself when I was angry, violent, or mean. It actually did hurt me to hurt others. It hurt far more than it did to be hurt *by* them.

Let me say that again to be clear: We think it hurts when other people hurt us, and it does. But compared to how it feels when we hurt others, that pain is insignificant. I realize that this notion runs counter to conventional wisdom, but how's that conventional wisdom working out for you so far?

Conventional wisdom tells you that if you could only get other people to behave, to love you the right way, to be nice to you, then you would be happy. We are conditioned to believe that our happiness depends on how other people feel about us and how they treat us. Out of that come individuals who are desperately seeking approval, and are willing to lie, manipulate, and cheat in order to get it.

Sure, it feels good, like a warm bath, when someone else loves us or thinks we are great, but that feeling only lasts for a short time. Then, like any drug, the effects wear off, and we go looking for the next fix. Pretty soon we need more and more approval in order to feel okay about ourselves. We learn how to get approval from other people, usually by manipulation, but we don't learn how to get it from ourselves.

If you don't think you manipulate other people to get approval, take a look at all the times that you've smiled when you really wanted to give someone a well-deserved piece of your mind. Or recall all the times you said yes when you meant no. All of that was manipulation. Don't get down on yourself for it. Most of us have been taught manipulation by people who were taught to manipulate. This does not mean they were bad people; they just didn't know another way.

But there is a *much* better way. You want love and approval from other people because it makes you feel good. It's better, however, to skip the middleman altogether and learn how to give love to yourself.

We started this section by talking about the radical idea that what hurts us the most is the pain we cause, not the pain we receive. We want to blame everyone else for our pain because we are taught to believe that other people have the power to make us feel good or bad. If we feel bad, we believe it must be someone else's fault. The truth is that no one can hurt you the way you can hurt yourself when you are unkind to others.

How does this relate to learning how *not* to take things personally? When we believe that our happiness lies in the hands of other people, everything they say or do feels incredibly personal. If I need your approval to feel good, and you say or do something that makes me think that you don't approve of me, it's going to devastate and overwhelm me. It is only when I understand that *I* am the one who has the most power to affect my own happiness that I can let you have your life and opinions without feeling that I need your approval.

When my happiness is within my own control, I can focus on doing the things I need to do to be happy, and the most important of those things is to be kind to other people.

You know those fights that feel like they are life-and-death battles? When a little time goes by, most of us forget what the other person said to us, but we remember, with cringing regret, the cruel and cutting things *we* said, and we desperately wish we could take them back. In the long run, those are the moments that eat away at our happiness, undermine our self-esteem, and chip away at our self-confidence.

Although we can't take the offensive words back, we can clean up our past by making amends to the people we have hurt. That is true even if they are no longer alive. In my own case, I wrote apologetic letters to deceased persons I had offended. For me, making amends has contributed more to my overall happiness and sense of self-worth than anything else.

Now it's your chance to take back the power that you have unknowingly given away. Your happiness, self-esteem, and joy have never been dependent on the actions or feelings of anyone else. If you had a way to approve of yourself and love yourself, you wouldn't need the love or approval of anyone else. That is a blessed state indeed. It doesn't happen in a day, but you are on the path. We will continue to learn about taking back the power to create and maintain our own happiness, but for now it's enough to mull over these radical new concepts.

In the Real World

Right before I sobered up, I signed a large contract for a job out of town—my biggest contract to that date. I entered into the contract full of fear, and with the attitude of "This will either make me or break me." My attorney had advised me to redline several areas of the contract with a letter of explanation. One of those areas pertained to complying with the production schedule, which was not yet posted.

As often happens with large projects, this one was delayed for nearly six months because of red tape. Then, as the project progressed, so did the production schedule. Because I had fifty men on the job, we were ahead of our weekly forecast. But even with manning the job properly and staying on or ahead of schedule, the project manager kept pushing me to go faster.

Because I had redlined the part of the contract pertaining to the schedule, no matter how hard he pushed me, he had no legal right to hold me in breach of contract. He never gave me a twenty-four-hour notice to perform, nor did he threaten me with any legal documents. However, I was seeing the handwriting on the wall. He was slow in paying me even as he was becoming more and more demanding. At that point, I had been sober for six months, but wasn't really sure how to deal with all of this.

In the past, I would have become angry and threatened to pull my guys off the job, which would have led to further complications. As was suggested to me by men wiser than myself, I started corresponding with the project manager in writing and began negotiations to terminate my contract amicably. After two weeks of negotiations (which at times were highly unpleasant), we arrived at an agreement that we could both live with.

The project manager's company owed me approximately $120,000, but in order to close the deal, I had to walk away from $30,000 of that. At that point in my life, making that decision was just smart business. I was starting to learn that I did have choices.

Part of my ability to make better decisions was that my self-worth was no longer tied to how other people saw me. Previously, if someone attacked me or threatened my business, I felt that they were attacking my innermost being, which was why I always felt that I had to come out with all guns blazing to protect myself.

Gradually, it mattered less and less what other people thought of me. Even money became less of a concern. Slowly, my own self-worth was starting to become the most valuable currency in my life. In the past, I had been so dependent on other people's opinions of me that I would violate my own sense of my self-worth in order to "win" their approval.

We all have that feeling inside that tells us when we are off course. When we start a fight or an argument, something inside us is sounding an alarm. But if we feel that we are desperate to win the fight because we need the other person to validate us, we ignore that alarm, and every time we do that, we both violate and undervalue ourselves. But that seems like an acceptable price to pay when we are fully vested in other people's images of us. It is only when we step back and learn how to build our self-confidence that we realize the cost was much too high.

Sometimes, changing our character defects can be as simple as choosing our battles. Unlike previous unpleasant situations, in my dealing with the project manager I asked myself different questions. Instead of getting angry because my ego-façade was being threatened, I asked myself, "Is it really worth the fight? How much will this battle interfere in my life, in my relationship with my wife and children? How much will this battle disrupt my own peace and serenity?"

Was it easy to walk away from $30,000? Absolutely not! Was it easy to let the project manager think I was weak or a quitter by walking away from that money? Nope. But not having it did not break me financially, and not having to fight over it gave me more peace and serenity than money could ever offer.

The truth is, I never had the power to change the way the project manager thought about me. He could think I was the most powerful, awesome man in the world, or the weakest loser ever, and I couldn't do a thing about it either way. When we are constantly living in someone else's head—and we know we're doing that when our internal dialogue is centered on what that other person might be thinking or feeling—we have abandoned ourselves. I was getting tired of abandoning myself.

But I did not develop my defects and maladaptive coping skills overnight, so I couldn't expect them to magically disappear. I had to slowly replace my defective behaviors with new and positive ones. Too many people believe that all one has to do is ask God to remove their defects, and it is done. I only wish it were that simple. But it's not. We have to do the work.

As I went about my daily business, situations would arise that in the past I would react to with a negative response, which almost always resulted in a negative outcome. It was as if my Higher Power were saying to me, "Okay, Randy, you want *me* to remove your character defects? How are *you* going to handle this situation differently today?"

I had to stop, think, and respond with the opposite of whatever action I would have taken in the past. Some of those previously negative situations were as simple as saying no when I meant no. As simple as that seems, for many people, especially survivors of sexual abuse, this can be one of the hardest things to do.

The process of change starts with baby steps, and having a good support system is important. In my own case, I had A.A. When I got to Step Five, which involves admitting "to God, to ourselves, and to another human being the exact nature of our wrongs," or what we call "sharing my inventory" with my sponsor, he pointed out to me the areas that he believed were my defects and my assets. Many traits that I believed were character assets were, he said, actually defects. The problem was that society also regards many of these traits as manly, such as manipulation, intimidation, selfishness, and self-centeredness. Furthermore, traits that I thought of as defects were, he said, actually assets, such as emotional vulnerability, ability to admit weakness, expression of feelings, and compassion.

My sponsor had me make a list of my character defects and assets in side-by-side columns. When I had completed this, I saw that my defects far outweighed my assets. But as I went through the two lists with my sponsor, he pointed out that I had a lot of assets that I hadn't put on the list—such as being a good husband, loving father, and hard worker. In fact, when we finished adding to the asset column, it was far longer than the defect column. This experience taught me that I had previously been unable to see myself clearly through the clouded lens of my low self-esteem.

Whenever you remove something negative, it leaves a void that must be filled by something positive. Otherwise, it will very likely be filled by something even more negative. Once I realized what my character defects were and was willing and ready to remove them, the work began. While some of those defects were easy to replace, such as coming home grumpy from work and taking out my frustrations on my wife, others were more difficult, such as constantly criticizing myself.

I had to remember that although some of those character defects had partly served me well by keeping me alive in the past, they were now causing more harm than good. As I traveled down this complex road of recovery, I had to be patient with myself. If I made mistakes, I had to love myself rather than beat myself up. Most of all, I had to remain willing to change.

Discovering Constructive Coping Skills

When I first walked into the Betty Ford Center for treatment, my counselor told me right up front that I had to develop healthy new coping skills. To this, my immediate reaction was anger.

Wait a minute! I thought. *I come into treatment and A.A. to get fixed, and you tell me I have to fix myself?! How am I supposed to cope? How am I supposed to relieve my anxiety? Damn you!*

But I was actually ready to do whatever it would take to change. Real change didn't come at once, but I started to sense it within a couple of weeks, when I began to understand how to replace my destructive coping skills with constructive ones.

What do healthy coping skills look like in the real world? Constructive coping skills can be anything at all, so long as they make you feel genuinely good about yourself—not just distracted, or high on approval from others, but truly peaceful. In general, constructive coping skills help you to relax and bring you into the now. Here were mine:

- Cycling.
- Hiking.
- Meditating.
- Playing a musical instrument.
- Playing with a beloved pet.
- Practicing yoga.
- Surfing.
- Walking on the beach.

Making these a part of my life and replacing the old, familiar ones of almost four decades was one of the hardest things I have ever done. It takes daily practice and a lot of fist-clenching patience. I knew that I needed help, and I trusted the men and women who suggested that I trust in a Higher Power. Although I was still angry at God, I started praying. At first, I just repeated some of the prayers from *The Big Book* of A.A., and slowly started asking God to help me with my daily challenges.[47] The habit of praying last thing at night and first thing in the morning helped to keep me centered throughout my day. Gradually, I began to talk to God as if He (or She) were an older, wiser sage.

Now, you may be thinking, *Randy, you don't understand the things I've done. God will never forgive me. God will never listen to me.*

I know that feeling, because I used to think the same thing. The way I got around that may work for you, so you're welcome to try it. Just tell God whatever is on your mind. If you're angry at Him, tell him that. If you think praying is a joke, tell him that. Get it all out. Just be consistent in your praying.

The more I prayed, the better I felt, and slowly my anger toward God dissipated. I started to get relief from my anxiety and fears, and was staying sober—something I had not been able to do on my own, no matter how hard I had tried.

Next, along with praying, I began to meditate daily. Praying, my spiritual counselor taught me, is talking to God, whereas meditating is listening to God. The hardest part for me was finding the willingness to sit quietly and still, but I gradually learned how to do that as I listened for the answers I was seeking. Most of the time, it only took five to ten minutes of meditation before those answers started coming to me. Initially, I wanted to return to my "do-do-do" habits of running from my pain by worrying about work and tomorrow. After all, my worrying was itself an escape from the fear and shame I carried around inside me. I felt comfortable with that fear and shame, so this new way of calming myself still felt foreign.

My sponsor, a relentlessly peaceful guy who went by the nickname "Way Spiritual Dave," suggested for my morning meditation that I imagine I was at the beach with a hot air balloon, into whose basket I would put all my worries about life and work. Then I could release that basket into the universe. The more I practiced that meditation, the easier it became to give my worries over to a power greater than myself. After all, the worrying had never fixed a single problem anyway.

---

[47] Alcoholics Anonymous, *The Big Book*, 4th ed. (New York: Alcoholics Anonymous Worldwide Services, 2001).

COPING MECHANISMS

At first, this practice only gave me a minute of relief. But then, that increased to an hour, and eventually to an entire day. Remember, everything is a process that takes time, so no matter what, be consistent in your prayers and meditation practices, because if you are not, your recovery process may only be delayed.

Even in the depth of my addictions, I had always taken care of my body. I worked out all the time, which proved to be one of my better coping skills, since it helped me to release my anger. I could go into the gym and quietly take out my aggression by working out, and no one ever knew about it.

Exercise has an added benefit as well, which I was not aware of until after I started working toward a real recovery. Exercise releases three neurotransmitters—serotonin, dopamine, and norepinephrine—which are known as the "happy chemicals." The release of these chemicals is what causes that relaxed, upbeat mood that you feel after spending an hour or so in the gym—that rush of pure, unadulterated euphoria, also known by runners and cyclists as the "runner's high."

If you don't like being around a lot of people, or just need time to be with yourself, other excellent ways to cope with stress and anxiety include cycling, running, and hiking. Yoga is also an excellent way to combine meditation and exercise into one supercharged positive coping skill.

Another very effective coping tool for me was (and still is) playing my classical guitar, which, like any instrument, takes a tremendous amount of concentration. Playing is a great way for me to turn my focus from worries to my music, thereby bringing me into the now.

But if I am worried or distracted when I sit down to play, my guitar instantly tells me, because I have trouble staying focused on reading the music, and the sound reflects that. Playing my guitar is a great way to assess my state of mind. Sometimes I think I'm fine when I'm actually upset somewhere below my conscious awareness. A few minutes with my guitar let me know where I am mentally and emotionally, but a few more minutes are usually enough to make me more positive, happy, and centered.

These days, I use playing my guitar as a form of meditation. While playing, I envision myself sitting on top of a mountain high over the ocean. I love to feel the warm sun and sea breeze on my face, taking in the sweet smell of the air, much as I did as a teenager, when I would sit on the side of a hill overlooking the coast—a refuge where no one could hurt me.

The more relaxed I am, the safer I feel, and the more easily the music flows softly and flawlessly from my guitar. This has taught me to release my worries and fears about yesterday and tomorrow, and stay in the moment, in the now.

One of the most important skills that I have developed is technically not a skill at all. I surround myself with healthy people. Initially, I developed new relationships in the recovery world with people who loved me until I could love myself. Healthy men in recovery surrounded me and walked with me through my fears, guiding me toward healthy situations and positions that helped to increase my self-esteem. It is vital to my well-being that I have healthy relationships with like-minded people.

All of these positive coping skills have helped me enormously to boost my confidence. Every time I use a positive coping skill, I increase my own happiness and self-esteem from the inside out. Not only do I relieve my anxiety, release my aggressions, and take care of my body, but I also teach myself in the most powerful experiential way that my happiness and self-esteem are truly in my own control.

Originally, as I left my old coping skills behind, that meant, to a large degree, that I was leaving my old life behind. So much of what I did and what I thought I was, was centered around constantly shoring up a façade that I wanted people to see. When, for the first time since my father had died, I began to learn how to be *myself*, so much of what I thought was "me" was really just part of an act designed to win approval from people around me. This new, more secure me realized that I had to have healthy men and women around me to bounce my ideas off, since my thinking could still be skewed.

Whether male survivors of sexual abuse are formally in recovery or not, we are—first and foremost—men, so the last thing we want to do is admit we need help and ask for it. However, we must do both, or we will fall back into our old behavior patterns and return to the maladaptive coping practices that no longer work for us.

When I started on this journey of recovery, I was very careful about the people I chose to have around me. The ones who helped me to develop new positive coping skills got to know the real me, learned what I liked and didn't like, and never introduced me to coping mechanisms that didn't work. But this went two ways. To let them see the real me, I had to let my guard down, which was not easy. But I made real friends for perhaps the first time in my life. And all of the new coping skills I learned really worked for me—the real me, whom I had hardly ever let anyone see before. I finally got the love and approval I had always craved from others after I learned how to give it to myself.

I started on my recovery journey with a set of unhealthy coping mechanisms, which, although they helped me to survive, were behaviors I had learned from unhealthy people and no longer worked for me. Just as I had to find what *did* work for me, so you will need to discover what works for you. There are so many different types of healthy coping tools out there that finding the best fit for yourself is just a matter of staying open-minded and continuing to try new ones until you discover your perfect fit.

You might like going to the gym with a bunch of muscle heads around you. Or perhaps you enjoy yoga or taking a hike. My goal in the beginning was to find just one new skill that would help me to cope with the "growing pains" I was having as I was becoming a new man. It is a lot less overwhelming to find and replace one skill at a time than to try to replace all your old maladaptive coping mechanisms at once. However, at a bare minimum, I suggest that you start praying and meditating every day.

Learning these new coping skills and having healthy men and women in my life—not only physically, but also spiritually and emotionally—allowed me to walk into my home at night in a good mood. For the first time, I was able to enjoy my wife without dumping all my toxic garbage on her. I stopped making her responsible for my happiness, and stopped treating her like an emotional vending machine, into which I could drop the right coin in order to get the response I wanted. Now that my happiness was coming from inside, I could focus my attention on her and how her day had gone. I actually started to get to know her, and was present and attentive in ways that I had rarely experienced before. Needless to say, being this "new me" had a highly positive effect on our relationship.

Today, I continue to use all the positive coping skills I have developed over the years. I pray and meditate daily, I go to the gym three or four times a week, I ride a hundred-plus miles a week on my bike, and I play my guitar every day. All these activities have become engrained in my psyche in the same way that all my old maladaptive coping mechanisms had. Using positive coping skills keeps me safe and spiritually and emotionally healthy.

Now I can actually be grateful for my old "bad" coping behaviors, which brought me to a point where I was willing to enter recovery. The very fact that you are reading this book is an acknowledgment, conscious or not, that *you* may be willing to begin your own recovery. The first step in the process is to reach out for help. Eventually, if you stay on the path of recovery, you will come out on the other side into a bright new world.

In your search for coping skills that work for you, just remain open-minded, flexible, and patient. The process is a marathon, not a sprint. Change hurts, but it will never hurt you as badly as you were hurt in the past.

Chapter 5: Spiritual Abuse

As a child abuse and neglect therapist, I do battle daily with Christians enamored of the Old Testament phrase "Spare the rod and spoil the child." No matter how far I stretch my imagination, it does not stretch far enough to include the image of a cool dude like Jesus taking a rod to a kid.

—Chris Crutcher[48]

I am often asked what exactly spiritual abuse is. Many people resonate with the idea of spiritual abuse, but have not had the chance to explore the parameters of this unique type of abuse. It is important to understand it, and to know its possible repercussions, so you can address the specific issues you might be dealing with.

Spiritual abuse is difficult to define because there are so many different religions and belief systems out there—and, sadly, just as many ways that those teachings can be twisted so they become abusive. In fact, in my research, I have found that every "expert" has his or her own definition of what exactly spiritual abuse is. However, the one constant I have found in the various definitions is that it involves the abuse of power and the misrepresentation of information by a spiritual leader or leaders, especially to individuals who are vulnerable and most in need of support.

Below is just one of many definitions of spiritual abuse. I choose to include it here, since it directly addresses the key component of abuse—the misuse of power. Ken Blue, a motivational speaker in religious and business circles, compares spiritual abuse to physical and sexual abuse:

> Abuse of any type occurs when someone has power over another and uses that power to hurt. Physical abuse

---

[48]Chris Crutcher, *King of the Mild Frontier: An Ill-Advised Autobiography* (New York: HarperCollins, 2003), retrieved from http://www.goodreads.com/quotes/968221-as-a-child-abuse-and-neglect-therapist-i-do-battle/.

means that someone exercises physical power over another, causing physical wounds. Sexual abuse means that someone exercises sexual power over another, resulting in sexual wounds. And spiritual abuse happens when a leader with spiritual authority uses that authority to coerce, control, or exploit a follower, thus causing spiritual wounds.[49]

In some cases, spiritual abuse is inflicted intentionally; in others, it is inflicted unintentionally. Unfortunately for the survivors, the end result is usually the same: broken individuals who no longer trust other people. In most cases, having been abused spiritually, they are not inclined to turn to a Higher Power for comfort. That can be devastating to their personal healing and their progress toward real happiness.

When I began my own recovery, I wanted nothing to do with any kind of God. I believed that, at best, He didn't care what happened to me, and at worst, He actually protected abusers. After all, that was my experience. The pastors and leaders of my church not only knew what Jack was doing, but they covered up for him, as a Deacon of the church, using quotes from the Bible to make *me* the evildoer.

As I saw it at the time, God took away my father and brought Jack into my life, despite all of my anguished pleadings with Him.

The elders of the church would come over to the house, late at night, drag me out of bed, and pray over me, hoping to cast out whatever demons were supposedly possessing me. My mother even told me that I was Satan himself. Not once did any of them ever ask what was going on with me. Not once did any of them ever ask if something were going on in the house that they should know about. To them, I was just another out-of-control, demon-possessed teenager.

Even if the elders had asked me these questions, I probably would not have said a thing. Why should I have trusted them? They already thought I needed to be exorcized—not the best way to build a bond of trust between a child and adults.

A common source of ongoing shame for me—as for all sexual abuse survivors—was the thought that I "should" have told an adult. In my own case, when I was sixteen, I did, in fact, ask my grandmother—my father's

---

[49]Ken Blue, *Healing Spiritual Abuse: How to Break Free from Bad Church Experiences* (Downers Grove, IL: InterVarsity Press, 1993), p. 559, retrieved from http://dallascult.com/?page_id=559/.

mother—if I could live with her. But when she said that wasn't possible, without giving any further explanation, I was afraid to tell her about the sexual abuse, for two reasons. One, I was terrified of the physical abuse that would follow if Grandma complained to my mother or Jack. And two, I was afraid that my mother and Jack would prevent me from ever seeing Grandma again.

So what *is* spiritual abuse, and what can we do about it now? Spiritual abuse damages the central core of who we are. It leaves us spiritually discouraged and emotionally cut off from the healing power of God. It rapes us of our innocence, dignity, integrity, and spirit. It does the opposite of what God and religion are intended to do.

Instead of feeling that I was loved and whole, no matter what, I felt that I was less than nothing because I was being abused both sexually *and* spiritually. The essence of the child within me had been crushed. The church had wounded that free-spirited kid I had been.

The Legacy of Spiritual Abuse

I grew up in a "Christian" home. From the outside looking in, my family appeared to be a carbon copy of the Cleavers from *Leave It to Beaver*. We lived in a nice house, we were well groomed, and we went to church every Sunday and Wednesday. My mother was a member of the choir, and Jack, as I've said, was a Deacon of our small community church.

In many ways, I enjoyed being a part of the church's youth group, and for a little while, that group was good for me because I was a part of something. I felt safe, loved, and accepted. Plus, there were girls.

I also got to go away to youth camps, which took me out of the house and away from Jack. We went hiking, snow skiing, and surfing, and I loved playing guitar for the group. And again, there were girls.

For a time, the youth group offered me solace from the uncertainty of living in a highly dysfunctional home. It offered me a place of acceptance, safety, and fun.

But then, one night, the pastor, whose name was Dick, came over to the house to counsel my mother and Jack, as he often did, and just to socialize with them and watch TV. Usually, the socializing would come first, and then the three of them would go out to Dick's "office," a 1972 blue Ford Maverick, to do the counseling. But on this night, Dick said to me, "Randy, you come with me and Jack."

A rush of confusion came over me as I thought, *Uh oh! What does he want with me? I hope Jack hasn't told him anything.*

But I just followed them outside and got in the back seat, while Dick got in behind the wheel, and Jack sat in the front passenger seat.

As soon as they closed their doors, they both turned around to look at me.

"Randy," Dick said, "Jack's been talking to me about what's been going on between the two of you."

I immediately felt a wave of shame wash over me. I'm sure my face turned bright red. As I sank down into my seat, I thought to myself, *I'll kill you both!*

I started sweating as a huge knot formed in my stomach. Although I wanted to disappear, there was a tiny spark of hope that I was finally going to get the help I had been craving for the past three years, ever since I was twelve.

"I just want to tell you, Randy," he continued, as calmly as can be, "that it's part of growing up, natural and normal, and doesn't mean that you will be gay."

Jack was smirking at me this whole time. I wanted to run, but felt trapped in the back seat of the two-door car.

Then Dick said a prayer, he and Jack got out of the car, and I headed straight to my bedroom, avoiding eye contact with my mother, trying to be as invisible as possible—even to myself.

As I sat on my bed, I thought of all the things I wished I had asked:

"If it's a part of growing up, then why does it have to be kept a secret?"

"Why don't we go in the house right now, and tell my mother what's been happening?"

"If it's a part of growing up, then why isn't it happening to my brother Richard?"

Those questions ran in circles in my head for the next thirty-plus years as I struggled to understand what had happened to me. But in that moment, all I knew was that a man of God was telling me that what Jack was doing to me was just fine.

To this day, I don't know what that pastor was thinking. He seemed more concerned that I would think I was homosexual than with the child abuse that was happening. I couldn't understand it. That sense of isolation and rage only deepened the effects of the sexual abuse on my psyche.

Dick's words made it a thousand times harder for me as an adult to finally tell someone about the abuse. Those words isolated me, not only from God and religious leaders, but from everyone. After all, if God himself judged me and thought I needed exorcisms, what hope did I have for my fellow human beings to accept me?

After getting this implicit approval from the pastor, Jack grew less restrained, and the sexual, physical, and emotional abuse intensified. If God was okay with what was happening in my home, I decided I was not okay with God.

What I experienced at the hands of the leader of that church was almost worse than the sexual abuse itself. What Jack was doing tore away my self-respect, but Dick's spiritual abuse destroyed my ability to connect with a Higher Power for comfort or healing.

In the same way that sexual abuse can be devastating because it leaves the child no safe physical space to go to heal from the trauma, spiritual abuse denies the victim any soul-based solace. When sexual abuse and spiritual abuse are combined, the result can be crushing. Whenever I was in church or participating in church activities, my mother and Jack were model Christians. But at home their true colors came out in fits of rage and violence.

Even on the nights that I spent peacefully watching TV, playing pong, or doing homework, there was always the underlying fear that something bad could happen at any moment.

Parents who abuse their children spiritually often pass down a legacy of spiritual abuse. Because spiritual abuse is often less talked about than male sexual abuse, many people don't recognize it as abuse. To them, it is just the "way we were brought up." Because of this, spiritual abusers often see no harm in what they are doing. As in my case, parents often spiritually abuse their children out of their own frustration and lack of knowledge of proper parenting skills. The hardest part of dealing with spiritual abuse is that, most of the time, parents truly believe that they are doing what is best for their child. They don't understand the long-term ramifications of their actions.

Frustrated parents, like Jack and my mother, often quote scriptures or spiritual teachings to their children in an effort to control them. As I grew up, there were two scriptures in particular that became ingrained in me. The first was, "Honor your father and your mother, that your days may be long in the land that the Lord your God is giving you" (Exodus 20:12). That scripture kept me stuck and angry until very recently. How is it possible to honor your father and mother when they are not doing honorable things to you? Respect, honor, and trust are earned, not given.

Yet, so many parents will defend their abusive actions by quoting scripture, especially passages that are backed up with words of fear about a punishing God.

The second scripture that my mother, Jack, and our pastor lived by was, "Do not withhold discipline from a child; if you punish them with the rod, they will not die. Punish them with the rod and save them from death" (Proverbs 23: 13–14). To have religion used as a justification for the beatings I endured left deeper scars on me than all of Jack's rods, belts, and fists.

To this day, I don't believe that love had anything to do with the beatings I endured at my stepfather's hands. The only way I can understand Jack's behavior is that he may have beaten me in order to excise his own self-hatred. But whatever his reasons, conscious or unconscious, his beating me and justifying it with religion only pushed me further away from the church and God.

It wasn't until recently that some of my psycho-spiritual scars started to heal, when one of my psychology professors explained the "rod" passage to the class like this: A shepherd uses his rod to gently guide his sheep back onto a safe path. If they start to wander off, he simply guides them back with a nudge from his rod. He doesn't beat them, for if he did, they would only run away.

I have raised three children, and not once have I laid a hand on any of them. There has been no legacy of abuse in my family. All three of my children have become respectful and respected adults. I finally understand that neither the Bible nor God advocates child beating. That was a twisted representation passed on to me by hurt people. I understand now that people's hypocrisy and misuse of power is not God's doing. But when I was a child, the message I received was that God was definitely not on my side.

Co-morbidity in Spiritual Abuse

Spiritual abuse is rarely found alone. Like many other diseases, it usually displays signs of co-morbidity, or association with other diseases. For example, spiritual abuse is all too often associated with sexual abuse.

The most infamous recent examples, of course, are those of the Catholic priests who abuse young boys and use their position as spiritual advisors to keep the youths from speaking out. It is a truism that the children who most need a loving intervention in their abuse are the least likely to get it—especially from their primary caregivers.

In my own case, my rebellious behavior and my alcohol and drug use were all direct results of the sexual abuse. Yet, to Dick, Jack, and my mother, I was just another out-of-control teenager. Because my mother and Jack were such "wonderful" people when they were around the other members of their church, their word was gold—a position that all too many abused children find themselves in.

If you are the one being abused, you probably look like the "crazy" one, or even get labeled as abusive yourself due to your behavior, which is fueled by rage, shame, and fear. But when most people see an angry or violent or rebellious teenager, they don't immediately think, *That child is acting out in disruptive ways. Perhaps there's a deeper issue here.* In fact, the majority of people only see the surface behavior and are inclined to sympathize with the parents rather than with the victimized child.

This is a tough situation to face as a child, which usually leads to a great deal of resentment, frustration, and mistrust of authority figures. Many of us internalize the lie that there is really something wrong with us, when in fact we couldn't be more normal in terms of how a child *should* react to trauma.

If you have internalized the destructive messages that you heard as a child, I want you to know that they are not true. You were *not* a bad kid, you did *not* deserve to be abused, and you are *not* responsible for the abuse. If you acted out with violence, addiction, or other maladaptive coping skills, you were only trying to save your own life the best way you knew how—and you were completely "normal" for doing so. There is nothing wrong with you, and there never was.

Children trust adults and caregivers until they are mature enough to realize that older people do not always *deserve* to be trusted—no matter how many biblical passages they may quote. It is difficult enough for a child to disbelieve an adult's negative messages. But it is far harder to be skeptical of God's own "messengers"—in the form of pastors or any other figures of authority, including one's parents.

The most common response to spiritual abuse from trusted elders is for a child to internalize the message that he is truly bad. Then, later, he turns on God and religion, rejecting what should have been the safest sources of comfort and solace. Speaking from my own painful experience, I despised

God by the time I was fifteen. Either I was evil and deserved all of the pain and shame of the abuse, or God was a bastard who let Jack hurt me and get away with it. Either way, I wanted nothing to do with religion or God.

Spiritual Leaders

Spiritual leaders have been given some type of spiritual training, whether by a priest, pastor, shaman, or guru, and spent time in the presence of God. However, they need not have a formal title. They can be our grandparents, parents, siblings, aunts, uncles, or anyone else with the ability to guide others through the problems and trials of life with love, peace, and kindness. Good spiritual leaders never condemn or shame others, and, most important, they practice what they preach.

However, many spiritual leaders are dogmatic in their teachings and hypocrites in their personal lives. They are closed-minded, authoritarian, and leave little or no room for individual experience or beliefs. They will often teach personal conviction as religious "fact" and can leave their followers with distorted beliefs about God.

Spiritual leaders can also be survivors of sexual abuse, since a big step in our healing is helping others to heal. In that capacity, it is important that we not push our beliefs on others, always remembering that spirituality is an individual and unique aspect of a person's life—an aspect that must be between an individual and his or her Higher Power. It is when we start to impose our own judgments on others, based on our inflated sense of self-righteousness, that spiritual abuse begins to be perpetrated.

The Power of Spiritual Abuse

Like abuse of any kind, spiritual abuse is about power. David Johnson, a senior pastor, and Jeff VanVonderen, a certified intervention specialist, state that "spiritual abuse is *always* a power issue. In order for abuse to happen, by definition, it has to come from a place of higher power to a place of lesser power. People in low-power positions can't abuse people in high power."[50]

When someone perpetrates abuse from a position of power, the victim is vulnerable because, if he does not comply with the abuser's demands, he fears that his spiritual and emotional needs, and perhaps even his basic

---

[50]David Johnson and Jeff VanVonderen, *The Subtle Power of Spiritual Abuse: Recognizing and Escaping Spiritual Manipulation and False Spiritual Authority Within the Church* (Bloomington, MN: Bethany House, 1991), p. 132 (emphasis added).

survival needs, will not be met. If the victim is a child or adolescent, he is reliant on his parents to meet his basic survival needs, which include food, shelter, clothes, and love. A victim of simultaneous sexual and spiritual abuse feels that if he does not give his power over to the abusive spiritual leader, these basic survival needs will not be met. In fact, he may even fear that his noncompliance with the abuse will lead his soul to burn in hell for eternity.

Being left homeless or denied food, sleep, or any other basic essential of life, including human connection and everlasting salvation, is truly terrifying. When threatened with any of these fates, a victim may crumble, handing his spiritual power over to someone who is *supposed* to protect, guide, and love him. All too often, however, an abusive spiritual leader knows this and deliberately chooses to use his (or her) power against the victim.

No matter what one's personal beliefs are, spirituality is about an intimate connection with a Higher Power. No one has the right to interfere with that relationship. Whenever someone gets between an individual and his Higher Power, attempting to impose beliefs on that individual's inner knowing, the person in a position of lower power has the right to ignore it.

We all know right from wrong, good from bad, moral from immoral behavior. It seems that the people who are most likely to commit sins are the ones who are also the most likely to cite religious "laws" in order to justify their manipulation of others. If the Bible says, "Obey your father and mother as you would your God," and a parent uses that to justify beating a disobedient child, then that parent is using the child's beliefs to manipulate him.

In my experience, the louder someone shouts that he is a good Christian, Catholic, Muslim, Buddhist, Jew, or whatever, the more likely it is that he is desperately trying to hide his own sins. A truly spiritual person tends to be quiet about his spirituality. He rarely tells other people what they should or should not do, since he is more interested in kindness and goodness than in laws and rules.

I was a happy-go-lucky kid who enjoyed life—until the abuse started when I was twelve. After that, I was not a perfect kid by any means, but I was not possessed by demons, either. However, the actions of the pastor and the church elders put me on a path on which, by the age of eighteen, I was swinging between murderous thoughts of killing Jack and totally depressed desires to kill myself.

Often, a victimized child experiences his life as already one of eternal hell. That can cause him to reinforce his false belief that he is inherently bad, and that, at some level, the abuse is his own fault.

Here is a spiritual abuse checklist:

- Do leaders in your church require you to consult with them before you make any significant decisions?

- Do you find yourself periodically questioning your spirituality or standing with God?

- Have you been preoccupied with checking out others in the congregation to see who is living up to the rules and who isn't?

- Are rules and standards that are not explicitly mentioned in the standard religious texts considered as coming from God, with your salvation or spirituality linked to following them?

- Are minor actions, such as cutting or not cutting your hair, indicators of your spirituality?

- Has the initial joy you felt when you first found your spiritual leader, group, or church been replaced by worry and anxiety?

- Do you often feel that you're not doing enough or are not good enough to live up to what is expected of you by your spiritual leaders?

- Do sermons or meetings uplift you and give you strength, or do you feel sad, discouraged, or depressed afterward?

- Has your view of God changed so that you now see Him as a harsh taskmaster, eagerly waiting for you to mess up, so that He can chastise you or cut you entirely out of the group?

Chapter 6:
The G–d Word

Religion is for people who are afraid of going to hell. Spirituality is for people who have been there.

—Vine Deloria, Jr., Sioux elder, author, and activist[51]

The first time I walked into the Betty Ford Center, I had a real problem with God. As I sat through my first lecture in the West Auditorium, I looked up and noticed the word *God* jumping off the wall at me in bold print and underlined. Immediately, I knew that there was going to be trouble—that this recovery process would never work out if God had to be part of it. Still, I sat with gritted teeth, remembering that I had promised to try, and that trying included being willing and open-minded to learn new ways of living.

I fully understand and respect any reservation readers may have about God. Many A.A. groups replace the word *God* with *Higher Power* because religion and religious leaders have spiritually abused so many people. To be honest, I still have some trouble with organized religions myself, although I have returned to the Christian faith of my childhood. One of my favorite sayings is the quote that opens this chapter.

I consider myself spiritual, not religious. Although I refer to my Higher Power as "God," if you choose to call your Higher Power "Coach" or "Papa" or "Boss," or prefer to regard the ocean or sky as your Higher Power, that works, too.

Recovery is tough, and working the Twelve Steps of A.A. was difficult for me, even with all the love, support, and wisdom I was surrounded by during my journey. I can tell you with absolute confidence that I would not have made it without all the help and support I received—and that includes the support from God.

---

[51]Retrieved from http://www.goodreads.com/quotes/160879-religion-is-for-people-who-re-afraid-of-going-to-hell/.

In the beginning, I was not ready to use the word *God*, so I used *Higher Power* instead. When I did, I thought of the feeling I got from surfing or hiking. Nature stood in for a deity until I was ready to heal from the spiritual abuse of my childhood. But even choosing to rely on the strength and steadiness that I had always found in nature was critical to my success in recovery.

When we are hurt emotionally or spiritually, we tend to retreat within ourselves. When the people we trust the most to love us and take care of us are the very ones who hurt us, we start to have trouble trusting others. When people hurt us in the name of God, we withdraw from God, retreating into a world where we rely only on ourselves.

This Me-Against-the-World theme is only reinforced by society, especially for men. There are many cultural references to the macho loner as an iconic hero. Songs praise him, movies idolize him, and books romanticize him. But the truth is that going at life all by ourselves is difficult at best. If we turn to other people, they inevitably let us down, sooner or later—not because they are bad or untrustworthy, but because we have unrealistic expectations of them.

Because survivors of sexual abuse tend to be so wary of trusting other people, when we do find someone we can trust, we dump decades of baggage and expectations onto that person—who is often an unsuspecting spouse. Not only is it unfair to unload all of our emotional pain on another person, but doing so is painful and costs many survivors their marriages or closest friendships. Human beings are not meant to go through life alone. We are social beings by nature. However, we certainly are not meant to be each other's Higher Power, either.

In order to heal, we've got to stop trying to do everything by ourselves. When we turn our life over to God, however, we understand Him, we want to know that God can handle it at least as well as we can.

Step Three

Every recovery program—at least those modeled after A.A.—have twelve steps. Step Three involves making a decision to turn our will and lives over to the care of God as we understand God.

Is it possible to really know who God is? For myself, I say yes. However, I know that there are plenty of people who will disagree with me and not believe in God. That is fine. I used to feel the same way. However, there is a commonality in how we all understand God. Let's be clear about one thing: I "religiously" avoid anyone who insists that God is vengeful, angry, or only likes one group of people. That has the work of Man written all over it, and I heard plenty of Man's versions of God when I was a child. To me, God is omnipresent and radiates love and compassion to all people, regardless of who they are, what they do, or what they have done. It is people who radiate love and compassion that I choose to look up to today.

I can tell you this with certainty: without God or a Higher Power in your life, the journey of recovery will be extremely difficult. I could not have made it without my Higher Power, which I call God. Try not to get too hung up on the names and minor differences between what people mean when they say the word *God*. Come up with your own definition for the God that you would want to follow, and let that be your Higher Power.

Spirituality is hardwired into humans. We've relied on mythology and stories about the afterlife and the spiritual world ever since we first started lighting fires in caves. Human beings have always needed some kind of spirituality, which may take the form of science, nature, or a religious deity. But whatever it is, when we embark on the journey back to our own wholeness, we need the kind of help that other human beings are just not capable of giving.

I knew that A.A. is not a religious organization, per se, but I prepared some choice phrases for the first person who dared to say anything even remotely religious to me. Much to my surprise, I did not need any of those phrases. People in A.A. were talking about God and how pastors, priests, and churches had wounded them in much the same way that I had been wounded. The priests and pastors sounded like the same kind of people I had known in my past, but the way the other people in A.A. were talking about God was totally different. They actually seemed to have found a loving, kind, and caring God, and they were happy about that. They were not fake-happy, like Jack and my mother, who put on the Good Christian costume when they were around other Christians. These folks in A.A. were authentic and profoundly connected to something great.

At 6:00 A.M., one Monday morning at an A.A. meeting, the people were smiling and laughing, confidently sharing their most vulnerable secrets. No one shamed them, no one responded with anything but understanding and quiet compassion. When I left, at least a dozen people said to me, "Keep coming back, Randy. Let us love you until you can you love yourself." That invitation is what kept me coming back.

A week into my treatment at the Betty Ford Center, it was time for me to have my first meeting with my spiritual counselor, Greg. I had already been introduced to him by my case manager, so I knew that he was a loving spirit in his fifties. When we met privately, the first question Greg asked me was, "What is your experience with God, Randy, and how do you feel about God? How do you *really* feel, good or bad, without your worrying about my judging you? Tell me everything."

As a survivor of sexual abuse, I found it incredibly difficult to take that first step to trust someone else. In fact, if it hadn't been for the half a dozen A.A. meetings I had already attended, I never would have trusted Greg enough to tell him the truth. But I was beginning to believe that it was possible that these people were different, that they wouldn't hurt me or abuse my trust in them.

Anyone who has not survived trauma and made that first step cannot understand how much courage it really takes just to open up to another human being. But it is as necessary as it is painful. We need one another to truly heal. Eventually, we come to see that it is by keeping secrets and shutting people out that we perpetuate the abuse, living in a deep and painful shameful darkness.

For an hour, I told Greg exactly how I felt about God, religion, and the church, but to my amazement, he didn't fight with me. He didn't argue. He didn't try to persuade me of anything. He just sat there taking notes, occasionally shaking his head and silently acknowledging my pain.

When I was done ranting, Greg looked at me with empathy and said, "I can see why you're upset, and you have every right to be upset. We have a lot of work to do."

He didn't condemn me for my feelings or words. He never said, "Randy, grow up and get over it!" Instead, he gave me understanding and compassion. For the first time in my life, a man with spiritual authority had modeled true spirituality for me. I was intrigued.

I don't know if Greg is aware of how much he did for me that night. In fact, I myself never realized how much he helped me until just *this* moment. Had his reaction been anything other than what it was, I probably would not be writing this book.

Before I left Greg that night, he told me a little story about how people in A.A. will put their keys under their bed before they go to sleep at night. When they get up in the morning, they have to get down on their knees to get the keys, and while they are down there, they stay and pray. I had not prayed sincerely in years, figuring that the desperate "Hail Mary's" did not count that I sent up from the foxhole only when I was in trouble.

Something about the way Greg told the story and the way he treated me that night stuck with me in a good way. While I didn't throw my keys under the bed that night, I did get on my knees the next morning. I didn't really know how to pray or what to say, so I simply told God that I had no idea how to pray, but that I could no longer live the way I had been, and I was asking Him for help.

Since I didn't have any prayers of my own yet, and I wasn't ready to go back to any of the Christian prayers, I repeated the Third Step prayer every morning:

> God, I offer myself to Thee—to build with me and do with me as Thou wilt. Relieve me of the bondage of self, that I may better do Thy will. Take away my difficulties, that victory over them may bear witness to those I would help of Thy Power, Thy love, and Thy way of life. May I do Thy will always.[52]

Ever since that first day on my knees, unless I have been sick or otherwise incapacitated, I have gotten down on my knees and repeated that prayer. While it has not been easy, and I have put in blood, sweat, and tears along the way, I believe that my reconnection with my Higher Power has been the key to helping me stay sober all these years.

The God of Your Understanding

Little by little, I started rebuilding my own idea of God. The key for me was being allowed to discover the God of my own understanding. I didn't have to buy into my mother's God or Jack's God.

In treatment, I was required to participate in several workshops. At the time, there were eight of us in the Intensive Outpatient Program. When it came time for us to meet as a group for our first spiritual workshop, to be led by my spiritual counselor, Greg, I wasn't yet healed enough not to be automatically wary. However, I had come to trust Greg and was willing to give him the benefit of the doubt as he launched into an introduction that I had never heard before. As he stood in front of a big whiteboard, he asked us what our concept of God was, what He looked like, and what He felt like.

Every one of us had an image of a vengeful God, who kept track of all

---

[52]Alcoholics Anonymous, *The Big Book*, 4th ed., p. 63.

our sins in a big book, and threw lightning bolts at us because he was an angry, cruel, and punishing God. It was a relief to know that I was not the only one who felt that way. In fact, it was a *huge* relief.

But Greg wasn't done yet. Next, he asked us what we *wanted* from God in our lives. Then he handed me a pen and asked me to write people's answers on the board. Words that I had long since stopped associating with spirituality started flowing from my marker: *loving, kind, compassionate, caring, funny, happy, discerning, friendly, forgiving*—and the list grew until the whiteboard was full of nothing but positive attributes.

When we finished that task, Greg walked toward the door, turned, pointed to the whiteboard, and said, "*There* is your new God."

In that moment, I saw the words of Step Three in a new light: "We turn our will and our lives over to the care of God as we understand him."

Suddenly, I realized that how I choose to understand God is in *my* power—that the God on the whiteboard could become my God in truth, right there, right then. My heart and mind had become open, and my hope for a better life increased exponentially.

The work I did at the Betty Ford Center was only the beginning of my search for a God I could understand. I had years of religious indoctrination about God, so it took a while to undo my tangled feelings and beliefs about spirituality. Although I wanted to believe in the whiteboard God, the word *God* had so many negative connotations attached to it for me, some of them deep in my unconscious, that it was difficult for me to accept Him. I had been so deeply wounded spiritually for so many years that I had a lot of healing and unraveling to do before I could start fresh with God. I was really angry at Him for not rescuing me from the pain and abuse in my life, and I didn't know how to process that anger.

Getting Honest About God

Part of what I had to do to reconnect with God was to get honest with myself and others. Many terrible things had happened to me in my life, but to be truthful, I had also received a great deal of kindness from other people. Therefore, I had to stop blaming God for everything that went wrong in my life. I realized that God had *never* hurt me; it was *people* who had hurt me. In fact, there was always a spiritual presence surrounding me, even in my darkest moments, which helped me to make it through.

In truth, I should be dead now, ten times over. I can't count the number of nights that I lay in my bed after taking massive amounts of cocaine and drinking way too much alcohol, my heart beating so hard and fast that it hurt. During many of those terrible nights, I called out to the God I despised, begging Him to let me make it through the night, vowing to change my ways. All those times that I had driven intoxicated, weaving in and out of traffic, could have been so much worse.

By the grace of God, I have been helped more than I have been hurt. When I began to realize that, I started to ask genuine questions, confronting pastors about theological contradictions that confused me. Most of those pastors just stumbled over their words, or fell back into some mechanical justification that didn't make any sense to me. But some of them answered honestly from the heart, and their words rang true.

I read books on Buddhism, Taoism, Hinduism, and other spiritual philosophies, seeking out all the information I could about God. I also spent countless hours talking with God as I hiked and meditated. I didn't just *want* serenity and peace in my life; I *needed* it. As I dealt with my anger and pain, I was working hard on myself, recognizing my faults and making amends for my wrong actions. Nevertheless, although I was staying sober, I still hurt emotionally and spiritually most of the time. Clearly, I needed the peace that the books and my mentors assured me I would find with God.

Admitting that I needed help and could not do everything on my own, I started a spiritual practice of getting down on my knees every morning to ask God to help me to stay sober. For several months, my prayers were just words. But with time and honest, openhearted searching for my own spiritual center, a measure of peace did finally come to me. And with that came the sense of well-being that my mentors had promised. God didn't just magically fix me, but my starting to heal that deep spiritual wound inside me helped to remove a great deal of my obsession over drugs and alcohol. Nevertheless, I still had to do the work, and lots of it.

Whether or not one is an alcoholic, recovery is not at all magical; it requires real effort to work the steps. But that has been the best work I have ever done in my life. Instead of building a business or erecting more walls around myself, for the first time in my life I have been doing the work that has helped me to accept and love myself. What God did in this process was give me a foundation for healing.

Human beings have an innate need to connect with a spiritual power. When we cut ourselves off from that source, we die on the vine. Healing my deep spiritual wounds gave me the courage to work through all of my issues, and still gives me strength, knowledge, and a deep wisdom that I can rely upon whenever I falter.

My journey to reconnect with God has been a long one. It is only because of A.A. that I have been able to heal from the spiritual abuse that cut me off from God and religion for decades. It was only in being allowed to question and challenge the God I grew up with that I was able to find the loving, kind, and caring God I have today.

I live near Rancho Mirage in the California desert, where the Betty Ford Center is located. Like thousands of people in recovery before me, I have spent countless hours hiking the desert trails. However, there is one mountain that is fondly called the "Magic Mountain" by people in recovery because so many of us initially think it will take a miracle to reconnect with God, when in fact it may only take a few hours of communing with nature on that mountain.

Like so many people in recovery before me, I would hike that trail and talk to God about whatever I was unsure of in my life. I asked questions that I had been carrying around for decades. For example, why did my father have to die when I was just a twelve-year-old boy? Why was I molested? Why didn't God help me?

The answers I received in the quiet of my heart focused on the fact that God had never left me. He had been with me through all of the terrible times, and He would continue to walk beside me now. I started to see that the quiet voice inside me could be right. I was still alive, and I was on a journey to true healing and well-being. The way I had come to be on this path was less important than the fact that I was here.

I started to recall earlier profound contacts that I had had with God. For example, when I was fifteen, I lay on the ground one morning, bleeding to death after crashing into a ditch on my motorcycle. I could hear the soft, gentle voice of God whispering in my ear that I was dying.

"But keep fighting for your life, Randy," God said, "and you'll make it."

Then, in defiance of all the odds and to the amazement of all my surgeons, I lived through an exhaustive surgery that the doctors were sure I would not survive. My right kidney had exploded like a raw egg, but my liver, spleen, and other major organs had miraculously come through untouched.

One night in my forties, I called out to God as I lay in bed after snorting a sixteenth of an ounce of cocaine and drinking a quart of Jack Daniel's. My chest felt as if it were going to explode, and death was an almost palpable presence. But I lived through that night, only to wake up the next morning to drink and use again.

Then there was the night that I was drunk, totaled a car, and jail seemed inevitable. But then, after I made a heartfelt plea to God, the other driver told the sheriff that the accident had been his fault. To my amazement, the officer allowed me to drive home, still drunk, with no legal consequences.

As I looked back over all these memories, I started to realize that some benevolent presence had always been right there with me, and that maybe, just maybe, it was me who had turned my back on God.

Shortly after I completed the program at the Betty Ford Center, I was coming down the hill from a beautiful evening hike near my home, when a profound insight came to me. In A.A.'s *Big Book*, there is a passage that tells us to quit playing God and let Him direct our lives in order to have a full recovery. "Most good ideas," it states, "are simple, and this concept is the keystone of the new and triumphant arch through which we pass to freedom."[53] I am a stonemason by trade, so this passage seemed particularly apt to me.

A keystone is the stone at the top of an arch. So long as it is placed at the top of the arch solidly and properly, the arch will never fail, for it simply cannot collapse inward on itself. For proof of this, look at the ruins in ancient Greece and Rome, where often the only things left standing are the arches, unscathed and still solid after time and decay have destroyed all other traces of the buildings.

In order for me to remain sober, my keystone had to be turning my will and my life over to the care of God. I had nothing to lose, for nothing else had worked, and my willpower was fading. I certainly didn't want to return to the emotional and spiritual hell of my old life. Now that God had revealed Himself to me in ways I couldn't ignore, my spiritual journey had begun.

Thirty-one years prior to entering treatment, I had turned my back on God. While my life on the outside looked as if I had everything together, spiritually I was bankrupt. My morals and values had gone right out the door, and I was doing things I had sworn I would never do. When I entered treatment, I finally found people I could talk to about my feelings—people I could tell how angry I was at God, who would then assure me that that was okay. I needed to be able to talk with people who understood how I felt without judging me or telling me I was going to burn in hell for the ways I was thinking.

The Betty Ford Center and Alcoholics Anonymous allowed me to do

[53] Alcoholics Anonymous, *The Big Book*, 4th ed., p. 62.

that. While people in A.A. did not always understand the effects on me of the sexual and physical abuse, they did understand the mechanisms of spiritual abuse.

Finding God did not come quickly or easily for me, although I suppose for some it might. However, the path to spiritual recovery is a good one to be on, for you will find healing where you thought there was no hope. The Third Step is hard. But for your courage, you will be repaid many times over in compassion and healing.

A Spiritual Church

Alcoholics Anonymous helped me to get sober and gave me a life I could never have dreamed of having. A.A. allowed me to seek and reconnect with God—as I understand God. I learned how to be of service to my community, family, and friends. A.A. taught me how to use my childhood trauma and pain to help other men.

But even after seven years in the program, I felt that something was still missing for me spiritually. I wanted to be closer to God, and that was not happening in A.A.

Just at that time, my wife, Cathy, was starting to make friends at work and around town. One such friend was Marlene Ruttenberg, with whom Cathy developed a sisterlike relationship. In December 2011, Marlene asked Cathy if she would like to come to the Christmas program at her church.

Cathy had always been a spiritual person, but because of my attitude toward the church and her codependency, she had not been to church, aside from weddings and funerals, for the duration of our marriage. However, when she asked if I would like to go to the Christmas service, too, I was pleased that she had found a friend and wanted to go to church with her, but I was not yet ready to take that step.

When Cathy came home from the program, she was really excited about the experience. The people there, she said, reminded her of the folks she had met at A.A. meetings that she had attended with me—open, warm, and welcoming—and the pastor tied scripture to actual situations. I was happy for her, but I was still not ready to go to church. I had already come to terms with God, but I still felt a lot of resentment toward churches and organized religions.

Just as Deborah, my therapist, had originally suggested that I go to A.A., but without insisting on it, Cathy did the same with the idea of my going to church. When and if I was ever ready to go back to church, she said, I would probably really like Destiny Church.

Three months later, in March 2012, Marlene told Cathy about a series of talks on relationships, called *The Lion and the Lamb*, which the lead pastor of Destiny Church would be presenting. Marlene thought that Cathy and I would like it, but if I were still not ready to go to church, we could watch the series online. I smiled and nodded politely, but inside I blew it off.

Eventually, Cathy persuaded me to watch the series online with her. She had been a supportive and loyal wife throughout my recovery, so how could I say no to her? She had even attended A.A. meetings with me every Sunday morning and Wednesday evening for five years. It was time for me to support her and her spirituality.

One night as we sat down for dinner, I asked Cathy to pull up *The Lion and the Lamb* series on her iPad, so we could watch Pastor Obed Martinez's message during dinner instead of our regular TV show. What I saw and heard was a pastor talking about scripture in terms of real-life situations actually experienced by couples. He wasn't preaching but teaching as he delivered a message of hope and love. What I did *not* see or hear was a pastor preaching fire and brimstone and condemnation. Just as Cathy had said, the service was much like an A.A. meeting, only more spiritual and uplifting.

Over the next two weeks, we watched the whole series. When it was over, Cathy asked me what I thought of it, and if I would consider going to Destiny Church with her. I told her I was very impressed with Pastor Obed, could feel my heart and soul starting to change, and would genuinely consider it. The thought of going back to church still made me cringe as I realized exactly how much spiritual damage had been done to me by the church of my childhood. But I was yearning to learn more, to grow closer to God.

The decision to give Destiny Church a chance came to me all at once. One day, I was simply overwhelmed by the desire to be a part of a loving spiritual community. Also, it occurred to me that, as an adult now, I could just walk away if the pastor became abusive in any way. I was so excited that I called Cathy at work, and asked her if she wanted to go to church that very night. She was shocked but elated.

As is my habit, we arrived half an hour early. Standing around in the atrium, I was fidgety and nervous about what to expect. Were the members of the congregation going to look at me funny? Were they going to judge me? This was a casual church, Cathy said, so I could wear shorts and sandals. That made me feel a little more at ease.

When Marlene and her family arrived, that made me feel even more comfortable. Marlene introduced us to other members of the church, and, just as at A.A. meetings, we were welcomed with open smiles. After the warm and friendly ushers let us into the sanctuary, they seated us right up front in the second row.

It was immediately obvious that the church was a converted commercial warehouse, and the energy in the room was positive and loving, not stuffy and uptight. The service started with thirty minutes of worship—not the hymns of my painful childhood, but modern Christian rock music.

To be honest, I was still skeptical about this whole experience, and it occurred to me that the people seemed to be somewhat brainwashed. I couldn't wait for the music to stop so that I could hear the pastor's message and decide if this place was really a sanctuary, or just another well-disguised hell masquerading as a House of God. Despite my discomfort, I stayed put. It was as though God had his hand on my shoulder, keeping me in my seat.

Pastor Obed's message was excellent, but I was still plagued by my childhood demons. Nevertheless, I was intrigued enough to want to come back. In fact, I even started attending services when Cathy couldn't come with me. Only God knows how many times I wanted to run as I tried to work through my discomfort. But there was some kind of energy in this church that I liked. I was experiencing a peace and serenity that I had never experienced before. I felt the presence of God that I had felt in my quiet meditation times. I had found the presence of God that I was craving.

Destiny Church has several spiritual leaders on its staff, one of whom is Rabbi Brian Bileci. That is another thing that attracts me to Destiny: it does not condemn other religions. Nor does it turn away homeless people, alcoholics, or drug addicts. Just as at A.A. meetings, everyone is welcome, and everyone is treated equally.

I am sharing my religious experience, not to try to convert my readers, but to impress upon you that, as bad as religion can be, it can also be wonderful. However, if you are recovering from spiritual abuse, it is important not to rush into a place of worship. Take your time, wait until you are ready, and be discerning about the place you choose. When it is right, you will know it.

THE G–D WORD

Another Spiritual Leader's Reaction to Sexual Abuse

Cathy and I had been attending Destiny for about a month when we were at an evening service with Rabbi Brian delivering the message. At one point, I had to use the restroom, so I went out to the one in the atrium. However, when I tried to return to my seat, I couldn't get through the packed crowd in the sanctuary, so I remained in the atrium to watch the end of the service on the TV monitor that was provided for the overflow.

I was leaning up against the wall, watching just as Pastor Brian was saying that God had a word for someone in the congregation. A boy, the pastor said, had been molested at the age of twelve, and because of that abuse he had turned his back on God and walked away from Him.

A wave of emotions immediately washed over me. As Rabbi Brian was revealing what God was telling him, I slid down the wall, sobbing. How did the rabbi know about me? How did he know what I was feeling? How did he know the struggles I was having? The emotions that I had been so good at controlling for so many years, I suddenly lost all control over. I couldn't help it. I just sobbed and sobbed.

Pastor Sergio, who happened to be in the atrium, came over to me to ask if I were okay. I told him that the twelve-year-old that Pastor Brian was talking about was me. Pastor Sergio comforted me until the service was over, and then introduced me to Pastor Brian, who was greeting departing parishioners at the side of the church.

There was no time for a prolonged meeting, but I did get to tell Pastor Brian that *I* was that twelve-year-old, and he prayed for me. A week later, I met with Pastor Brian in private, and finally an authority figure of the church apologized to me for the actions of the Christians who had abused me as a child. Although I was resistant and uncomfortable, he just hugged me and prayed for me and for the child within me who was so badly and wrongfully hurt by the church and people who were supposed to have protected me.

No shaming. No condemnation. No doubt. And absolutely no condoning of the abuse.

Thanks largely to that event, Cathy and I dedicated our lives to Christ, were baptized together hand-in-hand at Destiny Church, and have been faithful members of the congregation ever since. I had found the missing link in my spiritual walk.

However, I still struggled with my past. I might be standing during a worship service when overwhelming feelings of shame would suddenly overwhelm me. I would feel so vulnerable that all I wanted to do was run out of the church. No one was saying or doing anything to cause me to feel that way. Just being in church was flooding my senses with memories of being abused as a teenager. However, in time, and with the help of God, all of those feelings faded away.

I learned in A.A. that people are people. No matter which religious denomination they might belong to, and irrespective of whether or not they are in A.A., people will never be perfect, especially me. I learned that hypocrisy lives not only in the church, but also in A.A. meetings, our homes, and our workplaces. In fact, in many ways I had been hypocritical myself.

Way Spiritual Dave, my A.A. sponsor, taught me to keep my side of the street clean, no matter what, and to walk away from every confrontation and disagreement, leaving the other person's integrity intact. I owe my life to A.A. and the people who unconditionally loved me back to life when I could not love myself. A.A. allowed me to find and develop a relationship with God, one that is better than I ever imagined. For that I am eternally grateful.

It was the members of Destiny Church and Pastors Obed, Brian, and Sergio who truly displayed the love of God that made it possible for me to continue to grow spiritually. My life has flourished and continues to flourish beyond my wildest expectations. Thirty-plus years ago, I walked away from the church and turned my back on God, vowing never to set foot in church again. Today, I'm so glad I broke that vow, and I am grateful that that season of my life has passed.

The path to recovery tests our limits and forces us to turn to a Higher Power for the strength to continue. I am living proof that it is possible to turn even the most frightening God into a kind and loving friend. You can, too.

Chapter 7: Hitting Bottom

When this ultimate crisis comes..., when there is no way out, that is the very moment when we explode from within and the totally other emerges. It is the sudden surfacing of a strength, a security of unknown origin, welling up from beyond reason, rational expectation, or hope.

—Émile Durkheim[54]

I am often asked what the hardest part of my recovery was, and without question it was looking at myself in the hard light of day, without excuses, without defenses or justifications, and taking responsibility for my wrongdoing. Before that, I got really good at evading responsibility. The way I saw life, everything that went wrong was always someone else's fault. If there were no one else to blame, I would blame my own behavior on the fact that I had been abused. I could find ways to blame anyone for anything. If that failed, I could always blame God. The only one who consistently escaped my censure was *me*.

I thought I was terribly clever—a pro at being "right." I could harass, harangue, shout, bully, or manipulate anyone into buying into my sob story, which made me out to be the victim of every situation. The problem was that I was destroying my credibility with myself in order to look good to other people. I was trading my own self-respect for the respect of others: that is a very bad trade.

Recovery has helped me to understand that the one person whose good opinion I cannot live without is me. But I cannot have a good opinion of myself unless I live up to my own internal standards. In the past, it

[54]Durkheim (1858–1917) was a French sociologist and social psychologist. He is quoted here from David Rich, *How to Be an Adult in Faith and Spirituality* (Mahwah, NJ: Paulist Press, 2011), retrieved from https://books.google.com/books?id=22Wp65TgCPsC&pg=PT102&lpg=PT102&dq=When+this+ultimate+crisis+comes.../.

didn't matter if I could fool everyone around me—I couldn't fool myself. Deep down, I knew I was responsible for the bad choices I was making, but I thought that playing the victim would keep me from facing the consequences of my own poor decisions. I was afraid that if I ever owned up to the things I had done, I would not be able to live with myself. But ultimately, living in a perpetual state of victimhood felt even worse. I couldn't live with myself either way.

A Drastic Change

For most of my adult life, I lived on self-will alone, pushing through my fears about not really knowing how to be a man, husband, father, or citizen. I was just getting by day-to-day. When I ran out of answers, I faked them. When that stopped working, I turned to drugs and alcohol. Everything was always about me, but nothing was ever my fault.

At the age of eighteen, I walked away from the church and God, deciding that God had absolutely nothing to do with my life. I refused to owe anything to a God who, I believed, had betrayed me. I was determined that God should get no credit for all my near misses from the drug overdoses and reckless driving, although my survival during those years was nothing short of miraculous.

Then, one cold December night in 2003, my life took a drastic change. Like all of the nights before it, that night started out all about me. I was a successful entrepreneur, and although not a millionaire, I could buy just about whatever I wanted whenever I wanted it. I had everything I thought I wanted most out of life. Yet, I was still miserable. No amount of money, toys, cars, houses, trips, or admiration could fill the void in my soul. All the drugs and alcohol only temporarily numbed my unhappiness, and so I needed more drugs and booze to kill the pain. If truth be told, however, there are not enough drugs and alcohol on the planet to anesthetize the emptiness I was dealing with. In fact, the drugs and alcohol only turned me into an angry and rageful person.

Two weeks before Christmas in 2003, a good friend of mine invited Cathy and me to his Christmas party. A lot of our friends would be there, as well as some very influential members of the local business community, which made me feel that I had finally achieved the social status I had been so desperately trying to attain.

We had a great time at the party, and I had had more than a few drinks by the time it started to wind down. As we were saying our goodbyes, I kissed a female friend on the neck instead of the cheek. It was an innocent goodbye kiss, but Cathy did not see it that way. When she mentioned the kiss as she drove home, since I had had too much to drink, I tried to persuade her that there was nothing behind the kiss, but Cathy wouldn't listen. By the time we pulled into our driveway, less than half an hour later, she was fuming, and I was calling her every name in the book.

Listening to my verbal abuse as she sat in our driveway, my heartbroken wife switched off the car engine, turned in her seat, and slapped me. I was stunned, for she had never hit me before. In a rage, I stormed out of the car, rushed over to the driver's side, and yanked open the door. As Cathy raised her hand to slap me again, I put up my arms to block her. Then we struggled for three or four terrible heartbeats, and the next thing I knew, Cathy was on the ground, looking up at me with tear-streaked cheeks, cradling her left arm.

With my blurry, alcohol-infused vision, I looked up and saw my daughter, my son, and my son's girlfriend standing on the doorstep, watching this scene with horror. As I pushed past them, my daughter angrily told me to leave mom alone. I turned toward her and told her to get out of my way, or she would be next.

Writing these words now fills me with a cold, sick feeling. There are many things I have regretted in my life, but none more than the actions that made my wife and children look at me with the terror-filled eyes of loved ones who have been horribly betrayed by someone they once trusted completely. My disappointment in myself burns to this day. Although Cathy and my children have forgiven me, at times I still struggle to forgive myself. If you have ever doubted that it is the wounds that we inflict on others that hurt us the most, I hope you don't have to learn that truth the same hard way I did.

However, on that night, cocooned in the numbing blankets of alcohol, all I could feel was rage. Grabbing my truck keys and tearing out of the driveway, I left my devastated family to pick up the pieces.

I roared down the street to one of my favorite watering holes, The Beer Hunter, to get something to eat and, of course, a few more cocktails. When I returned home around midnight, the entire La Quinta police department appeared to be in my front yard. Through my alcohol-induced fog, I remember calling out to God for help. But enough of my conscience was still intact to let me know, even in my drunken stupor, that I didn't believe I deserved it. When I stumbled out of the truck, I was certain that this time I would be going to jail.

When I asked one of the officers about Cathy, he told me that she had been taken to the hospital with a possible fractured elbow. At the time of this incident, the laws had not yet changed, so it was not mandatory that I be taken to jail, and Cathy didn't want to press charges. That did not please any of the officers, who were all staring at me with contempt in their hard, cold eyes—contempt that I knew I deserved. But once again, I was not given a field sobriety test, nor was I even asked if I had been drinking that night. For the umpteenth time, I had avoided any legal consequences for my actions. Once again, it seemed as though my prayer to God from the foxhole was being answered. However, I could not avoid the fact that I had hurt my wife and terrified my children. Before that night, I had never laid a hand on her, or any other woman.

Before the officers left, the one female officer at my house warned me not to call the hospital or try contacting my wife, and said that I was lucky that I wasn't going to jail. In no way did I feel lucky that night. In fact, that was the darkest, loneliest night I endured after my father died, four decades earlier. I couldn't bear not knowing how Cathy was, so I called the hospital anyway, only to have a nurse refuse to tell me anything about my wife's condition. The nurse also let me know in no uncertain terms that I was not to call back. I was alone, imprisoned in a dark world filled with nothing but my own shame and self-hatred. I have never been in prison, but I spent that night in a mental prison filled with torment and pain that I wouldn't wish on my worst enemy.

The next day, a Saturday, Cathy returned to our home and our life together, which I had shattered. The police had referred us to a domestic counseling center, so on Monday morning I made the call, and that afternoon Cathy and I walked into the facility.

Many times in the past, when I had behaved badly, I had retreated into the "victim mentality," throwing the blame onto other people in order to avoid feeling shame and regret. I was a pro at twisting the facts of any situation until I came out as the wronged party. This time I couldn't do that. Not only did the staff at the facility make it unmistakably clear that I was far bigger and stronger than Cathy and very much in the wrong, but my wife's red eyes and the sling on her arm made it impossible to hide from the truth of what I had done.

Emotional abuse was easier to deny. I could tell myself that Cathy had started the fight when she slapped me. But I couldn't shield my mind from the ugly truth that I had frightened her terribly when I knocked her to the ground. She was there next to me, hurting both physically and mentally, which I could see clearly because I was no longer drunk. The remorse I felt as I watched her wince every time she moved her arm cut me nearly in half. It was like a hot, dull knife stabbing into my stomach over and over again.

At one moment, when Cathy looked over at me and smiled, I was devastated. In the face of her love and forgiveness, there was no place for me to hide from myself. I had become a monster. I didn't deserve her love at that moment, and I didn't deserve to get off without any legal consequences.

I was starting to believe that I was responsible for getting myself into trouble, and maybe I had to change. But even that wasn't enough for me. I wasn't done with creating disasters.

The Affair

On November 11, 2004, I met a woman named Susan (not her real name) for lunch at The Blue Coyote restaurant in Palm Springs. I knew that Cathy was going to be out of town all day at a business convention, and I was hoping to start an affair with Susan. The meal started out innocently enough, with both of us munching away at a bowl of chips. Susan was nursing a beer, and I was sipping an iced tea, using the excuse that I was going to be working out later that day. But as the afternoon wore on, I gave in to that irresistible urge to have a beer. After all, what harm could one beer do? Before I knew it, a six-pack of beer was down my throat, and tequila was pouring freely between me and Susan. Soon things started to get pretty loose between the two of us.

Cathy had called me several times during the day to see how I was and to ask what I was doing. Every time she called, I lied, telling her that I was just having a few beers with some employees. When she called around 4:30 to tell me she was on her way home and was just passing through the city of Riverside, about ninety miles away, I thought to myself, "Good, I still have an hour or so to spend with Susan and enough time to get home."

Twenty minutes later, Cathy called to tell me she was passing through Palm Springs and was almost home. I needed to get there first to shower and change clothes. The race was on. As I was weaving in and out of traffic down Highway 111 in my Ford F250 with 38-inch tires and a 6-inch lift, a compact car made a sudden lane change in front of me. Despite all my efforts to avoid a collision, I could not. The car I hit was totaled, but thankfully no one was hurt. I remember thinking, *This is it. This time I'm screwed for sure.*

There were witnesses who had seen my erratic driving, not to mention the fact that I was about a bottle of tequila over the legal drinking limit. When I called Cathy to tell her what was happening, she said, "This time you're going to jail, and don't call me." That's when I learned that she was still in Riverside, and, being highly suspicious of my avoidant behavior throughout the day, she had tried to cross me up and catch me in a lie.

After she hung up on me, I looked around at the scene on the highway. I could smell the burning rubber on the asphalt and hear the metallic voices on the police radios. At that moment, I prayed the familiar alcoholic's prayer from deep down in the foxhole: "God, please help me, and get me out of this one, and I promise I will...."

To my shock, the driver of the car I hit got out of his vehicle and told the police officers that it was *his* fault that I had hit him. He stated that he never saw me coming and made a lane change without looking. I had six different police officers approach me at separate times, coming within six inches of my face to ask me questions, so I knew I was cooked. I could practically feel the cold steel of the handcuffs clicking shut around my wrists. After some discussion among all the officers and witnesses, one of the officers approached me, handed me my driver's license and registration, and said, "Drive home safely and have a nice night."

I stood there, dumbly staring at my license and registration, wondering why I wasn't being steered headfirst into the back seat of a black-and-white.

There had been other similar incidents with law enforcement over the years, but this one was close enough to shave me. My family and friends had tried to broach the subject of my drinking after other close calls, but, like every other addict, I minimized everything, denying that my problems were related to my drinking or using. However, after this incident, even *I* had to admit that they might be right. Still, unbelievably, I wasn't done. It was going to take a bit more for me to hit bottom.

After that, I thought I was leading a charmed life, and nothing could touch me. But as it turned out, something could. It wasn't the many near misses with the law; it wasn't even my many brushes with death; it was Cathy and my children who ultimately brought me to my knees.

Although once again I was Mr. Life of the Party and Mr. Successful

Businessman, I was hurting emotionally more than I ever had before. Nothing was helping the pain anymore—not drugs, alcohol, success, or money. So, like many other survivors of sexual abuse, I tried to fill the gnawing ache in my soul with the high of an affair with another woman. *That*, I thought, *will fix all my problems.*

One Friday evening, after yet another quarrel with Cathy while I was intoxicated, she got up the courage to call me a "lazy alcoholic." That's all I needed to hear. Two seconds later, I was out the door and calling Susan, whom I had not seen since our rendezvous at The Blue Coyote a month earlier. She told me to come right over. After spending the whole weekend with her, I returned home on Sunday afternoon and told Cathy I was moving out.

I will never forget the desperate look in her eyes as she dropped to her knees, wrapped her arms around my legs, and begged me not to go. Then, in a flash, she stood up and told me to get out of her house *now!*

If I went, I would be walking away from a twenty-one-year marriage to a woman who was the love of my life. But in that moment, I was willing to throw away everything that I truly cared about. I packed a suitcase and moved in with Susan.

However, from day one with Susan, I was filled with guilt and remorse, and could not even fall asleep as I lay beside her in her bed. Nevertheless, I rationalized this restlessness, just as I had justified the uneasy feeling in my stomach when Jack began molesting me, by telling myself, *I just don't know Jack yet. As I get to know him, the uneasy feeling will go away.*

As time passed, I started to realize just how out of control my life had become: I was losing whatever ethics and morals I had left, and I was about to destroy my marriage, which would have taken my home and my children with it. The thought of losing the people who truly loved me broke some barrier inside me. I couldn't bear the idea of losing them. I had always told myself that I would never let things go this far. Nevertheless, that's exactly what I was doing. One minute, I was ready to run out the door; the next minute, I was afraid Cathy wouldn't take me back.

As I continued to lie awake every night next to this new woman I had been so desperate to have, I kept wondering if I were really going to piss away twenty-one years of marriage for a woman I barely knew. I was so filled with pain, guilt, and remorse that I silently cried myself to sleep, holding myself still so as not to wake the woman next to me.

On December 31, 2004, I was scheduled to have surgery for a hernia

I had developed from working out. Susan and I had planned to drive to my cabin in Pine Cove after the surgery to recover for a couple of days. She would take time off from work to take care of me. The day before the surgery, she arranged for us to spend a day at a spa with a nice room at a hotel. After massages, we returned to our room to get ready for dinner.

While Susan was in the shower, I was lying on the bed, filled with overwhelming grief and remorse. But I called room service and drowned out the voices with a few more cocktails. Then I pasted a smile over my heartache, and off to dinner with Susan I went.

In the middle of dinner, I felt my phone vibrating silently in a way that told me I had a text. Glancing down at the phone surreptitiously, I saw I had a message from Cathy. Excusing myself to go to the restroom, I went into a stall and read the following words: "Randy, your children and I belong with you at the hospital tomorrow, not that other woman." I immediately called her, and wound up spending the next half-hour with her on the phone. When I came out of that stall, I knew I had to end it with Susan that very night.

When I returned to the table, Susan immediately grabbed my cell phone out of my hands and started going through it. Our evening and our relationship were about to come to an abrupt end. When she discovered that I had been talking with Cathy, she was not happy, to say the least, and began to make a scene. After calming her down by telling her that Cathy and my kids were just concerned about my surgery, I paid our bill and we left the restaurant.

As we were walking toward my truck, Susan snapped at me once again about the phone call. That was all I needed. I took off for my truck, called Cathy to tell her I was on the way, and left Susan stranded in the parking lot in disbelief with no money and no way home—although I didn't know that at the time. It was just another jerk move on my part. In my desperate attempt to stop hurting, I was harming everyone who dared to get close to me. Although Susan knew she was sleeping with a married man, she couldn't know that I was also an alcoholic with four decades of pent-up rage and shame.

As the night progressed, and I moved back in with Cathy, I received several hostile texts and voicemails from Susan—and rightfully so. I was every bit the scumbag she said I was. But all I knew at that point was that I was a scumbag who was getting a second chance with my wife, and had to take it.

HITTING BOTTOM

Affairs do more damage to more people than one might realize. Susan's seven-year-old son, "Adam," had been bonding with me after being more or less abandoned by his biological father. (I haven't gone into that, because that's a whole other story.) Furthermore, taking a chance on trusting me, Susan had introduced me to her entire family, so now my sudden departure had eroded her credibility with her family members. The damage to my own family was even worse. Cathy's self-esteem had plummeted, so that now she doubted her self-worth as a woman and a wife. In addition, I had sent my children the worst possible message: their father was abandoning them because they weren't good enough for me to stay.

I am not writing all this to wallow in self-pity, for I'm certainly not enjoying putting this story down in black-and-white for the world to read. I know there are many other men out there who have been hurt like me, and because of that hurt, they hurt others. We all live our lives comparing how broken we feel on the inside to the shiny masks that other people present to the world. We compare our insides to other people's outsides, forgetting that they are pretending, too.

I wish I had had an older man to talk to at the time, who could have told me how broken he had been about wrongs he had committed, so I wouldn't have felt so alone in my own brokenness. We are all broken in some way, while trying to pretend to the world that we aren't. But we just end up feeling isolated and "terminally unique," as if we aren't okay, we aren't normal, and there's something terribly wrong with us that isn't wrong with anyone else.

The truth is that we are *not* terminally unique. We are all original combinations of brilliance and brokenness, having done things of which we can be proud, and other things about which we are deeply ashamed. No matter how deep a foxhole we have dug for ourselves, climbing out is possible. I have climbed out of my hole, and you can climb out of yours. Never believe that you are too broken to get better. It just isn't true. Never believe that you are the only one who is broken. That's not true, either.

Having an affair is never good, but it happens a lot, especially with adult male survivors of sexual abuse. If it has happened to you, it's not the end of the world, and there is hope. However, there is work that must be done, and lots of it. Part of my recovery from abuse was to recognize that I had become an abuser, and to accurately name my victims and make amends to them for the harm I had caused them. Although I was not yet in a twelve-step program, Deborah, my therapist, pointed out to me where and how I had become an abuser in my relationship with Cathy. Deborah explained to me that my anger was sending both my wife and my children into a state of fear that no one deserves. Whenever I got angry, I would start calling Cathy names, which crushed her self-worth as a wife, mother, and human being. All the anger and name-calling that I had endured as a child I was now casting down upon my wife. Hurt people *hurt* people!

Believe me, I wish I had chosen some other way to get to a place where I was willing to face the root causes of my problems, but ultimately it was the affair and my broken home that put me on a therapist's couch. I had always resisted the idea of therapy. My whole life had been invested in projecting an image of myself that essentially said, "I'm just *fine*, thank you very much." But when Cathy agreed to give me another chance, I decided it was time to try something different, because what I was doing was no longer working. Cathy and I were committed not just to getting better for each other, but to getting better for ourselves as well.

I think being committed to each other and ourselves was one of the most important factors that contributed to the positive outcome for both of us. Today, our marriage is better than ever. I am deeply in love with my wife, and extremely grateful for my life, and I do acts of kindness that help me to love myself more, each and every day.

Once I began therapy, I started to work on the issues in my life that I learned were a direct result of all my abuse—and the ultimate reason I had had the affair. Concurrently, Cathy was doing her own work with her own therapist. After working on ourselves for about six months, we were ready to work on our marriage together. For the next year, we worked diligently and relentlessly on mending our relationship. However, alcohol and drugs were still part of my life—not to the extent they had been, but they were still interfering with our growth individually and as a couple.

A High and Dry Drunk

Being clean and sober is one thing. Being in recovery is another. Many people will quit alcohol and drugs, but their lives remain in shambles. They still find themselves with a multitude of legal issues and insurmountable financial problems, their families are alienated from them, and their marriages are in a state of disarray. Relapse is common among these individuals because they often think that, since their lives are still unmanageable, it must not have been the alcohol or drugs that were the problem. Their lives remain unmanageable because they have only quit alcohol and drugs, and they have done nothing to resolve the underlying issues. That was a part of my story, too.

While I was in the Betty Ford Center, I had to create a timeline of my life, from my earliest memories right up to the present. As I was doing this, I recalled a two-year period between 2000 and 2002 when I decided to quit drinking just to show my wife and children that I could. For those two years, I remained abstinent, but that is not the same as remaining sober. I was what is known as a "dry drunk." That is, I was not drinking, but my behavior was becoming increasingly worse. I became angrier, more judgmental, and much more arrogant, and the people around me did not like me very much. The fact is, I didn't much like myself.

The underlying issue, my sexual abuse, had not been dealt with, and my way of self-medicating had been taken away from me. I was white-knuckling it every day. Things had changed alright, but they had changed for the worse. My life had been easier to handle when I could work myself into exhaustion every day and collapse into bed at night.

Vacations in particular became far more stressful, especially at night. For example, whenever Cathy and I went camping with friends, I would be fine with everyone drinking for a little while, but there would always come a point in the evening when I became immensely uncomfortable. As the campfire popped and crackled, I would listen to everyone laughing and having a good time, but be unable to laugh and have fun myself. The same people I had hunted with or hiked with during the day, I could not deal with at night, when conversations tend to become more intimate and personal.

At bottom, I couldn't handle the stress of just being *me*, for that had never been good enough. I could handle taking action, such as shooting or racing, but the moments when I just had to be myself left me shaking like a child. Sometimes I even ran away to literally pull the blankets over my head. In those moments, when everything was quiet, I felt that everyone around me could see my shame and brokenness.

Drinking Again

I'll never forget the evening in 2002 when I started to drink again. In some ways, it was similar to my first experience of drinking when I was back in high school. At the end of a long day of deer hunting, while my buddies were pouring the traditional end-of-the-day round of Jack Daniel's, I rationalized that I could join in. After all, I had not had a drink in nearly two years, so I had proven to everyone, including myself, that I did not *have* to drink. Besides, what could one little drink do to me anyway?

When I asked my friend Jimmy to pour me a Jack and Seven, he looked stunned, reminding me that I had not had a drink in nearly two years. When I insisted, he resisted me at first, but eventually poured me a drink with a great deal of reluctance. Unfortunately, that one drink led to two, two led to three, and you know the rest. That one drink started me back on a four-year run that nearly cost me everything I loved.

Alcohol gave me an artificial sense of confidence, which I hadn't experienced since my father died. Although that confidence was a shabby copy of the real thing, when I drank I was able to interact with people in ways I couldn't when I was sober.

After I started drinking again, I justified it by telling myself that it was so I could continue to maintain the business relationships that were crucial to my financial success. At that point, I had reached a level of economic success that I never thought possible. Being successful in business was a way to compensate for feeling broken from my abuse. Spending money and buying the latest gadgets made me feel powerful and important, which compensated for the feelings of helplessness and inadequacy that had been festering inside me since I was twelve.

When I had stopped drinking in 2000, my business was suffering because of my frequent withdrawals. When I started drinking again, I transformed back into that work-hard, play-hard Randy that my clients enjoyed being around. Ironically, I was miserable, but my business was prospering again.

Turning Around

My life wasn't turned around this time by another melodramatic scene, with hurt people shouting and crying. Rather, it was turned around when God whispered softly in my ear, "Randy, you need help, and you need it *today*."

I made a commitment then and there that I would stop drinking. I had "quit" several times before, but each time I had returned to the bottle. However, I could tell that something was different this time. In part, I had hit bottom and was sick and tired of it. I knew that if I did not quit drinking and take care of the underlying conditions that were a direct result of my sexual abuse, I would probably lose my wife and children. This wasn't like previous times when I had hurt Cathy, but she had forgiven me. By

HITTING BOTTOM

now, Cathy had had enough of my abusive behavior, and was insisting that something had to change, and change quickly.

Chapter 8:
Getting Clean

There is no better high than discovery.

—Edward O. Wilson[55]

In order to heal, I had to get clean and sober. There was no more evading or denying that truth. I had to deal with my childhood, and I couldn't do that while I was still drinking alcohol and taking drugs. My marriage was on the line, but I had come to realize over the year of therapy that my very *life* was on the line, too.

Ever since Jack had started abusing me, I had been living a half-life, going from shadow to shadow, escape to escape. Back then, if I lined up all of the moments that I had actually lived without running away from my feelings, I would still have been a teenager.

While I was still drinking and using, I had tried to work on my abuse issues several times, but to no avail. When the various therapists and the psychiatrist had asked me how much I drank alcohol or used drugs, I lied through my teeth. "I only use drugs recreationally," I said, and "I only have a couple of drinks on the weekends." On several occasions, I showed up at my appointments after taking cocaine, but still insisting that I didn't have a problem, and my therapist never realized that I was high. The truth is that "not having a problem" was my biggest problem.

So long as I was drinking and using, it was impossible to get out of the victim role. So long as I was drinking and using, I was delusional about what was causing my pain, and I was in total denial about my responsibility to others and myself. So long as I was drinking and using, every problem was someone else's fault. After all, I justified to myself, how could my problems be my own fault? I had a beautiful wife and family, a fancy house, expensive cars, and a million-dollar business at which I showed

---

[55]Retrieved from http://www.goodreads.com/quotes/458476-there-is-no-better-high-than-discovery/.

up every day to work. Me have a problem? Me an alcoholic? No freaking way.

Deep down inside, I knew I was full of enough excuses to cover a football field. But I rarely let myself get that honest. Most of the time, I was completely invested in maintaining the image of myself as the Ultimate Man's Man: successful, self-sufficient, and strong.

If anyone pressed me, I had my defensive story all ready to go. On rare occasions, when a close friend might question my drinking and drug use, I had the victim card ready to play. I didn't tell anyone what had actually happened, I just hunched my shoulders, glared, and said something to the effect of, "Well, if what happened to me had happened to you, you'd be drinking and using, too." And that was that. No one pushed beyond that.

Like most addicts, I argued with myself about what I thought other people were thinking of me. I made up conversations about what I imagined my friends and acquaintances were thinking, and then I defended my actions in made-up conversations that were only an exercise in futility and stupidity. I don't know what the people around me were thinking, but I did know deep down that what I was doing was very wrong. Believing that others were judging me, I spat back all the defense and justification I could muster. To put it mildly, I was hard to be around. I was touchy, sensitive, defensive, and unpredictable.

Victims excel at being victimized, and I was a pro at it. I became so difficult to be around that people started to avoid me. Then I would feel victimized all over again. I would whine to anyone who would listen to me, "People don't understand.... No one keeps their word to me.... He's just a fair-weather friend." I never took a close look at myself and at what I was doing to push people away. Everything unpleasant was always their fault.

All this is not to say that I was never abused. As a child, I was certainly a victim of sexual abuse. To escape the spiritual and emotional wasteland that the abuse left in its wake, I turned to alcohol and drugs. Eventually, however, victims turn into victimizers if they don't face the pain and learn healthy, compassionate coping skills.

Every time we light up a joint or pour another shot, we know that there are alternatives to drugs and drinking. To escape the victim-victimizer cycle, we must take responsibility for our own actions. When I lift a bottle to my mouth and swallow, *I* am doing those things, and no one else. I am also responsible for any and all consequences that follow.

There is an ongoing debate about whether or not the propensity for alcoholism is genetic—and if so, to what extent genetics affects behavior. According to the National Institute on Alcohol Abuse and Alcoholism, the picture is mixed:

> Many scientific studies, including research conducted among twins and children of alcoholics, have shown that genetic factors influence alcoholism. These findings show that children of alcoholics are about four times more likely than the general population to develop alcohol problems. Children of alcoholics also have a higher risk for many other behavioral and emotional problems. But alcoholism is not determined only by the genes you inherit from your parents. In fact, more than one-half of all children of alcoholics do not become alcoholic. Research shows that many factors influence your risk of developing alcoholism. Some factors raise the risk, while others lower it.[56]

Risk Factors

One factor that raises risk is, of course, sexual abuse. I'm no expert and certainly no scientist, but I am an alcoholic with a genetic history of alcoholism on my mother's side of the family. I experienced all of the factors—genetics *and* childhood trauma—that increase the risk of alcohol use turning into alcoholism.

While it may be true that there is a genetic component to my alcohol and drug abuse, I want to be clear that, in recovery, there is a fine line between a reason for something and a justification for it. My genetic predisposition to being an alcoholic does not give me an excuse to drink. Neither does my childhood sexual abuse give me that excuse. I cannot heal and move on without taking full responsibility for my own actions.

But I also cannot heal if I overcompensate by taking *too much* responsibility. I don't want to escape from responsibility by slipping into victimhood, but I equally don't want to cripple myself by shouldering more responsibility than I truly have. I accept the idea that I might have

---

[56]National Institute on Alcohol Abuse and Alcoholism, *A Family History of Alcoholism: Are You at Risk?* NIH Publication No. 03–5340, Reprinted June 2012, retrieved from http://pubs.niaaa.nih.gov/publications/FamilyHistory/famhist/htm/.

been partially predetermined to turn to drugs and alcohol because of my genetics, but I know that my recovery is more powerful than that genetic predisposition.

My genes may lessen the responsibility that I had as a teenager who fell into alcohol and drug abuse, but they do not excuse the actions of the adult Randy, who had a choice between drinking and getting help. I became an alcoholic, at least in part, due to my genetics; I drank because of my environment. Today, I stay sober because I am committed to my recovery and my happiness.

Getting clean is essential when it comes to learning how to effectively reparent yourself. Just as you cannot parent a child responsibly if you are acting out your addictions, you also cannot reparent *yourself* in a consistent, loving, and effective way. It was not until I admitted that I had a problem that I was able to get help. In treatment, it was not until I stopped holding on to my victim story that I was able to grow up enough to learn how to reparent myself. Staying stuck in victim stories, insisting that there is always someone else to blame for unwanted outcomes, makes it impossible for me to find the inner power to develop appropriate responsibility in order to create my own outcomes.

"Shoulding" on Others

Victimhood is an attractive addiction. It feels good in the moment. We get all puffed up in our ego-state with self-righteous anger and blustery pride, and then start blaming other people. Chronic victims of abuse are unwilling to look at *themselves*, but it's only when we examine our own behavior that we can start to heal. Every time I blame the world or other people for my own problems, I try to find at least three ways that *I* might be at fault.

Recently, when I was talking to a friend, the subject of mothers and motherhood came up. Because that is still a sore trigger for me, I took an immediate nosedive into a gigantic pile of smelly "shoulds." For starters, mothers should love their children, protect them, and always be gentle and kind. Fortunately, my friend, who is a fellow survivor, gently reminded me that I was starting to "should" in public. "It's so easy," he said, "to be certain of what everyone else should do. But it's really difficult to apply that certainty to ourselves." It is not easy to look at ourselves, but there is a powerful freedom that comes when we do.

After countless months of meditation, journaling, and speaking to my mentors, I discovered several character defects in myself, one of which was my dislike of my mother for all the ways she had abused me. But then I realized that my mother had grown up in a highly abusive family herself, and that insight led to the beginning of my forgiving her. I understood that if it is a mother's job to love her child, it is equally the child's job to love his mother. But for several years, I not only disliked my mother, I actually *hated* her. The cold hard truth is that the best I was able to do during that season of my life was grudgingly wish her well in order to preserve my own peace of mind.

When I turn the "shoulds" around on myself, a different perspective comes into focus. Without all the "shoulds," I am free to live my life. I can choose to walk around carrying a load of "shoulds," and suffer the attendant unpleasant self-righteousness, or I can lay that burden down where it belongs, at the feet of my God. I am then free to focus on my own shortcomings.

There are two things that make a "should"-free life a happier one:

1. When you come off your self-righteous high horse from which you criticize everyone, and instead accept others for who they are, you will be a happier person yourself, and people will be glad to be around you again.

2. When you realize that you cannot change others, but only yourself, you get to be the hero of your own adventure story, in which no one has any power over you except *you*.

It takes courage to accept responsibility for your own happiness, but the rewards are everything you truly want: self-confidence, self-acceptance, joy, peace, and lightness of being. Life on the other side of the victim story is good. Getting there requires slogging through some mud, but it's well worth the effort.

Alcoholics Anonymous

On February 1, 2006, I was getting ready to go on a hunting trip for wild boar in Central California. My idea of manliness had been so twisted that I made a habit of doing the most dangerous things I could think up. Hunting trips were a combination of pleasure and pain for me. On the one hand, I love the outdoors and the excitement and challenge of hunting, for camping and backpacking with my dad are still some of my most treasured memories. On the other hand, the hunting trips became an opportunity for me to prove that I was better than everybody else.

Four years earlier, I had blown two years of abstinence at a campfire after a long day of hunting. This time, although I had been in therapy with Cathy for a year to repair our marriage, I was still drinking. Before I left on this trip in 2006, I stopped by a liquor store to pick up a half-gallon bottle of Jack Daniel's for the trip. When I started packing at 10:00 A.M., I opened the bottle and began drinking.

Twenty minutes later, I saw that the contents of the bottle were down by a good 25%. That was the first moment that I questioned my ability to stop drinking anytime I wanted. In that same moment, I heard the same soft, gentle voice that I had heard at the age of fifteen, telling me to fight for my life as I was lying on the ground bleeding to death after a motorcycle accident. This time that quiet voice was telling me that I needed help. Clear as day, I heard the words, "Your get-out-of-jail-free cards are all used up. You need help, Randy, and you need it *now*."

Unlike the shaming, belittling, screaming voices in my head that I tried to drown out most of the time, this was a soft, gentle, loving voice. After listening to it, I called a friend, knowing that, if nothing else, he would hold me accountable to my personal commitment to stop drinking. He told me to get A.A.'s *Big Book* that very day and to call him in the morning. I did neither and ignored *his* call the next morning. Instead, I had decided that although it was time to get help, I was going hunting for the weekend and was bound and determined to enjoy those three last days of drinking.

The following Tuesday, February 7, 2006, two days after returning home from the hunting trip, I proudly told my therapist that I had quit drinking. Although she was happy for me, she strongly recommended that I go to Alcoholics Anonymous. She explained the difference between abstinence and sobriety, and knew that I would not get sober unless I got real help.

I felt besieged, first by my friend and then by my therapist. A.A. was definitely out of the question. I was not one of *those* people. I was a successful businessman with a wife and family. I still had my house and all my toys. I even had great credit. I was not a loser living under a bridge. I told myself, I'm not an alcoholic, I just have a drinking problem.

Thankfully, my therapist did not shove A.A. down my throat, she just asked me to consider it. Of course, she asked me to consider it for three straight weeks. I was not drinking, but I was becoming more and more anxious, growing ever more miserable with each passing day. My body hurt, I was agitated and angry all the time, and I felt that I had no escape from my negative thoughts and dark emotions. Something had to change. I didn't want to drink, but I was tired of feeling horrible. I would come home from work and literally crawl into my recliner, shaking and rocking. My anxiety increased a hundredfold, and as time went on, if someone so much as looked at me the wrong way, I wanted his head on a platter—preferably from tearing it off with my bare hands.

Fridays were the worst days of the week, because Friday was date night with Cathy. In the past, by the time she got home from work, I would have done a line or two of cocaine and tossed back a cocktail or four to get ready for a night of dinner and drinks on the town.

The second Friday after I quit drinking and taking drugs, Cathy walked into our home to find me curled up in a ball in my recliner, sweating and shaking. When she asked me what was wrong, I told her I needed a drink—and badly. But I had promised her and myself that I would stop drinking, so I asked her to please just sit with me and help me through the withdrawal. Therefore, on that Friday, date night was in our darkened living room, with Cathy holding me as I shook, cried, and gritted my teeth.

Over the course of the next few months, there were many other nights like that. After several similar Friday nights, I decided that something had to give, because if this is what being sober was going to be like, I wanted nothing to do with it. There used to be a billboard on the freeway near my house, which said, "This year, thousands of men will die from stubbornness. Get a prostate exam." I can imagine couples driving by that billboard, with the wives sagely nodding and the husbands pointedly staring straight ahead.

Certainly, no one had ever accused me of being eager to change, so it took three weeks of sleepless nights of sweating it out alone in the wee hours of the morning for me to admit that I might, under perfect conditions, just possibly consider going to an A.A. meeting.

In Deborah's infinite wisdom and experience handling my touchy ego, she suggested that, if I didn't want to go to A.A., maybe I should look into going to the Betty Ford Center.

Still refusing to admit that I was an alcoholic, I wasn't ready yet to be one of "those people," but I was willing to consider being one of the "special people" who seek treatment at the Betty Ford Center. After considering Deborah's suggestion for a day and a night, the next morning as I sat sobbing in my office, looking at the Betty Ford Center website, I called Cathy to ask her to stop by on her way to work to check it out with me. I could no longer deal with the pain, I said, and needed help *now*. In less than half an hour, we made the decision to call the center to begin my journey into recovery.

I want to be clear here: you do not have to go to a treatment center to get sober. I have seen plenty of people, including my sponsor and his wife, who have fifty years of combined sobriety between them, get and stay sober by simply walking into an A.A. meeting. In my own case, however, I needed to go to a center because paying for treatment would help me to stay committed.

However, the very first time I walked into the center, I wasn't sure what to expect. More than once, I had imagined going through some kind of program that would include massages, art therapy, and talking about my feelings, so that, eight weeks later, I could drink like a gentleman. Clearly, I was still delusional enough to believe that I wasn't really an alcoholic. I just had this tiny, little, inconsequential problem with alcohol.

Thankfully, the wonderful people at the Betty Ford Center had seen my kind before. When I told the intake counselor what I had in mind, she smiled and nodded her head, then patiently explained the two principal kinds of programs at the center. First, she said, there was the inpatient program, in which the participants agreed to remain at the facility for ninety days, working on sobriety under the controlled environment in the center. Second, there was the Intensive Outpatient Program, which met Monday through Friday from 5:00 P.M. to 9:00 P.M., for eight weeks. That gave the patients the advantage of being able to work on their recovery in a safe environment, while participating in their regular life at the same time.

Against the advice of the intake counselor, who felt that the severity of my childhood sexual abuse would be best served by the inpatient program, I decided to go with the outpatient approach.

"After all," I said, "I've got a business to run."

"Fine," she replied. "We're not going to make you do anything you don't want to."

I soon found myself learning how to deal with my problems in real time. I wasn't isolated in a bubble where nothing went wrong and then sent back to the real world after just a few weeks or months. Thanks to this program, I had peers I could call during the day to help me through the hard times, and I had a small group to look forward to on weekday evenings.

In case you think that the Betty Ford Center only caters to movie and rock stars, let me clear that right up. Yes, celebrities with addictive problems do go there for help, but the vast majority of patients are just everyday folks—people who get up every morning, go to work, and support a family, or even stay home with their children, taking them to and from school, baseball and soccer practice, and attending PTA meetings. In any case, I soon discovered that the work is the same, whether the meetings are held in a dusty old church basement with rickety folding chairs or in a well-lighted, beautifully appointed, and fully staffed center.

However, I also originally suffered from the glamorous misconception. *If I go to the Betty Ford Center*, I figured, *I'll be treated like a rock star, whereas if I go to an A.A. meeting, I'll be treated like an ordinary loser who can't hold it together.*

What I didn't know then was that the center would be where I would face my spiritual abuse and learn to reconnect with God, whom I had rejected when I was a teenager. Peter only denied Christ three times before the rooster crowed in the morning. Over the previous thirty-one years, I had denied God countless times.

Yet, somehow, I had escaped any legal consequences, and I still had my life, my family, and my business. Nevertheless, I was spiritually and emotionally bankrupt. I no longer had any idea who I was or what my purpose was in life.

In nearly every addiction treatment center that follows a twelve-step program, the steps are posted on a wall. As if that were not intimidating enough for a newcomer, the word *God* is not only included, but it is printed in bold type, and practically jumps off the wall at you. Or at least that's how it felt to me. Step Three states, "We made a decision to turn our will and our lives over to the care of God as we understand him."

On my first day, as I stared at the twelve steps printed on the wall, I thought, *Now we have a problem. If God is a part of this program, I want nothing to do with it, period. Besides, I came here for the glamorous Betty Ford treatment part. I didn't sign up for any A.A. program.*

I decided to ignore the big bold letters.

Fortunately, it appeared that God was optional in the program. The people in charge made it clear that *everything* was optional, so I could take what I liked and leave the rest. I was desperate enough to take them at their word.

Because I had a lot to lose, I needed treatment and recovery to work. Cathy, my children, my business, and what was left of my self-respect were all on the line. Drinking was no longer an option. After all, no one had forced me to get sober—not a judge and not my wife. I had made that decision on my own, and was determined to see it through. I was too stubborn and proud to fail at anything, and that included staying sober. But without drugs or alcohol, my emotional pain was nearly unbearable. So I ignored the words on the wall, and focused on doing only what my counselor requested of me, one day at a time.

In my initial assessment meeting with my counselor, whose name was Melissa, she told me some of the requirements I needed to follow during treatment. I had figured that, as an outpatient, I would be in control of my own schedule. That was true to some degree, but there were consequences of varying severity for not following the guidelines.

The first thing my counselor told me was that I was required to attend a minimum of three A.A. meetings a week. I stared at her, certain that she was kidding. She wasn't. I couldn't believe my ears! I just sat there, glowering at her and sending mental daggers toward Deborah, who hadn't told me about this part.

I never signed up for A.A.! I thought.

And there was no opportunity to play hooky, either. Melissa handed me a "court card" that had to be signed by the secretary of the meetings I would be attending.

I was so busy fuming that I barely heard the next part: that I also had to call at least three male peers a day to check in with them.

When I opened my mouth to tell Melissa exactly where she could shove her "mandatory meetings," I realized that I was utterly and completely exhausted. All of the fight was drained out of me. Puffing out my feathers and causing yet another scene seemed harder than sprinting up Mount Whitney. I was done fighting. In that moment, I realized that I was actually willing to do whatever it would take to have a better life. Finally, I had surrendered.

I hadn't had a lobotomy or anything like that. I was still me. So I put off going to those despised meetings as long as I could. It took some forceful encouragement from Duke, a friend of twenty years, who confided in me that he was also in A.A. and an alumnus of the Betty Ford Center. Duke was, and remains to this day, the kindest, wisest person I know. When I tried to apply my negative judgments to him about the kinds of people who go to A.A., the fallacy of my thinking was immediately evident, for Duke was successful, kind, and honest.

Nevertheless, I went to my first A.A. meeting with my guard fully up. Although my butt was in the chair, I was slouched down, remembering all the times I had shown up at church after not going for several weeks. Back then, the elders and Jack would inevitably make some sarcastic comment when I arrived, shaming me for my absence.

For the first three weeks of those meetings, I hovered in a state of fear, delusion, pain, and confusion. I would go to work and fake my way through my days, doing my best not to unleash my anger and anxiety on my employees or clients. Eventually, between doing the work at the A.A. meetings and the Betty Ford Center, I became less angry and anxious, and started to be more likeable.

No matter what path you choose—whether it be A.A., an inpatient program, or an outpatient program—if you *want* to stay sober, you will. If you don't, you won't. But if sobriety is what you desire, then you *must* be willing to do the work as laid out in A.A.'s *Big Book*.

The twelve steps contain solid recovery practices. Any competent therapist or treatment program will put you through the same process. But you cannot cherry-pick the steps you like and just follow those. To be successful, you must complete *all* twelve steps—and in the order they are numbered.

Technically, the twelve steps in A.A. are just "suggestions." However, they are suggestions in much the same way that putting on a parachute before jumping out of an airplane is a suggestion. Other people may see the steps as suggestions, but I followed them to the letter, because, as they say in A.A., I was sick and tired of being sick and tired. I didn't want to party anymore. I didn't want the ego-based highs and lows. I didn't even care if people liked me or thought I was cool or macho. All I wanted was to have some peace and serenity in my life. It was a bad place to be stuck in, but a good place to start my recovery.

Recovery

After the initial detox period, getting clean and sober isn't so bad. However, *staying* clean and sober can be difficult. Quite frankly, in today's world, simply not drinking or using appears to be good enough for most people. The trouble is that their wives want to leave them, their finances are in shambles, and they are constantly fighting legal battles. There is nothing wrong with their behavior or way of life, they say. It's just the way they are. However, I wanted more out of life. I was financially successful, spiritually bankrupt, empty on the inside, and miserable. Avoiding alcohol and drugs was not enough to fix what was broken inside me.

Eight weeks at the Betty Ford Center gave me a great foundation for my recovery. I was able to talk openly about my sexual abuse, the loss of my father, and my anger at God, and had my feelings validated for the first time. I learned that there were others with issues similar to mine. I was not alone.

Although the rules of treatment required me to start going to A.A. meetings, I didn't go to only three a week. In my usual fashion, I went to *ten or twelve*. At those meetings, I learned that alcoholics are not just winos under bridges. They are everyday people: business owners, mothers, fathers, mayors, doctors, lawyers—and *me*. In a matter of weeks, I had grown tired of carrying around my huge ego. No longer did I care if others thought I was one of "those people." I was starting to feel better, I wanted more of that, and I wanted it right away.

When I entered treatment, I was willing to do whatever it took to change my life. Along the way, I surrendered to the fact that I was an alcoholic and could never drink again. But if I couldn't drink, how was I going to deal with my underlying issues? How was I going to anesthetize my feelings of shame and my sense that I was less than good enough?

As it turned out, I wasn't and couldn't. I had to walk through the shame and pain without any anesthesia. I had to travel into the depths of my mind, where I had stored those memories under layers of drugs, alcohol, and denial, falsely believing that if I could just make the sexual abuse and my memories of it disappear, eventually they would somehow magically vanish.

If you already know that isn't how life works, you're leagues ahead of where I was when I entered treatment. I had to unpack all of that old baggage, and I had to do it sober. But I had support that made all the difference: I had the love of my wife, Cathy, the help of my therapist, Deborah, and the encouragement of my sponsor, Way Spiritual Dave.

I also had one more thing: my back was firmly up against the wall. I knew that if I chose not to do the work that was necessary for me to heal, I would certainly drink again. If I did that, I knew deep down that I would most likely take my own life, either by my own hand or by drinking-induced recklessness. I have seen too many survivors resume drinking because of their unwillingness to do this work, and I have seen too many survivors commit suicide because of the immense pain that comes up while doing this work.

This is not an easy journey that can be completed quickly. It can be extremely difficult, and I will most likely be traveling on it for the rest of my life. Remember, recovery is a marathon, not a sprint, so you should have realistic expectations about it. There is no "cure" for surviving sexual abuse, and nothing will make the memories go away. But in time, you will learn to carry the effects more easily, to let them enlighten you instead of depress you. Every day, you have the ability to improve. True recovery is a return to a normal state of health in body and mind. It involves regaining control of something that was stolen or lost: our childhood innocence.

When we become clean and sober, and *only* then, can we start doing the work necessary to recover. Not until we become rigorously honest with *ourselves* will we discover just how much of our life was stolen from us. I believe that a hidden gift of abuse and surviving the pain associated with it is that we can learn how to actively seek tools to handle adversity and turmoil as well as develop the discipline and skill to lead kind, compassionate, and wise lives. When we choose to walk through the fire of the recovery process, we are no longer only surviving—we are learning how to thrive.

I discovered early on that if I wanted anything in life I had to work for it, and what I wanted now was for my life to change. I hated leading a life of fear that was filled with chaos and turmoil, but in order for that to change, I had to put in a lot of effort. Fortunately, I didn't have to do that alone—and neither do you! From day one of my recovery, there were trustworthy people ready to stand by my side. These were men and women who had walked the road before me and knew where most of the pitfalls were. Just as their mentors had had the experience and expertise to guide them through the recovery process, so these individuals had the experience and expertise to guide me.

Embarking on the twelve-step journey was daunting for me. When I walked into the rooms of A.A. for the first time and saw all the steps written out on the wall, I thought they were sure asking a lot of me. It would be hard enough just to embrace the challenges of Step One.

Step One

We admitted we were powerless over alcohol—that our lives had become unmanageable.

In the following pages, I provide a brief outline of my experiences in A.A. in relation to Step One. Hopefully, a fellow survivor's experience and perspective will make that first walk into A.A. a little less intimidating for you.

Step One and I did not exactly get off to a glorious start. I don't know about you, but admitting that I'm powerless over anything doesn't exactly make my Top Ten list of Stuff I Like Doing.

What do you mean, I'm powerless? I said to myself. *I'm a man, and a powerful one at that. I'm running a million-dollar business. I'm raising a family. When I want something, I go after it and get it. Don't tell me I'm powerless!*

For most survivors of sexual abuse, powerlessness is one of the worst feelings possible. When we were abused as children, it was our sense of powerlessness that created most of our long-term pain. I spent decades building up a façade so that the world would think I was powerful and untouchable. I even persuaded myself that it was true. But here was some puffed-up personal growth group forcing me to ask myself questions I couldn't answer. No one challenged my doubts, and it was a good thing they didn't, because I might have left and never returned. But all the members who shared on that first day did so honestly and with a total commitment to their own growth. The honesty I heard in that room about the shortcomings and struggles of others made it impossible for me to ignore my own.

I got the feeling that while the others were glad I was there, it didn't really matter to them if I agreed with them or even if I came back. They were going to get better with or without me. That was a sobering realization. No one was going to fight with me or even engage with me. The format is brilliant. People are invited to share their experiences, strengths, and hopes around whatever issue is the focus of the meeting. There is no crosstalk, arguing, or dialogue of any kind.

As I listened to the other members share experiences that sounded an awful lot like my own, it often seemed to me that they could read my mind. I would be struggling with something that day, and someone would share about the same issue. Because the stories were so similar to my own, I started to accept that I was no longer alone. When human beings become honest with themselves, I realized, our problems are a lot alike, and we tend to come to the same wise solutions when we aren't too busy defending our egos.

Randy, I asked myself, *if you're so powerful, how come you can't control your drinking? How come you have to use intimidation and manipulation to get what you want?*

At first, I didn't much like that voice, but thanks to the group dynamic, and the honesty and vulnerability of the other members, I quickly realized that I wasn't the first person to ask questions like those. Hearing other people admitting that they were powerless helped me to admit that I was powerless, too.

Soon after that first meeting, I completed at home an assignment called the Powerlessness Exercise, which had been given to me by Way Spiritual Dave, my sponsor. If you would like to do this exercise, here is the guideline Dave had me follow for the process:

Powerlessness

At some point in your history, you became alcoholic, became powerless over alcohol, a mood-altering chemical. It happened over a period of time. Define the process as it happened to you by answering the questions below. You will discover how your disease affected you and changed you so that you compromised your basic values.

1. What did you drink, how much, how often? How and when did this change as time went on?

2. Growing tolerance: Did it take more to make you feel good? Did it finally take more just to make you feel normal? Did you gulp drinks? Order stiffer drinks? Protect your supply? Hide your supply at home, in the car, at your job? What hangover symptoms did you have?

3. Growing preoccupation: thinking, planning, or scheming how to drink or set up situations to drink. Were you preoccupied with drinking even when sober? When and how? (Daytimes, vacations, increased drinking time.) Did your other activities then get in the way of your

drinking? Did you increase your drinking during times of stress? (Job/family/personal.) Did you begin to drink at particular times more regularly? (After work, weekends, before going to bed, before leaving the house, morning drinking.)

4. What accidents did your drinking cause? What dangerous situations did your drinking get you into?

5. How and when did you attempt to cut down or control your use of alcohol? How did you feel as a result of your attempts to control or stop your drinking?

6. Loss of Control: You used alcohol and then it started to use you! That's when you lost control. Give specific examples on each of the following:

FAMILY: Broken promises, drunken embarrassing behavior in front of your family, sacrificing family for your drinking, physical and verbal abuse of yourself and your family.

LEGAL: Drunk driving, drunk and disorderly conduct, divorce, jail, bankruptcy, and theft.

SOCIAL: Loss of friends/hobbies/community activities? Problems with sexuality?

JOB: Were you absent? Lose promotions? Were you fired from your job or threatened with that? Did you quit your job(s) due to your drinking? What were the impacts of going to work hung over or drinking while at work?

PHYSICAL: Were you hospitalized, or told by your doctor to cut down on your drinking? Were you using alcohol and/or other drugs as a medicine to sleep or relieve stress? What were your withdrawal symptoms? Did you have blackouts?

GETTING CLEAN

Here is what I wrote down when I reviewed the Christmas party experience from several years before:

> Cathy and I attended a Christmas party where lots of drinking was taking place, especially by me. At the end of the evening, as Cathy and I were leaving, I kissed one of our female friends on the neck. On the way home, Cathy and I got in a heated confrontation, which continued in front of our children when we got home. At one point, as Cathy tried to slap me, I threw up my hands to block her, but only succeeded in knocking her to the ground. When my fourteen-year-old daughter protested, I told her to shut up or she would be next. Then I left the house to get a bite to eat and have a few more drinks.
>
> When I arrived back home, a couple of hours later, there were six La Quinta police cars in front of my house. It turned out that my son's girlfriend had called 911, and Cathy had been taken to the emergency room. One of the police officers told me that I was not allowed to call the hospital. All my weapons had been removed from the house and put into safekeeping for ten days. Worst of all, my daughter wanted absolutely nothing to do with me.

When I completed my list, which took up five pages of consequences, I realized just how powerless and unmanageable my life had become.

It is important that you have a good sponsor or therapist to walk you through the steps, which must be done in a particular order to get you through the process safely. A main tenet of A.A. states: "When your own house is in order, the answers will come. But we cannot transmit something you have not got." All too often, people who have not done their own work try to walk others through the steps, which usually results in doing more harm than good. Find someone who has walked through his own fire to earn wisdom. Mentors who have walked a path similar to yours are more valuable to you than a thousand well-meaning people who haven't. A.A. makes some bold promises, but I can tell you, as an alcoholic and a survivor of sexual abuse, they do come true.

A.A. Promises

If we are painstaking about this phase of our development, we will be amazed before we are halfway through. We are going to know a new freedom and a new happiness. We will not regret the past nor wish to shut the door on it. We will comprehend the word *serenity* and we will know peace. No matter how far down the scale we have gone, we will see how our experience can benefit others. That feeling of uselessness and self-pity will disappear. We will lose interest in selfish things and gain interest in our fellows. Self-seeking will slip away. Our whole attitude and outlook upon life will change. Fear of people and of economic insecurity will leave us. We will intuitively know how to handle situations that used to baffle us. We will suddenly realize that God is doing for us what we could not do for ourselves.

Are these extravagant promises? We think not. They are being fulfilled among us—sometimes quickly, sometimes slowly. They will always materialize if we work for them.[57]

---

[57] Alcoholics Anonymous, *The Big Book*, 4th ed., pp. 83–84.

Chapter 9:
Secrets and Silence

Anything that's human is mentionable, and anything that is mentionable can be more manageable. When we can talk about our feelings, they become less overwhelming, less upsetting, and less scary. The people we trust with that important talk can help us know that we are not alone.

—Fred Rogers[58]

On a macro level, secret-keeping perpetuates the scourge of child abuse. On a personal level, it perpetuates the feeling that the child has done something wrong. More than almost any other demographic, boys who have been sexually abused are unfairly stigmatized by society. Almost without exception, men who were sexually abused as children carry a deep sense of shame and unworthiness, feeling that they are somehow broken and tainted because they were abused. This "thought-virus" about male sexual abuse is unfair, untrue, deeply painful, and reinforced by the idea that abuse needs to be kept secret.

The definition of sexual abuse that I find the most beneficial to the healing process comes from author Judith Lewis Herman, who wrote that "any touch or other behavior between the child and adult which must be kept secret will be considered abuse."[59]

That definition fascinated me when I first heard it, although it actually seemed somewhat too inclusive. I thought, *Surely there are times when a child keeps a "good" secret, and every secret a child has regarding contact with an adult can't be abuse.* But then I thought about it some more and applied Herman's definition to my own experience. Then my thought

---

[58]Fred Rogers, *Quotes*, retrieved from http://www.goodreads.com/author/quotes/32106.Fred_Rogers/.
[59]Judith Lewis Herman, *Trauma and Recovery: The Aftermath of Violence—From Domestic Abuse to Political Terror* (New York: Basic Books, 1992), p. 35.

became: *If there was nothing wrong with what Jack was doing to me, why couldn't I tell my mom? If there was nothing wrong with all the physical abuse, why did I have to keep it a secret?* The more I talked with other survivors, the more I realized that there was a common thread between all our stories, and that thread was centered on this idea of secret-keeping.

I have yet to find an example of a long-term secret that was *not* abusive in nature when it involved a child concealing *anything* to do with an adult. The child often carries the burden of this secret into adulthood, unconsciously allowing it to become heavier and more painful with each passing year. Of course, there are good secrets and bad secrets, but most children don't understand the difference between the two. Abused children in particular almost never get the chance to discover this difference. When a child takes on the burden of protecting an adult at the expense of his own well-being, shame sets in alongside the secret, and it often becomes impossible for him to distinguish between the secret and shame.

Fortunately, adult survivors of sexual abuse can unlearn this early programming by learning the truth about secrets and discovering the link between bad secrets, abuse, and toxic shame.

Good vs. Bad Secrets

According to the Kids Safe Foundation, a good secret is something that feels good to know and has a time limit. At some point, a good secret won't be secret anymore. Common examples of good secrets are surprise gifts or parties. Bad secrets make you feel anxious, scared, confused, or ashamed. Without question, all secrets involving abuse are bad.[60]

One of the saddest facts about child sexual abuse is that almost every abused child, especially in cases of incest, is manipulated into staying silent. Perpetrators threaten or cajole their victims, or misrepresent the abuse, in order to keep their crime a secret. But then, at some point, the victims begin to believe that the abuse is *their* secret, not the abuser's. They feel that *they* are to blame. They are broken, evil, bad, and dirty, so the abuse *must* in some way be their own fault. This false belief can take a deep hold, coming as it does during our most impressionable years, and therefore can be exceedingly difficult to undo.

Here are some of the most common threats and manipulations that sexual abusers use on their victims:

---

[60]Kids Safe Foundation, *A Child Who Keeps Secrets: An Easy Target for a Predator!* Retrieved from http://www.kidsafefoundation.org/a-child-who-keeps-secrets-%E2%80%A6-an-easy-target-for-a-predator/.

- Don't tell or I will hurt you and your family.

- You can't tell because no one will believe you.

- We can be "special friends," but you have to keep it a secret.

- If you tell, people will know you're bad.

Whether the perpetrator threatens physical harm or twists the abuse into some kind of special favor, in both cases the abuser tends to be highly skilled at making the victim feel complicit in the abuse via secret-keeping. When we victims become adults, we can see this shameless manipulation for the poison it is, but as children we tended to trust and believe our adult caregivers. Some of us will even take our secrets to our graves because, at some level, we still believe the words of our abusers.

When the abuse was physically arousing for the victim, keeping the secret often intensifies the feelings of shame and complicity, making it even more difficult for him to heal in later years. But it cannot be stated enough that even if you were physically aroused, you were not complicit in the abuse—and it was, in fact, still abuse. I know too many men who feel ashamed about having enjoyed some of the abusive situations they experienced. Many of them truly believe that they were responsible for creating the abuse. While some victims do seek out attention from their abuser, a child is *never* responsible for what an adult chooses to do. Children can never give consent, for they are utterly dependent on the approval and care of the adults in their life. If you sought out the attention of an abuser, even knowing that that would most likely involve intimate violations, you are just like many other survivors.

Abuse rarely happens in healthy, loving, supportive families. For many victims, the attention they receive at the hands of their abusers is the only positive attention they ever get. It is completely understandable why an abused, frightened child would seek out an attentive abuser, no matter what price he has to pay for that attention. If that is how you feel, I understand. I did that myself. When the abuse started, Jack was the only father figure I had in my life. I had just lost my beloved biological father, and my mother had, if anything, grown even colder since his death. Jack was always available for me when I needed kindness, support, and understanding. However, I had no idea he was actually grooming me for the fast approaching abuse.

All I knew was that I felt safe, loved, and happy when he paid attention to me. Later, when what he wanted from me became clear, it didn't seem like that much of a price to pay. Often what he did to me felt physically good, and he didn't hurt me. After I hit puberty, he stimulated my body to orgasm many times. This does not mean that I wanted to be abused. I didn't. It felt good, and there was nothing I could do about it.

God created our bodies to be aroused when we are touched in certain areas. Our bodies don't know that we are being abused; they just know that the stimulation feels good. That is very confusing to us and carries more shame than any other secret we carry.

In one extreme case, "Jordan," after admitting to his sexual abuse survivors group that it felt good when he was being sexually abused, then went home and wrote a suicide note. Fortunately, he checked himself into a mental health facility instead. That is how much shame this secret carries. Luckily, Jordan is doing very well today.

After keeping Jack's secret for months, I started to believe that the abuse was my fault. As time passes, we start to believe our own internal dialogue. Even if the abuse ended decades ago, or the abuser is out of our lives, or even deceased, we take up the mantle of secret-keeping, creating our internal rationalizations for keeping our secret. We tell ourselves it's because "other people wouldn't understand," or "society isn't ready," or "it's not the right time," or "it's just part of growing up."

But all the rationalizations in the world will not dissolve the shame that comes with keeping this kind of secret. We can tell ourselves any kind of "rational lie," but the truth is that most of us are deeply and miserably ashamed that we were abused. Most of us have spent years rejecting ourselves because of the abuse, telling ourselves that we were somehow bad or broken, and are now terrified that if other people knew, they would agree with our self-condemnation. We project our self-hatred, fear, and shame onto the people nearest to us, and we hide away our secret, letting it eat away at our self-esteem, our relationships, and our happiness.

For most survivors of sexual abuse, it is only after they work on themselves and achieve some kind of inner stability around the abuse that they are able to tell someone else about it. So long as we feel that we have to keep our abuse a secret, we are telling ourselves that it was in some way our own fault, and therefore something to be ashamed of.

It is heartbreakingly common for male survivors of sexual abuse to be so terrified of what other people will think if they knew about the abuse that they even rationalize the abuse away. Many male survivors normalize the abuse; something that is often all too easy to do when it comes to incestuous abuse. Incest can be especially devastating because the victim often keeps a secret to protect his family or the abuser.

When a child feels that he needs to keep a bad secret, such as being sexually abused by an adult, he might attempt to normalize the abuse in order to feel safe by thinking that it is just an ordinary part of growing up. The problem with normalizing abuse is that it doesn't get rid of the shame and emotional pain. Survivors who normalize their abuse get caught in a vicious cycle in which they still suffer the residual effects of the abuse. They are unable to get the help they need because they tell everyone, "My childhood was just fine, thank you."

While this kind of denial might offer some short-term solace to the child, it can make recovery much more difficult in the long run. If the victim has persuaded himself that he wasn't actually abused, he cannot admit to himself that he needs help to deal with the effects of that abuse. In other words, he has no choice but to continue blaming himself.

I have seen so many men suffer from almost unbelievable emotional torment because they refuse to let go of the idea that they were loved, or at least not hurt, by those who abused them—or by the adults (like my mother) who failed to protect them from being abused.

This book is *not* about assigning blame and hating or shaming people from your past. Just as there are many survivors of sexual abuse who rationalize away their abusers' guilt, so too, at the other extreme, there are many survivors who have gotten trapped in an endless cycle of blame and hatred, which only locks them into a state of perpetual victimization. However, although I am not advocating assigning arbitrary hatred or blame to your abusers, I do urge you to assign responsibility to them for their actions.

While you don't want to become trapped in the blaming-victimization cycle, if you are a survivor who got through your childhood by normalizing the abuse, you need to reassess those situations from an adult's perspective. If you don't, it's all too likely that you will continue to blame yourself, often without even knowing that you are doing it.

The Mother Role

A mother's role in abuse can often be confusing and possibly even just as damaging to the victim as the main abuse itself. At one extreme, she may instigate as well as participate in the physical, emotional, and spiritual abuse, stating that she was just being submissive to her husband and fearing for her own life. At the other end of the spectrum, the mother may be completely oblivious to the sexual abuse. However, she is likely to regard the physical and emotional abuse as just normal discipline.

Oftentimes, a mother will talk with her abused child in their alone times, holding him and telling him how much she loves him and wants to remove him from the abusive atmosphere. But because of the mother's own insecurities, she remains in the abusive household. More often than not, she does not know the intensity of the abuse, and therefore acts as if the cries for help are much like crying wolf. Because our mothers don't believe or protect us when we tell them the truth about the abuse, we interpret that as meaning that they don't love us. That may or may not be true.

I use this example, not only because it is incredibly common, but also because it is a perfect instance of how a child's black-and-white thinking can continue unchecked into adulthood, preventing the survivor from healing. Children don't understand the nuances of human nature. They think that either their parents love them or they don't.

It's terrifying for a child to live in a world where their caregivers don't love them, so they create elaborate justifications for abusive or neglectful behavior from the adults in their lives. These justifications protect the child's mind from more frightening alternatives.

As an adult, you can look back and understand that people are all imperfect, and that the more accurate story was probably that your mother loved you to the best of her ability, but her flaws led her to either directly or indirectly cause your abuse. This doesn't mean that you have to hate her. The fact that she was flawed and made mistakes doesn't negate the positive memories you may have of her. You don't even have to tell her that you have realized she was abusive or neglectful. That insight is for you and you alone.

The main thing is that you need to stop blaming yourself, and you can't do that when you're protecting your story about someone else. You've been carrying that burden far too long. It's time to lay it down and step away from it. You aren't a child anymore. You don't need to keep recycling the same story that served you when you were young. You are free to exchange that story for one that is more honest—and far gentler to you.

SECRETS AND SILENCE

Ending the Silence and Stopping the Shame

Secret-keeping is damaging on so many levels. This one act alone can keep you from getting help or even make you feel complicit in your own abuse. On a societal level, secret-keeping makes it easier for everyone to ignore the problem by protecting the perpetrator at the victim's expense. It even makes it easier for the perpetrator to abuse other victims.

Ending this culture of secrecy and shame around sexual abuse is crucial, but that does not make it simple. In many cases, survivors may be right to protect themselves from the additional pain that might be inflicted on them if they were to bring their secrets out into the open. It is important to choose your friends carefully and only confide in the ones you totally trust. You don't have to confide in the whole world. Even just telling one safe person—for me it was Cathy—can alleviate a huge amount of shame and pain. If you haven't told anyone about your abuse yet, I encourage you to find a safe person, a safe time, and a safe space to start this healing process. A kind, compassionate, and knowledgeable person, such as a therapist, spiritual counselor, best friend, or spouse, will understand that the abuse was not your fault.

Of course, having a confidant will not cure all your problems, but it can certainly be a step in the direction of recovery. In my own case, I told Cathy about my sexual abuse before we were even married. However, I carried the secret of being sexually abused into my first marriage, which resulted in a disastrous ending.

While my first wife, "Jane," knew bits and pieces about the emotional and physical abuse I had endured, she was totally unaware of the sexual abuse. I had a great job and was a great provider. However, my drinking was getting worse with each passing month, my self-esteem was plummeting, and the fact that I had put on sixty pounds was not helping either my self-esteem or my marriage. I was not the person Jane had married, and she was angry and confused about who I had become. My secret was killing me and literally destroyed my first marriage.

Telling Cathy about my abuse prior to us getting married was not something I had planned or premeditated, it just happened. We were sitting on the patio of a wine bar on the Southern California coast, talking comfortably about our lives, when suddenly the secret started rolling off my tongue. For years afterward, I couldn't figure out exactly why I had told her about the abuse. However, after lots of meditation and reflection, I know today why I told her. In part, it was a divine intervention. I didn't know it then, but God had placed Cathy in my life as my lifelong partner. I now know that carrying secrets into a marriage is a recipe for disaster. On a more superficial level, I came to realize that if I told Cathy about the abuse and she didn't leave me, she must truly love me.

Nevertheless, telling Cathy that I had been sexually abused did not save us from the many problems that we faced over the next twenty-two years. Yet, I am convinced today that Cathy's knowing about my abuse helped her to understand that many of the problems we had in our marriage were a direct result of me being sexually abused, and that kept the marriage alive. It was twenty-two years after I told her about the abuse that we entered into therapy together and directly addressed the issues stemming from my abuse.

If you don't feel that there is anyone in your life to whom you can safely tell your story, you can tell *me*. Just go to my website at www.courageoushealers.org and fill out the contact request. I will be honored to hear your story.

Where Does Secret-Keeping Start?

Secret-keeping often starts with the desire to protect loved ones with our silence, but as we develop the habit of keeping secrets, we run the risk of becoming even more secretive. This only reinforces our false belief that we have something to be ashamed of, something to hide from others. Over the years, we harm ourselves by keeping secrets we should share.

When we have one big central secret, such as sexual abuse, we can become so accustomed to the pain of hiding it that it then becomes easy to keep other "secrets." The sense of shame and fear can become overwhelming. The more secrets we keep, the more overwhelming they become.

When secrets become magnetic—that is, when they pull other secrets in and become stronger with each new addition, we can feel "terminally unique," as if we were the only person in the world who has ever been this "bad." We feel that no one could possibly understand that we are all alone and that people would revile us if they knew our secrets.

Toxic shame, the feeling that you are bad or wrong, thrives in the darkness of secrecy. Over time, my secret-keeping expanded from concealing my abuse to concealing my drinking and drug use, and finally and worst of all, to concealing my extramarital affair. Eventually, my shame monster spent so much time in the darkness that it became enormous, like a great slavering beast that would kill me if I ever let it out. It didn't matter that a part of me knew that the abuse wasn't my fault; my shame felt huge and powerful. As I started my healing process, however, I discovered that the shame began to wither as it was exposed to the light of openness and compassion.

When, after working with a therapist and getting clean and sober, I found the courage to be open about my sexual abuse, I dealt a mortal blow to the shame monster, which had terrified me for decades. There are still days that I have panic and shame attacks, but the negative emotions don't come close to the old overwhelming fear and pain of the past.

Normalizing Abuse

What keeps so many survivors trapped in self-blame and shame is that, in the vast majority of situations, it's horribly scary for a child to be angry at an adult caregiver or authority figure, even when that individual is abusive. Children are entirely dependent upon adults for all their basic needs, including food, shelter, clothes, and connection. Therefore, if a child realizes that his abuser is emotionally unstable, that can easily throw his whole world into even more frightening and unpredictable instability.

By normalizing the abuse, the child attempts to gain a degree of control over it. The first step in this process is often to assume blame for the abuse. If the child decides that he is "bad," that gives him, in his own mind at least, the opportunity to control the abuser by being "good" in the abuser's terms.

In other words, if the child assumes the blame for his own abuse, he gains a sense of control over his environment. Instead of living in a state of near-constant panic, he can construct rules that make him feel temporarily safer. Although those rules are untrue, the child who imagines that he has some control over his world feels better than he would if he concluded that he is at the total mercy of a sick and unpredictable adult.

The degree to which a child will carry out this rationalization depends on the severity and duration of the abuse. That is one reason why one-time incidents of rape/molestation by a stranger can be easier to heal from than incest. Children are resilient. When given a safe and loving home, most of them can recover from even the worst traumas. But when home itself is unsafe, the child has nowhere to heal and no adult to whom to turn for help.

In such cases, the repercussions of abuse get turned inward, so, in the absence of true love and safety, the child may construct fantasies in which he normalizes his home life in order to survive on a basic level. In this fantasy world, because the adults cannot be the "bad guys," since that is fundamentally terrifying to a child, he makes *himself* the "bad" guy. This internalized fear and anger can then fester and grow into toxic shame. He feels safer keeping his secrets than risking opening up to other people. The longer he keeps his secrets, the longer he feeds himself the destructive programming that he should be ashamed of what happened to him.

The "cure" for toxic shame is to share your secrets with at least one other person. However, you must choose that person well. First and foremost, he or she must be loving, safe, supportive, and wise. When we open up to loved ones and see our past through their eyes, we can begin to understand that it was *always* the abuser, *never* ourselves, who should have been ashamed. When others see us as blameless, innocent victims, we can start to see ourselves in that light, too.

"Grooming"

It is not uncommon for perpetrators to "groom" their victims, taking time—perhaps up to five years—to win their trust. In the absence of a father in a young boy's life, a perpetrator—often an uncle, cousin, or family friend—will slowly interject himself into the boy's life, filling the father's role. The process may look something like this:

The perpetrator will start to show up at the boy's baseball games, encouraging him as a spectator. As time goes by, the perpetrator may start to take the boy out for pizza or ice cream after the game. Because 93% of perpetrators are either a family member or family friend,[61] this behavior doesn't raise any suspicions. Once the perpetrator has gained the trust of his innocent victim, and of everyone else who is a part of the boy's life, that fateful day arrives when the perpetrator makes his move. For example, the two of them may be in a tent on a camping trip, far away from any other people. Therefore, when the adult starts molesting the child, the boy has nowhere to run or hide, so he just submits to the abuse.

A perpetrator will often make his child victim feel special by giving him extra attention and by praising him for his "grown-up" ability to keep a secret. In reality, of course, the child is keeping the secret out of fear that he will lose the special treatment—or worse yet, that his family may be

---

[61] Sexual Assault Response Services of Southern Maine, *Sexual Assault and Rape Statistics, Laws, and Reports*, retrieved from http://www.sarsonline.org/resources-stats/reports-laws-statics.

harmed. A predator will take ruthless advantage of this.

In my own case, Jack insinuated himself into my family over the course of a few years at a vital time in my life when I was highly vulnerable. My mother and father had divorced when I was ten. For the next year, I continued to see my father, whom I adored, every other weekend. Then, one day, my mother told my brother Richard and me that our father was ill—that he had contracted yellow jaundice from drinking water in the Kern River on a fishing trip, and that we would see him again when he got better.

Around that same time, my mother met Jack. Thus, at precisely the time when my father could not be with us, Jack could. Within a year, he was literally our second father. Aside from his superficial charm, he had a house with an ocean view in Laguna Beach and knew people in Apple Valley, including Roy Rogers. Every weekend, Richard and I either had the run of the beach or the run of the valley, so we were in heaven. We were two boys who terribly missed their father, and Jack was kind, supportive, and more than willing to play with us. In very little time, he had won over not only my trust, but my mother's and Richard's as well.

What my mother and Jack knew that Richard and I did not was that my father did not have yellow jaundice, but in fact was dying of colon cancer. Then, one Sunday, after a weekend in Laguna Beach, my mother, Richard, and I drove home through a severe rainstorm. Looking back at it now, perhaps it was an omen of what was coming. The date was January 12, 1969. When we got home that night, the phone rang as soon as we stepped in the door. It was Betty Welch, our neighbor across the street. After talking to Betty, my mother said she would be right back.

Richard took all this in stride, but I was nervous about being left alone in the house with all that lightning and thunder raging outside. I still remember the smell of the rain and the sound of the thunder as it roared with each flash. As I looked out the window, I finally saw my mother and Betty coming this way, and my first thought, for some reason, was that I had done something wrong. Perhaps that was because my mother had punished me so often for things I hadn't done.

As soon as they came into the house, my mother and Betty pulled up chairs in front of Richard and me, and with cool, measured words, my mother told us that our father had died earlier that evening.

The roaring in my ears immediately eclipsed the thunder and lightning outside. Emotions that I am unable to name to this day ripped through my chest. All I knew was that every beat of my heart hurt, and that every breath seared my lungs.

I don't remember much about the days before the funeral. But I do remember that Jack held my hand throughout the church service while I was crying. Although I knew that he could never replace my father, I was grateful to have a man in my life who was kind and supportive. In the weeks after the funeral, I started to come to terms with the loss of my father. The pain didn't go away, but I was just beginning to carve out a new life for myself.

Then, a month after my father died, I was walking home from school on a perfect sunny afternoon that stretched in front of me like a golden promise. When I entered the house, I was expecting it to be empty, and was looking forward to a snack and playing flag football with the neighbor kids, as I did on most weekday afternoons. However, when I pressed my shoulder against the sticky lock that opened the door, I saw Jack sitting on the couch in the living room. I was surprised but pleased, thinking that a game of catch with Jack and my new mitt would be even better than playing football with my friends.

But instead of tossing me a baseball, Jack stood up, put his hand on my shoulder, and walked me into my bedroom. Then he sat down next to me on my bed, his big frame squeezing a protesting squeak from the box springs. Out of the blue, he started to tell me how sorry he was that my father had died. He knew I would have struggles over losing my dad, he said, but assured me that he would always be there for me. As we sat on the edge of the bed, he suddenly reached over, put his hand on my crotch, and started fondling me as he was talking. After a while, he took my hand and placed it on his crotch and had me fondle him, still talking all the while.

"This is what a father and son do," he said.

What we were doing didn't hurt. In fact, although I hadn't hit puberty yet, it felt good. There was no violence associated with it, so I thought it was okay, although I was a bit uncomfortable.

When we were done talking, with just a little fondling this first time, we went back into the living room, where I heard one of the most clichéd phrases in the English language: "Now, don't tell anyone. This is our secret."

Like almost all other abused children, I thought that having a secret with an adult whom I trusted and loved was pretty great. After all, I was a twelve-year-old boy who needed a father figure and craved a father's love. Thus, I believed that being a member of Jack's "secret club" just put icing on the cake. What else could a twelve-year-old boy want than a caring, loving father?

Over the years, I have heard many stories about sexual abuse. Common elements include a trusted friend or family member, a slow buildup to the abuse, and a lack of violence, at least at first. No one type of abuse is more or less painful than another; that really depends on the circumstances and the individual.

It is possible that Jack had been abused himself as a child, so he was just doing to me what another had done to him. In fact, in his own mind, his abuse of me may have been his twisted version of being a loving parent. But his secrets and the ones he was forcing me to keep had nothing to do with love.

Feeling Special

Feeling complicit in abuse because we liked feeling special can be particularly hard on male survivors of sexual abuse. In addition to feeling special, we may have had physical pleasure. There is a myth in our society that equates a male erection with consent and pleasure; if a male has an erection or ejaculates, it cannot have been abuse because he must have "enjoyed" it. That is just not true. No one can automatically control his body's reactions to pleasurable touch.

Nevertheless, this myth is insidious, in that it supports the idea that the abuse was, in fact, our fault—that we wanted it, and so we are to blame. Let me be clear, we were *not* at fault, nor did we want the abuse. Children cannot be complicit in sexual acts; they cannot give consent because of the fundamental difference in power between children and adults. Even if a child felt that he encouraged the abuse, it was still abuse.

Sexual abuse of children includes any sexually inappropriate acts with them, whether by force, persuasion, or encouragement. In addition to physical sexual contact, sexual abuse may include such non-tactile activities as:

- Making a child strip or masturbate in front of an adult.

- Intentionally engaging in sexual activity in front of a child.

- Not taking proper measures to prevent a child from being exposed to sexual activity by others.

- Exposing children to X-rated films or magazines.

- Encouraging children to participate in prostitution or child pornography.

The Rape, Abuse, and Incest National Network reports that 93% of abused children know their abuser.[62] In most cases, child abusers just look "normal," like everybody else. Most people are shocked when they learn that someone they know is a sexual predator. However, the fact is that a sexual abuser of children is far less likely to be a stranger to them than a trusted family member, friend, or coach.

As a child, I had no idea of the impact that being abused by a trusted adult would have on me over the course of my life. I didn't understand why something that was supposed to be good—namely, "affection"—felt so confusing. As much as I felt like a member of a secret club, I knew that something wasn't right. This was not the same as playing ball or picking up ice cream before dinner. At a deep level, this was terrifying in a way I had never experienced before. Although I was confused and frightened, if what I had to do in order to be loved was to keep these sessions a secret, I was determined to do that, regardless of my misgivings.

I had just lost my father and didn't want to take a chance at losing the father figure I had in Jack. There are very few things as important to a twelve-year-old boy as having a loving father figure. Although what Jack was doing to me had nothing to do with love, it was better, I felt, than not having a father at all.

Jack was not physically hurtful to me as part of the sexual abuse, although he did beat me on occasion, usually for arguing with my mother. Nevertheless, the "affection" and the beatings were not directly related. I suppose, in the back of my mind, the beatings were like the proverbial elephant in the room. In any case, as time passed, I grew steadily more afraid of Jack.

Survivors of sexual abuse often experience a mounting fear and anxiety around the relationship with the abuser that begins to eat away at their self-esteem and confidence. Soon after my abuse began, I realized that not only would I disappoint Jack and lose his trust if I "told" on him, but any attempt to expose these sessions could have a devastating physical

---

[62]Rape, Abuse, and Incest National Network (RAINN), *Who Are the Victims?* (2009), retrieved from https://rainn.org/get-information/statistics/sexual-assault-victims/.

and emotional outcome. Nevertheless, the burden of keeping my secret just grew heavier and heavier.

Most survivors of sexual abuse know the horrible sick feeling that comes when shame washes over them like a tsunami. We also know that we would do just about anything to avoid feeling that overwhelming shame. That is how and why the abuse becomes so confusing, especially for male victims. We need the loving, caring affection of a father figure, and are willing to do whatever it takes to get it, even if it hurts us.

The secrets have a tendency to pile up. As I grew older, emotional, physical, and spiritual abuse were added to the sexual abuse, and soon it felt like my secret life far outweighed the life I was willing to present to the outside world. My secrets just grew and grew, and with them, my shame mounted.

Over time, keeping secrets becomes easy and automatic as the fears about what other people will think grow ever more frightening. I knew I needed help, but I had become numb, and so I rationalized the abuse. After all, I had already been told by Dick, my pastor and supposed spiritual leader, that it was "a normal part of growing up," and it was only a small step to make myself believe that.

Aside from Dick's and my own rationalizations, Western culture as a whole inappropriately sexualizes young boys, and the double standard is clear: If a girl has sex at twelve or thirteen, in society's eyes she is either promiscuous or has been raped. If, however, a boy has sex at the same age, he is celebrated and admired—at least by his peers. But that admiration is devastating to boys who are being sexually abused. The message from society is clear: boys can't control their sexual impulses, so it's "cool" for them to have sex at a young age. Girls are vulnerable sexually, but boys are not. These societal messages conflict with the deep, gut-wrenching feeling that comes with sexual abuse. What generally happens is that the sexually abused child internalizes the gut-wrenching feeling as shame, never reveals the abuse to anyone, and the effects of that secrecy linger and fester.

When I decided to write this book, I knew it would mean sharing my story on a much more public scale than I had in the past. It's one thing to share from an A.A. chair, or from a therapist's couch. It's quite another to take a deep breath and print my story in black-and-white for the world to read. I decided to share my experiences on this broad scale to help others in my situation know that they are not alone. I hope you will follow the paths out of darkness and despair that many other survivors have taken to recovery. I have been where you are, I know your pain, and we can all walk out of the darkness together.

Escalating Abuse

Jack had a shiny orange 1969 El Camino with oversized wheels and rims that were so shiny you could see your face in them. It was one heck of a car, and Jack knew how much I loved it. When I was fifteen and had my learner's permit to drive, Jack would often invite me on "errands." Whenever my mother needed something from the store in the evening, when it was starting to get dark, Jack would say, "Come on, Randy, let's go. You can drive the El Camino." Even knowing what was coming after the first "errand," I would still be so excited to drive that car that I was willing to pay Jack's price.

At the store, Jack would run inside and return with the milk or whatever, and then he would lay out *Penthouse*, *Playboy*, and *Hustler* magazines on the seat next to me.

"Scoot over, Randy," he would say. "I'll drive so you can look over the magazines."

But then, instead of heading home, he would drive down by the river and pull over into some dark off-the-road turnout. By the time we reached the water's edge, I had acquired an erection from "reading" the magazines.

After parking, Jack would typically reach over and begin fondling me and put my hand on his erection and have me fondle him. Once we both ejaculated, we would clean up and head home. I guess, during the act itself, my hormones took over, but immediately after the ejaculation, the shame kicked in again. The drive home was when it got really tough for me.

We were supposed to have gone to the store for a quick errand—a thirty-minute round trip at most—yet we would have been gone for an hour or more. When we returned, I would slink into the house, a sea of shame covering me. If my mother asked why we had been gone for so long, I would rush into my bedroom and let Jack answer. But then I would feel that sick sense of shame, as if I had swallowed a lead weight. Every trip in the car made that weight a little heavier, until it was so consuming that I often felt that I was being buried alive.

I have often asked myself a question that I believe only a fellow survivor would understand, and it is my hope that it will help to answer similar questions of yours. The first time Jack invited me to go out on an "errand," what happened next was a total surprise. I was unsuspecting and truly believed that he was giving me some experience to prepare me for the driving test. I had no idea of his true intent.

After that first trip, however, I knew what was coming, so why did I ever get in that car again? It was, I believe, for the same reason that so many children get caught up in a long-term abusive relationship. Like them, I was unable to truly comprehend the malicious nature of my abuser. I kept hoping that the next time would be different—that we would just make a quick milk run, and then Jack would let me drive home through Capistrano Beach just to get some extra miles under my belt. But those rides never *were* different. They were a heavy price to pay for a father's "love" and "attention."

I wonder how many secrets Jack was carrying around with him. Had he been molested, abandoned, or beaten as a child himself? How many other boys—or girls—had he molested? As for my mother, I wonder how many secrets *she* carried, and who had hurt her? What was she afraid to speak about and why? I know the life we were living at the time was riddled with secrets—not only the secrets of my sexual and physical abuse, but also the physical abuse of my mother herself, for Jack occasionally beat her, too. Like most other survivors, I learned how to keep secrets and tell lies at an early age.

As I entered my late teens, I began to understand that what Jack was doing was not right. By then, I had a constant battle going on in my head: *Tell or don't tell?* Reaching out for help hadn't gone so well for me in the past. Dick, the pastor of the church, had virtually condoned the abuse when I was fifteen. Then, two years later, my mother called the sheriff on me because I had gone out surfing after she told me I couldn't. When the sheriff arrived, he took me into my bedroom, where I said to him, "You don't understand what it's like living in this house." Instead of questioning me about that, he said, without hesitation, "I don't care how bad it is living in this house. Until you're eighteen, if you're told to stay in your room, you stay in your room." The choice seemed obvious: it was best to just keep quiet.

Do I tell or do I not tell? is the question we all live with as survivors. In the face of violent threats, or the potential loss of parental affection, or even the possibility of being thrown into the foster care system, the answer seems obvious: *Don't tell!* For the vast majority of children, the reasons to remain silent far outweigh the reasons to tell.

Married with Secrets

I kept rationalizing reasons to keep the secret well into adulthood. When I was nineteen, I married my first wife, Jane, entering into the marriage with a bag full of secrets. She was aware that my family life had been somewhat abusive, but she knew nothing of the darkest secret I kept. That one never left me alone. I would drink all day at work to keep the secret buried even from myself.

Then I would go home to Jane, drunk and worthless. I tried to be a good husband—and I *was*—so long as I wasn't drinking. But at those times, I was reliving my secret shame over and over again in my head. In the company of others, I was just faking my way through a life filled with shame, and my secret was destroying my marriage. No one could ever figure out what was wrong with me, and I certainly never told them. I figured it was better for everyone to believe that I was a worthless, no good, screwed up kid, rather than finding out the truth.

Within a few years, secret-keeping destroyed my marriage to Jane. I can blame her, the alcoholism, or even Jack, but the truth is that the root of my problem was my own inability to break down the walls I had spent years building up. I tried to "fix" myself from the outside because I was terrified to look inside. First, I started exercising and soon became a health fanatic. I lost weight, gained muscle, and with that, an artificial confidence. But inside I was still brittle and broken. I even divorced Jane for no reason other than my reluctance to tell her the truth about my childhood. I was more invested in maintaining the "Randy is fine" façade than in anything else, including my marriage.

A few years after my divorce, I met the woman who would become my second wife. Cathy was beautiful inside and out, free-spirited and fun, yet responsible. When I was with her, I felt confident and good about myself. However, I had a secret that had already destroyed one relationship, and I didn't want to lose Cathy even more than I wanted to keep up the image of the Perfect Randy. It helped that Cathy had (and still has) a calming and peaceful spirit. After two months of indecision, I decided that if I wanted to keep her in my life, I had to tell her everything about my abuse. I had already let this secret destroy one relationship, and I was not going to let it destroy another. I remember thinking, *If I tell her now, I will know how committed she really is to our relationship*. Nevertheless, no matter how I tried to be rational about telling her, I was still terrified.

When I finally did tell her about Jack, the words came spilling out of me. But inside I felt sure she would never love me again and would always look at me as less of a man. When I finished telling her about the abuse, I was certain she was going to tell me that a "real man" should have been able to defend himself, and would have moved on already. However, she said nothing of the kind. In fact, she was compassionate, loving, and understanding, assuring me that we would work through this together.

Nevertheless, as we walked back to the car together that afternoon, I felt tainted and dirty despite her loving affection. After I had revealed my darkest secret to her, I just *knew* that she would never look at me again the same way. In fact, years had to pass before I fully believed that she meant all the kind things she said that day.

Today, I believe that one of the main reasons Cathy and I are still married is that I told her about my secret while we were still dating. Had I not told her when I did, I am convinced that our marriage would not have survived even one year, let alone thirty-plus. It was the kindest thing I could have done for both of us.

More often than not, the secret of sexual abuse is carried into a marriage because the victim has either repressed the secret or has decided that he is going to take it with him to his grave. In doing so, he creates a multitude of problems that can totally confuse his partner.

For example, at age sixty-five, one of the men in a sexual abuse group finally told his wife about what had happened to him years before. She responded: "Thank God! Now I know that I'm okay. Your behavior, the affair, and your drinking were making me feel crazy. I kept thinking that *I* had done something wrong. Now I know I'm okay, and *you're* the one with the problem." That was a vital turning point in the marriage. The wife could have chosen to walk out forever, but in fact she decided to stay and work on the relationship with her husband.

Survivors often believe that their secretive behavior is perfectly normal. But it is a way of coping that we developed as children, and does not serve us well as adults.

Finding a Trusted Listener

Even if the person you tell about the abuse is unconditionally loving and understanding, there is nothing easy about gathering your courage to tell your secret. That can be especially difficult if you are one of the many survivors who, like me, tried at some point to tell someone what was happening, only to have it be discounted, or even flat-out disbelieved.

Too many survivors have been told by unsympathetic listeners that the abuse was *their* fault. "You must have asked for it," they say. I have heard countless stories from abused kids who have sought help from some adult, only to have their story rejected and the abuse continued.

After experiences like that, it is understandable that I waited for more than a decade to try again. Sadly, this is the case for many other survivors as well. If we feel that we have already tried to reach out, only to be rebuffed, it can be that much harder for us to try again. If you feel that you would rather die than tell your secret, you are not alone. Without exception, every survivor I have ever worked with has told me that he believed, at one time or another, that his secret would die with him. Yet, every one of those men finally reached a point of desperation at which he knew that something *had* to change. Eventually, the pain of keeping the secret usually outweighs the fear of revealing it.

Today, if you are an adult, you are no longer a helpless, dependent child, and you deserve to have a voice. Most of us have at least one person whom we trust and can talk to about anything. Or anything except *that*. After we have kept *that* secret for so long, and are well aware of all of the negative messages that society sends out about male sexual abuse, it is understandable that we might be reluctant to reveal our secret even to that person.

If you feel safest with a therapist or counselor, start there. If you don't have such a person in your life, there are several helplines that specialize in sexual abuse trauma (see the Resources Appendix at the end of this book). If you choose to tell a trusted friend, let him (or her) know that what you are about to say is really hard for you, and you need his support. Let him know that you are not asking him to fix you, and do not want advice. All you need is to be heard by a sympathetic listener. Let him know that you chose him to talk to because he is a dear and trusted friend. But set boundaries before you begin to tell the story. Know that it is perfectly fine to stop at any point.

When I told Cathy about my abuse, I was not seeing a therapist. Looking back at that time, I'm sure it would have made it a lot easier for me to have worked with a sympathetic, objective, professionally trained individual to discuss all the mixed emotions and uncertainties I had about confiding in Cathy. But even after I opened up to her, it would have been helpful to have been seeing a therapist, because I don't think I would have tormented myself for so many years, wondering if I was man enough for such a beautiful woman.

A word of caution: I was blessed by how kind and compassionate Cathy was when I told her—but I only told *her*. With the rest of the world, I continued to carry this secret shame locked deep inside. The burden was lighter than it had been before I told Cathy, but feeling that I needed to keep the secret from everyone else still fed the shame that was eating away at my soul. It wasn't until twenty-one years into our marriage that I found the courage to enter recovery. After that, it took three years of intensive one-on-one therapy twice a week in order to tell anyone else about the abuse.

My hope for you is that your road to recovery will be shorter than mine. But short or long, what matters most is that you *start* on the healing journey. Unburdening yourself from the secret you have carried for far too long is the first step in the right direction.

Unfortunately, people can be ignorant and even cruel. When it comes to sexual abuse in particular, not everyone—including some therapists—understand its emotional and life-altering impact on the human psyche. Therefore, you must choose your therapist with great care. First of all, you can consult websites such as *1in6.org* or *malesurvivor.org*, which list therapists that have experience in this area. Then select one after interviewing two or three on the phone. Of course, you need to maintain a comfortable relationship with your therapist throughout your treatment.

A.A.'s *Big Book* says, "sometimes quickly, sometimes slowly."[63] For me everything happened very quickly after I found the courage to start talking about the abuse. But what worked for me might not necessarily work for you. One thing I will say with absolute certainty is that once you unburden yourself to even one kind soul, you will experience a peace unlike any other. The more you unburden yourself to the right people, the faster you will realize that you never had a reason to feel ashamed of your abuse. One hundred percent of the shame belongs to the perpetrator.

However, telling your secret is not a magic elixir. You may still be hit with waves of shame or regret, and there is still work to be done in order to truly heal from your past. This "teller's remorse" is natural and one reason why it can be helpful to have a therapist to talk with during the unburdening process, or at least someone who is farther along the healing path than you are.

I tell all the men I work with that they are going to have to walk

---

[63]Alcoholics Anonymous, *The Big Book*, 4th ed. (New York: Alcoholics Anonymous Worldwide Services, 2001), p. 84.

through the shame and pain at least one more time—sometimes even more often—in order to heal. But when they get through to the other side, it will have been well worth it. I also assure them that so long as they are willing to do the work, I will always be there for them, and I will *not* abandon them.

It is not just in our own lives that we need to speak up about male sexual abuse. Until society at large becomes more educated and understanding about this subject, survivors of sexual abuse will continue to have difficulty getting the help they deserve.

An Expert Speaks Out:
Mic Hunter, Ph.D.,
On Hiding in Plain Sight:
The Ever-Expanding Realization
of the Sexual Abuse of Males[64]

The Bad Old Days

In 1989, when I tried to find a publisher for a manuscript entitled *The Neglected Victims of Sexual Abuse*, I was informed by dozens of publishers that it was unreasonable to expect them to publish a book on the sexual abuse of boys, because boys are almost never victims of sexual abuse—that even when it does occur, it doesn't harm them significantly, and those rare few who are harmed can't be helped. When I finally found an editor who believed in the project, she told me that my proposed title, *The Neglected Victims of Sexual Abuse*, would have to be changed to *Abused Boys: The Neglected Victims of Sexual Abuse*, because sexually abused boys were so neglected as a topic at the time that without the new title, nobody would have any idea what the book was about.

In the Preface, I wrote: "This year, as in every year, tens of thousands of boys will be sexually abused in the United States. They will be damaged physically, emotionally, mentally, and spiritually. Every aspect of their lives will be affected. When they become adults, they will be plagued with sexual dysfunctions, troubled relationships, a poor sense of self-worth, and intimacy difficulties. Many will become drug addicts. Some will destroy themselves. Most of them will suffer from the effects of sexual abuse without ever realizing that they

---

[64]Copyright © 2014 by Mic Hunter. Reprinted here by permission of the author.

were victimized. When they read books or hear programs about sexual abuse, they probably will not hear about male victims. They will call what happened to them many things, but rarely will they think of themselves as victims. To add to this tragedy, those who seek professional help from mental health centers, treatment programs, and therapists will often be misdiagnosed: the symptoms of sexual abuse may be treated, but not the underlying cause. The stereotypes and myths that surround sexual abuse and males will prevent them from getting adequate help. Victimized as boys, they will be neglected as men."

A quarter of a century later, I am happy to write that what was once a taboo topic—the sexual abuse of boys—has become common knowledge. Thanks to media reports on abuse of boys by clergy, coaches, and teachers, the general public has learned that boys can be, and are, victims of sexual abuse. Whereas in the past, men came into therapy, not only unaware how the childhood sexual abuse they experienced was affecting their current functioning, but not even identifying what happened to them as abuse, it is now common for men to come into therapy already with an understanding that they were abused and that it had a negative impact on them. As a society, we have come to the realization that women, not just men, commit sex crimes against children. There are now many books about sexually abused males, as well as well-established organizations committed to assisting males with a history of sexual abuse.

Still Much To Be Done

What we once thought rare we now realize is much too common. In the 1980s, it was estimated that between 2 and 8 percent of boys experienced sexual abuse. Current research indicates one in every six boys is sexually abused (nearly 17 percent). The Internet makes child pornography much more widely available than in the past, and makes long-distance solicitation of children for sex easier than in the past.

Here We Go Again

Although we have certainly made progress on the issue of sexually abused boys, the issue of men as victims of sexual abuse has not advanced as much. It wasn't until 2012 that the Federal Bureau of Investigation included the sexual assault of men in its crime figures.

Currently, between 5 and 10 percent of reported sexual assault involves a male as a victim. The crucial word in that sentence is *reported*, because the crime of sexual assault in general is underreported; and when the victim is a man, even more so. In his book, *Male on Male Rape: The Hidden Toll of Stigma and Shame*, Michael Scarce observed: "We can easily believe that a child might not be able to defend himself against an adult, but the sexual violation of a man may come as something of a shock, for men have traditionally been expected to defend their own boundaries and limits while maintaining control, especially sexual control, of their own bodies. When this does not occur, when other men rape men, society tends to silence and erase them rather than acknowledge the vulnerability of masculinity and manhood."[65]

In 2006, when I contacted fifty publishers with *Honor Betrayed: Sexual Abuse in America's Military*, I was informed I was being unreasonable because the sexual abuse of military personnel by their comrades is rare; when it does occur, only women are victimized; in the rare cases that a male is the victim, he is a homosexual and shouldn't have been in the military in the first place; and that military personnel who are sexually assaulted aren't damaged to the degree civilians are harmed. However, by 2013 it had become painfully clear that sexual assault in the military does occur, is perpetrated against both men and women, and is damaging. Research indicates that at least 10 percent of male veterans were sexually assaulted while serving, and it was so traumatic that half of them left the military.

Here We Go Again..., Again

In 2014, the topic of sexual assault on college campuses began to be addressed in the media. In almost all cases when males were mentioned, it was only as perpetrators, never as victims. Experts who were interviewed advised parents to warn their daughters about the risks of sexual assault, and to discuss with their sons how to avoid being falsely accused of date rape, but the topic of males being sexually assaulted was absent from the discussion. The sexual assault of young males continues to be overlooked and minimized, particularly when it occurs as a part of hazing conducted by sports

---

[65]Michael Scarce, *Male on Male Rape: The Hidden Toll of Stigma and Shame* (Cambridge: Perseus Publishing, 1997), p. 9.

teams and fraternities. What would be considered a criminal assault if perpetrated by a stranger is explained away as nothing more than a harmless tradition when committed by teammates or fraternity brothers.

Conclusion

In my lifetime, I have witnessed significant changes in the way the sexual abuse of males has been understood. Much progress has been made, yet much more is left to be done. But I am confident that we have reached the point of no return: no longer will the abuse of boys and men be ignored. The fact that you are reading these words is proof of that.

About The Author: Dr. Mic Hunter has held Minnesota licenses as a Psychologist, a Marriage & Family Therapist, and an Alcohol & Drug Counselor. He is a recipient of the Fay Honey Knopp Memorial Award, given by the National Organization on Male Sexual Victimization, "for recognition of his contributions to the field of male sexual victimization treatment and knowledge." In 2007, the Board of Directors of Male Survivor announced the creation of The Mic Hunter Award for Research Advances. Dr. Hunter, for whom the ongoing award was named, became the first recipient.

Chapter 10:
Confronting the Perpetrator

The demon that you can swallow gives you its power, and the greater life's pain, the greater life's reply.

—Joseph Campbell[66]

As stated earlier, the Rape, Abuse, and Incest National Network reports that 93% of abused children know their abuser.[67] Almost all survivors of any kind of abuse or trauma think about confronting their perpetrator. We want to know why we were singled out, if that person is sorry for the pain he or she caused, and what made him or her do it.

This wanting to understand *why* is a natural response to betrayal. We are trying to make sense of chaos and pain. The desire for resolution can be heightened if the perpetrator was a *trusted* adult. The violation of a boy's most intimate boundaries by a trusted caregiver is one of the most devastating betrayals the child can experience. No wonder we often feel that we need an explanation in order to move on. But the truth is, we *don't* need an explanation. However, to help with the healing process, an apology from the perpetrator, as well as a genuine attempt to make amends, would be nice. The reality is that most victims never get their questions answered, never receive a sincere apology, and many never even receive validation that they were in fact abused.

If you were abused by someone, it is highly likely that your abuser was hurting, at the least, and mentally ill, at the worst. Most perpetrators are not capable of giving their victims answers to questions such as, "Why did you do it?" or "Are you sorry?" Expecting sanity from a sick mind is

---

[66]Joseph Campbell and Bill Moyers, *The Power of Myth*, retrieved from http://billmoyers.com/spotlight/download-joseph-campbell-and-the-power-of-myth-audio/.

[67]Rape, Abuse and Incest National Network (RAINN), *Who Are the Victims?* (2009), retrieved from https://rainn.org/get-information/statistics/sexual-assault-victims/.

a kind of insanity all its own.

I had to come to a place of accepting—*without* approving—that what happened to me happened. Eventually, I had enough recovery to know that I could either dwell on the unfairness, or on the semantics of abuse, or I could relegate it to the past, where it belongs. As author and practical philosopher Byron Katie says, "You know what I love about the past? It's over."[68] And it is. The abuse is over, and unless you re-subject yourself to it now, by dwelling obsessively on why it happened or how it shouldn't have happened, you are holding the keys to your own prison cell.

As a child, you were trapped, but that part of your life is over. Now you have to have the courage to free yourself. It takes guts to decide to step out of the past and get on with your life. We can grow comfortable in our victimhood. We get used to telling our victim story; and to some extent, we benefit either from the reaction of other people, or from our own reaction if we become self-indulgent. This isn't a harsh message. I wish you could hear me *say* it to you, instead of reading the words on a silent page. You would hear the love, compassion, and deep empathy I have for you.

We have to *want* our freedom and happiness *more* than we are afraid to lose the shelter of our victim story. After all, it's a terrible shelter, little more than a ramshackle hut that provides almost no protection whatsoever. When we feel that all we have is our story, we cling to it, too scared to let it go. But so long as we cling to that victimhood, we continue to place our healing power in the hands of our perpetrator. One of the most horrible aspects of incest is that, at some deep level, most survivors feel that they need their abuser to rescue them.

Whether you knew your abuser or not, most of you have obsessed over the idea of confronting him. Hell, I not only fantasized about confronting Jack, I plotted his assassination on a daily basis for thirty-plus years. If you are thinking about confronting your abuser, I strongly suggest that, in order to safeguard your own heart and mind, you already have some recovery in place, for it is imperative that *you* first be grounded in your healing journey. My advice is that you think twice before confronting your perpetrator. In fact, for most survivors, I don't believe it is the best choice. Sexual abusers are usually not the sanest or healthiest people in the world, so it's unlikely that you are going to get the response you want from a person who is mentally ill.

---

[68]Byron Katie, *Who Would You Be Without Your Story: Workshop with Byron Katie*, retrieved from http://sourceofenlightenment.com/Byron%20Katie%20Workshop.html/.

It's also interesting to know that, in general, once a survivor has enough recovery to handle a confrontation without reopening old wounds, that confrontation often becomes less important. If, however, you are still determined to confront your abuser, I have some suggestions. If you are working with a therapist, it is absolutely essential that you develop a plan to have a support system in place before you move forward. If you're not working with a therapist, find one before you contact your abuser. I would also advise you not to confront your abuser alone. If at all possible, do it in the presence of your therapist or a professional third party who can help if the situation escalates and starts to cause you pain.

In the brightest scenarios, a confrontation can be a cleansing and healing event. However, if things go wrong, you may jump back down the rabbit hole you have worked so hard to climb out of. Since this is *your* healing, it is vital that you take measures to safeguard your recovery in case things do not go well.

Examining Motives

The most important recovery tool to have in hand before you sit down with your abuser is a personal inventory of your own motives. When you think about confronting the abuser, you need to be honest with yourself about what it is you want from the confrontation. That can range (at one end of the continuum) from trying to establish a real relationship in order to heal the past, to a desire (at the other end of the continuum) to see the abuser suffer. Some of you may want an apology, or for the abuser to understand the impact of what he did. Some of you may just want validation of your memories. But what you all need to thoroughly understand is that, unless the abuser has had some kind of spiritual awakening or intensive therapy, he is sick, and the chances that you will get a healthy, loving response from him are slim to none.

It is important that you not expect to get a satisfying apology or a gesture of remorse from your perpetrator. That is most likely not going to happen. It is more probable that the abuser will minimize or outright deny that the abuse ever happened, or he may even blame *you* for it. Abusers typically do not like to be confronted or made to feel out of control. Child sexual abuse is *never* about sex; it is the control and domination that appeals to sexual predators. When perpetrators feel that their control is threatened, things tend to go downhill quickly. Perpetrators are also highly likely to be delusional about the abuse. It's entirely possible that your perpetrator does not believe that what he did to you was abusive.

Since the abuse took place during your formative years, many of your emotional patterns are based, to some degree, on the abuse. Strong negative emotional connections that go back as far as your childhood are much more difficult to overcome than the more recent positive ones that you have learned. I've been doing this work for almost a decade now, but any contact with my mother can still send me into a downward shame spiral, in which I feel as if she is sitting behind a control panel, and I am helplessly reacting. Most survivors who have abusive family members who are still alive feel this way. Abusive family members can be the single strongest trigger we have.

I have found, both for myself and for the men I work with, that it's far better, when meeting our abuser, to be overprepared than underprepared. In order to have a positive outcome from the meeting, you should focus on doing it for *yourself*, and not on any outcome that is dependent on what the abuser may or may not do. Before going into such a meeting, ask yourself the following questions:

- To whom do I want to talk, and why?

- What do I want to get out of it, and is that a realistic outcome?

- Can I handle being challenged by this person or arguing with him?

- Am I willing to lose contact, not only with the abuser, but also with people we both know?

- What is the worst-case scenario? Will I be able to handle that if it happens?

- If I get everything I want from the abuser, what will I have?

Best-Case Scenarios

One of the most positive outcomes of a confrontation with an abuser is that, when done right, the victim is the one in control of the situation— the very opposite of what you experienced as a child. When you control the balance of power between yourself and the abuser, you are sending a powerful message to yourself about your ability to stay safe, even from the person who once may have frightened or hurt you the most.

In direct contrast to your childhood experience, as an adult *you* set the boundaries, *you* determine the duration and location of the meeting, and *you* have the power to say *what* you want and to walk away *when* you want. Taking back control in this way can be extremely empowering. However, you do not want to set yourself up to be traumatized all over again.

Remember, while you can set the boundaries for the meeting, you cannot control the outcome. *No one* can make another person feel or do anything. Therefore, you definitely cannot make your abuser feel or do anything. So long as you go into the situation with reasonable expectations, and with enough recovery and healing to handle whatever the abuser may throw your way, confronting him can be a visceral, dramatic way to reaffirm your own power and establish your own boundaries.

Two of the most difficult aspects of healing from sexual abuse are creating healthy boundaries and building healthy, trusting relationships. For children who were sexually abused, boundaries were often violated, usually in highly manipulative and confusing ways. For survivors, then, establishing healthy boundaries as an adult can be like trying to learn a foreign language. For most children, when the most fundamental relationships are violated, trusting other people can be extraordinarily difficult.

When children are manipulatively groomed by someone they know and love, the grooming time can seem idyllic. For some of us, it may have been the first time we ever had a loving, attentive adult consistently in our lives. Our abuser often appeared to be, at least for a while, the healthiest and most loving person we knew. When he turned out to be our worst nightmare, our ability to trust our judgment was compromised. When we grow up and begin meeting truly healthy and loving people, we feel that we cannot trust them. After all, we trusted our abuser and learned later that he wasn't trustworthy. Abused children grow up with this double-edged sword. We are often desperate to be loved, but too terrified to trust the people who try to love us.

Seeking Love and Approval from Abusers

Many books, websites, and articles indicate that survivors of sexual abuse often experience an intense array of emotions, ranging from self-hatred to rage to depression. What many of them fail to mention is that these feelings often stem from an inferno of neediness, a black hole of insecurity and desperation to be loved. Some of the most painful and lasting effects of sexual abuse spring from this desperate desire for love and approval, which can run our lives well into adulthood, so that we often act out our frustration and longing in destructive ways.

I left home at seventeen, and basically cut Jack and my mother out of my life soon after that. But even knowing what he was and hating him for it, I still wanted his approval. When I was twenty-five, shortly after I first met Cathy, she and my son, Danny, and I were four-wheeling in the San Bernardino Mountains, an hour east of Los Angeles. At some point, I realized that we weren't far from the campsite where I had deer hunted with Jack and my family as a child, and because deer season had just opened, they might be in the area.

I hadn't seen my mother or Jack for some time, and neither of them had met Cathy. So after telling my wife-to-be what I had in mind, I headed over there. As if in a dream, I pulled onto the familiar road that led to the campsite. When I drove around the final bend, there they were! My heart skipped a few beats, my mouth went bone dry, and my palms began to sweat.

Memories came flooding back, both good and bad. Then I saw Jack's son-in-law from a previous marriage, "Jason," standing by his motor home, drinking an iced tea. He was one of the only members of my family who had consistently treated me kindly, so I immediately remembered an amusing incident with him that I had long forgotten.

Jason was a short, burly man with a full black beard that was bristly enough to serve as the business end of a hairbrush. At the time, I was thirteen or fourteen, and it was 3:00 in the morning. He and I were sleeping on cots around the campfire under the stars, tucked into our warm sleeping bags, when suddenly my cot started shaking. As I slowly awakened, I heard snorting, grunting noises, and was terrified because we had gone to sleep listening to bear stories. My first thought was, *Please don't let this be a bear!*

As the grunting noises got louder, I finally rolled over slowly, and froze when I saw a face covered with black hair just inches from my own. Jumping out of my cot, yelling loud enough to wake the moon, I was rewarded with Jason collapsing on the ground, laughing until tears rolled down his cheeks.

Seeing Jack and my mother on that fall day, sitting around with relatives at the old familiar campsite, set off a wave of rage in me. Even before Cathy, Danny, and I got out of the car, I wanted to leave.

What was I thinking?

The whole point of my trip to the mountains had been to be with Cathy and Danny. I would have sworn on a stack of Bibles that I wanted nothing to do with my old family. Yet, somehow, I had found myself driving into the old campsite, looking for something I felt I needed.

We received a warm welcome from everyone, including Jack. After a short visit, we were back on our way, but I had a sour taste in my mouth. I was much more physically fit than I had been the last time I had seen any of those people, I had a great job, and there was a beautiful woman at my side. Nevertheless, I felt sick as I realized that I had gone to the campsite because I had wanted to show all this off. Even after everything that Jack had done, and everything that my mother had failed to do, the truth was that I still needed their approval.

The pull on us to get our parents' love is an incredibly powerful one. Until we recognize it for what it is, that need for approval and affection silently runs us, driving us to perform at some impossible standard to offset the desperate insecurity that we feel inside. I was a workaholic from the time I was a young man. I drove myself to build my business, to make more money, and to get more, more, more. But no matter how much I gained, it was never enough.

I didn't really want the money or the success, although they made my life comfortable. What I really wanted was for the empty, aching hole inside me to be filled with the warm light of approval and love. Over time, not even the love of my wife, family, and friends proved to be enough to fill that void. Even if my mother and Jack had apologized sincerely and then loved me in the ways I had wanted to be loved when I was a child, *that* would not have been enough.

Abuse steals our ability to love ourselves, to look in the mirror and see a whole, lovable, perfect child. Much of the desperate pain we experience in our lives as survivors of sexual abuse comes from needing love and not knowing how to get it from ourselves. Until we learn how to fill ourselves from the inside, we will be trapped, because no matter how much other people try to love us, we won't believe them, since we don't believe that we are lovable. The only way to end that pain is to relearn how to love ourselves.

What I have discovered over the years is that loving yourself is just another way of allowing your own happiness to matter more to you than anything else. That can sound odd at first, because most of us have bought into the cultural conditioning that making yourself happy is "selfish" or even "narcissistic." Cultural conditioning would have us believe that we should focus on making *other people* happy, and that it is a bonus when what *they* want coincides with what *we* want.

Also, there is the assumption that "good" people find happiness by making other people happy. That is surely one of the most painful ideas that Western civilization has ever come up with. It fosters a world of codependent resentments, unspoken motives, and manipulation as a way of life. It is so much simpler, kinder, and easier to take responsibility for your own happiness. The alternative is to continue to put yourself last, with the unspoken hope that others will reciprocate. The trouble is, that makes us passive-aggressive and manipulative. We learn that it is not okay to ask for what we want, so we hint at it. We don't come right out and say it, because that would be selfish. Instead, we become expert at manipulating others into giving it to us. That ties everyone up into knots of frustration, hurt feelings, and resentment.

If there is anything you walk away with after reading this book, I hope it is the belief that you have the freedom to be happy. You alone have the power to make yourself happy. *No one else* can make you feel anything *without* your consent. But learning to love yourself again is not a straight shot from depression to joy, nor from rage to peace. There are steps along the way that have to be taken. Expecting to be able to leap from your worst to your best feelings in a single bound can actually delay your long-term healing. I strongly urge you to drop any hope that you will be able to make such drastic leaps quickly. If you hold on to that illusion, you will find that you are unable to sustain your new good feelings for very long. The frustration from that may lead you to feel that giving up would be a better option.

Letting Go of Anger and Rage

My abuse started when I was twelve, and I was forty-nine when I entered treatment. By that time, Jack had been out of my life for twenty-nine years. I think part of the reason I resisted treatment for so long was that I believed that therapy would mean having to forgive Jack and my mother for their abuse. Most mainstream religions will tell you that, in order to heal, you must first forgive. But I wasn't ready to forgive Jack or my mother.

To me, forgiving meant condoning the abuse, or letting them off the hook. I knew that my hatred and rage were poisoning me—while, ironically, having no effect whatsoever on my mother or Jack. But I was terrified to let those feelings go, for they had come to define me. Without them I didn't know who I would be.

When the abuse was actually happening, I spent many painful years trying to make it "okay," so that I wouldn't lose my family. But that meant making myself the bad guy, so I could maintain the fiction that there was nothing wrong with Jack and my mother. It wasn't until much later that I was able to become angry at Jack, instead of hating myself. Focusing that anger outside instead of letting it eat at me from the inside was a vast improvement over the black abyss of shame and depression in which I was mired.

It had been a struggle to find my anger—and now I was supposed to just let it go? Two of the most common side effects of sexual abuse are repressed anger followed by rage. My anger helped me to claw my way out of my blackest depression, and my rage protected me from the worst of my shame attacks. Although I hesitate to use blanket statements, I believe that women are more likely than men to internalize their feelings. They turn to depression and people-pleasing, whereas men are more likely to externalize their feelings by turning their anger into rage. In my own case, I was not ready to let my anger go, and I was certainly not ready to forgive.

There are still days when I am angry with Jack, my mother, and even God. In the past, my anger and rage could consume me for years. But now I have reduced those episodes from lasting for years to months, from months to weeks, from weeks to days, from days to hours, and from hours to minutes.

To help make the transition from feeling dependent on others for my happiness to being confident that I could take that responsibility into my own hands, I used the Emotional Guidance Scale.

The Abraham-Hicks Emotional Guidance Scale

Today, I have many tools to move out of anger, without falling backward into shame or depression. One of the most valuable of those tools is the Abraham-Hicks Emotional Guidance Scale:

1. Joy/Appreciation/Empowerment/Freedom/Love
2. Passion
3. Enthusiasm/Eagerness/Happiness

4. Positive Expectation/Belief
5. Optimism
6. Hopefulness
7. Contentment
8. Boredom
9. Pessimism
10. Frustration/Irritation/Impatience
11. Overwhelmment
12. Disappointment
13. Doubt
14. Worry
15. Blame
16. Discouragement
17. Anger
18. Revenge
19. Hatred/Rage
20. Jealousy
21. Insecurity/Guilt/Unworthiness
22. Fear/Grief/Depression/Despair/Powerlessness[69]

    As I started my journey of recovery, I was at the bottom of this scale, living in fear, depression, and despair (22). As much as I had gained materialistically, I had lost so much more as a human being. My father was taken from me by cancer when I was only twelve—and as if that were not bad enough, I was raped of my childhood innocence. I was full of negative feelings and had no idea, other than drinking and drugging, how to deal with them. When I first saw this scale early in my recovery, it gave me the glimmer of hope that I needed to continue on my journey. There was finally a light at the end of the tunnel, and all I had to do was stay on the journey, no matter how uncomfortable I became. As I started to ascend the scale, the light grew brighter with each rung of the ladder I climbed.

    Although the scale is arranged in numerical order, from best to worst, no two people move up the scale in exactly the same way. You may skip a step on the way up, and then go down two steps, but as long as you

---

[69]Esther Hicks and Jerry Hicks, *Ask and It Is Given: Learning to Manifest Your Desires* (Carlsbad, CA: Hay House, 2004), p. 114. Also available at http://www.discoveringpeace.com/the-abraham-hicks-emotional-guidance-scale.html/. ("Abraham" is the name given by Esther Hicks to a group of spirits ["non-physical entities"] she claims to channel.)

continue doing the work, your overall journey will be upward.

Although none of the feelings on the bottom two-thirds of the scale are desirable in and of themselves, insecurity (21) feels just a little better than depression (22). The pain and shame that we feel around the issues related to our abuse did not develop overnight. The chronic feeling patterns have been developing over decades. I have heard it said by many well-meaning people that "you can choose to be happy," but I haven't met anyone who could make a healthy, sustainable jump from depression (22) to joy (1) in a single leap.

Believing that we are somehow "choosing to be miserable," because we can't manage to grit our teeth hard enough to achieve happiness, is a painful thought indeed. Now, not only do we have all of the effects of our abuse to deal with, but we are also defective in not being able to choose to be happy. That is not the way such advice should be taken. No one can blithely leap from the bottom of the Emotional Scale to the top. What we *can* do is make small steps up the scale, one at a time. Eventually, we can move all the way up to joy just by shifting what we believe about ourselves.

Every time you consciously and deliberately move up the scale may not seem to be much of a victory, but you have achieved something far more important than a fleeting and ungrounded temporary happiness. You are teaching yourself that you, and you alone, have the power to affect your feelings.

Every time you find yourself in a depression (22) and you make the conscious choice to move from that state to guilt (21), you have proven to yourself that you can change your emotional state. From then on, it is just a matter of making the trip, at your own speed, up the scale.

At some point, I finally learned how to get myself from grief/depression (22) up to hatred/rage (19). If I forgave my abusers, I was afraid that I would lose the refuge in anger that I had found. That wasn't true at all, and I hope my experience will keep you from similar fears.

The problem about moving up the Emotional Guidance Scale is that it tends to make other people in our life more uncomfortable. When you're depressed and insecure, you are relatively controllable. You're quiet and you stay to yourself, mostly sleeping, crying, and being miserable. When you transition up the ladder, things tend to heat up. You learn that it's acceptable to be angry, but you don't yet know how to express that anger in a healthy way, so you get upset, shout, and stomp around. Well-meaning people often try to talk you out of your anger and back into your previous states because your anger frightens them. These people are not intending to hurt you, but they don't understand that sometimes you need to express your anger in order to move from the paralyzing hopelessness of despair into the better-feeling emotions.

If you are currently spending a lot of time around the middle of the scale, give yourself a pat on the back. I know it's not where you want to end up, but you have found the ability to move yourself in the right emotional direction, and that is a huge accomplishment. Once you can deliberately move from depression (22) up the steps to anger (17), you have everything you need to continue further up the scale.

No one likes spending time in the bottom two-thirds of the scale, but each of the emotions listed on it brings relief from the previous level. How many times have you tried to climb a ladder by starting at the bottom rung and trying to get to the top rung without climbing all the rungs in between? Climbing up the Emotional Guidance Scale is no different. Oh, you might be able to go from depression (22) to joy (1) for a short period of time, but I can say with certainty that that joy will be short-lived. In order to achieve true joy, we must walk through and feel each of the emotions on the scale. Blame (15) is more empowering than discouragement (16). Being overwhelmed (11) is more energizing than feeling fear (22). If you can get yourself all the way up to boredom (8), you will have experienced an enormous amount of relief.

I found boredom in a roundabout way. It wasn't that I became bored with my entire life; I just became bored with my story. When I was predominantly in the bottom third of the scale, telling my story made me feel crushed with shame and depression. While I was in the middle third of the scale, I felt strong but frightening waves of rage (19) and a life-affirming desire for revenge (18).

As I entered the upper third of the scale, I started to become bored (8) by my own story. It wasn't that I didn't honor the pain I had experienced. It was just that the drama of it all was starting to fall away. From there, it was just a small emotional step to the feelings that we all truly want to experience.

When we have finally settled into that upper third of the scale, we discover that there is a world of good feelings that we once thought were meant for everyone but us. After you have learned how to move up and down the scale, you will have the ability to turn contentment (7) into joy/

empowerment (1) whenever you want. Knowing that I can climb back up the ladder when I occasionally slip down it has made me eternally grateful for the existence of this scale. Other tools have been able to make me happy, or have momentarily moved me out of pain, but none of them has taught me how to do that consistently for myself.

Before I learned about the scale, the empowerment after a motivational seminar, the joy from spending good times with friends, feeling loved by someone dear to me, even feeling better after a therapy session were all dependent upon people and forces outside of myself. However, once I learned about the scale, and how to consciously direct my thoughts to make incremental jumps upward, I didn't need anyone or anything else to make me feel better. I began to realize that, in the past, there had been times when everything external had lined up perfectly—friends showed up, my wife said just the right thing, and so on—but I was still miserable. When we rely on external forces to make us happy, we are setting ourselves up to be disappointed. But when I look inside myself today, I find out what level I am on, start making incremental shifts to move up, and it works every time!

We would all love to "pass Go and collect $200," moving directly from despair (22) to joy (1), bypassing all the stages in-between, but expecting that to happen is just setting ourselves up to fail.

The best part about doing this work is that no one and nothing can ever take it away from you. You will have the most important tool in your recovery toolbox: the ability to shift yourself out of unwanted emotions and into more desirable ones.

Forgiveness and the Emotional Scale

Forgiveness is such a huge and crucial component of your healing that I dedicate an entire chapter to it (see Chapter 12, below). However, it is important to have a handle on the basic idea of forgiveness before you decide whether or not to confront your perpetrator. First, you need to understand how forgiveness fits into the scale.

All too often, forgiveness is misunderstood as self-righteous condescension that leaves you feeling like the "bigger person," and the other person feeling judged and humiliated. Feeling like the bigger person is just a case of our egos becoming temporarily inflated from some petty, small-minded gesture. It is destructive to indulge in these ego-inflations, because they are based on false pride. The only thing that condescension accomplishes is to throw us back into the miserable ups and downs of the insecurity roller coaster.

When I first started my recovery work, I wasn't ready to forgive Jack or my mother. But living in a world where the mere thought of my abuse could send me hurtling down the Emotional Scale from passion (2) or optimism (5) to hatred (19) or pessimism (9) is not what I wanted, either. I wanted to live in the top ten levels of the spectrum, and to do that, I needed to find a way to create some kind of peace around my thoughts about Jack, my mother, and their abuse.

For years, I wrongly thought that forgiveness is about the other person—that, somehow, if I forgave another individual, I was doing something nice for the person who hurt me, at my own expense. But that didn't sound like a good deal at all, especially when it came to Jack and my mother.

Forgiveness is not about me approving what Jack did, or trying to make my mother feel better about herself. Forgiveness doesn't have much to do with the other person at all. Byron Katie's definition, below, might be a bit extreme, but it helped me to spend more time in the top levels of the Emotional Scale, instead of vegetating at the bottom, where I had lived for so long.

"Forgiveness," says Katie, "is coming to see that what you thought happened, didn't."[70]

Now, before you think I am urging you to say that your abuse never happened, let me explain. The abuse was an isolated incident, or a series of isolated incidents, that involved your body and your abuser. But the damage that comes from sexual abuse is usually not physical. Rather, it is emotional, psychological, and spiritual. The damage is not based on the physical act, but on your thoughts about that act. I was repeatedly abused by Jack, and the physical and emotional beatings certainly hurt. However, the sexual abuse never hurt physically. What hurt emotionally and spiritually were the beliefs about myself that I internalized because of the sexual abuse. I believed that I deserved what Jack did to me, that no one could love me, and that I was irreparably broken and damaged by his abuse. In other words, I spent thirty-plus years of my life living in victimhood, believing that there was something intrinsically wrong with *me*. Otherwise, why would I have been singled out for this kind of punishment and shame?

---

[70]Byron Katie, *Who Would You Be Without Your Story?* (Carlsbad, CA: Hay House, 2008), p. 311.

CONFRONTING THE PERPETRATOR

When I came to understand the truth about forgiveness, I started to realize that I was wrong to be taking the abuse personally. I always thought that Jack hated me, and therefore there must be something wrong with me. The reality is that Jack had probably been abused himself, and later went on to become an abuser. I was just a kid who happened to cross his path. If it hadn't been me, it would have been someone else. I wasn't abused because I was a bad child; I was abused by chance. Jack seized the opportunity to take advantage of a hurting child. When I finally came to that realization, I stopped seeing myself as a flawed human being and was finally able to start loving myself.

In the beginning stages of my recovery, Jack wasn't the only one I felt I needed to confront. My mother had willfully ignored the sexual abuse for years and actively participated in the physical, spiritual, and emotional abuse. She was, and still is, cold and selfish. In fact, most of her family members are about as warm as a polar ice cap. For decades, I tried to drink and drug away the thought that there was something so bad about me that my own mother couldn't love me.

But her coldness and brokenness were not about me. She was cold and broken before I was born, and she's continued to be that way since I stopped being a part of her life. That emotional remoteness no doubt traces back to the fact that, as a child, she was physically and sexually abused by her own father and brothers. So although I always thought her cold behavior was about me, it was actually about her. The actions of other people toward us hurt us so much more when we take those actions personally. Yet, when we can be objective about them, they hurt a lot less.

What I needed so desperately from my mother was a sincere apology. I wanted answers. I wanted her to admit that she had deliberately kept me in an abusive situation, egging Jack on and encouraging his beatings—even actively instigating them. Most of all, I wanted to know why she didn't love me.

I did confront her once, asking her to tell me she was sorry. However, I didn't get any of that from her. Instead, what I got was more blame and more reasons why the abuse was *my* fault. The closest thing I got to an apology were her reasons for doing nothing: "I was molested as a child," she said, "and Jack threatened and beat me the whole time we were together. In the 1970s, women were supposed to be submissive. *No one would help us.*"

It took me quite a while before I realized and accepted that, barring some miracle, I am *never* going to get an apology from her.

Here's one of the paragraphs from a letter she wrote back to me after our conversation:

> There is so much you don't know about me and my past, and I am not sure you would care if you did. I, too, was molested several times when I was very young, and told no one until I was in my late forties or fifties. You asked me why I stayed with Jack when he was so mean. I could ask you the same question. Why didn't you tell someone?

I was four years into my recovery when I received that letter. Yet, even with all those solid years of recovery and working with a therapist on a weekly basis behind me, I still fell into a spiral of shame and self-loathing that lasted for a period of three months. After all, I had used those same words against myself for decades. I hated myself for not telling anyone, or for not telling the right person, so I believed the abuse had to be my own fault. There were few words that had more power to hurt me than the words my mother put in that letter. However, in reading it aloud with my therapist, I was able to see that the thoughts my mother was expressing had everything to do with *her* and nothing to do with *me*.

A sane person would never blame a child for being abused, because that child was too afraid to come forward. It takes a certain type of insanity to blame an abused child for his own abuse. Usually, that type of insanity is found in survivors of abuse themselves, since they internalize the self-hatred. They blame themselves for the abuse, telling themselves that they should have said something, and it's their fault that they didn't. The fact that my mother blamed me for my abuse shows how damaged she was from her own.

Again, I am not excusing her for abusing me or for allowing Jack's abuse. Nor am I excusing her for blaming me now, four decades later. Knowing that her letter is about her and not about me has helped me to stay out of those lower levels on the Emotional Scale. Although I may still get angry from time to time, I can more quickly reestablish my footing and understand that my mother hurts because *she* was hurt, and she hasn't yet learned another way to cope.

On some days, I feel compassion for my mother. However, that's a work in progress, and I am painfully making my way up the Emotional

Scale when it comes to dealing with my thoughts and feelings about her. At times, it's a halting, often exhausting process. I feel that I am barely hanging on to rage, hoping not to slip down into shame and despair. On other days, as I said, I feel a tiny sliver of compassion.

I don't think it can be overstated that the process of forgiving my mother is *not* for *her* sake. I am not celebrating the moments when I feel compassion for her because it helps *her*, but because it helps *me*. It feels better to experience true compassion for someone who has hurt me than it does to feel rage or bitterness toward her. Feeling compassion for another person helps me to feel strong and loving. On the other hand, feeling bitter breaks me down and makes me small and miserable.

It is important to note here that I am *not* talking about pity, which is a small-minded emotion that is just self-righteousness wrapped up in fake humility. Compassion is not pity.

My mother still believes that she did nothing wrong. In her mind, *I* am wrong to be angry and hurt. She actually believes that I am abusive toward her now because I don't choose to include her in my life. Her victim story is a powerful one, and her unwillingness to even see basic facts borders on insanity. As I said above, I will probably never get an apology from her, or even a warm and sincere gesture of love and approval. In fact, while I was in treatment, I remember calling her one time, wanting her to say something like this: "I'm really proud of you, Randy, and I'm here for you and Cathy if you need my help." Instead, I got this: "You didn't have a problem growing up. Oh, wait a minute..., yes, you did. Do you all talk about Jesus in your recovery meetings?"

I immediately hung up on her and didn't talk to her again for several months. Since then, I have come to see that her behavior toward me is not personal. In fact, getting hurt by my mother is no more personal than it would be if I fell down a flight of stairs or into a fire. I wouldn't get up and scream at the stairs, or cry because the fire didn't love me enough to put itself out before it burned me.

Yes, I wish my mother had been different. Even now, a part of me wishes she would change. But I can look back through my own adult years and remember how the people I loved the most, especially Cathy, wished the same thing about me. I was incapable of changing until the pain became so great that I was willing to face it. Until I was ready, I couldn't change, so why would my mother be any different?

In large part, who I am today was shaped by my mother, for in many ways our behavior is modeled for us by our parents or caregivers. The behavior my mother modeled for me taught me how *not* to parent my own children. As I worked to be the best parent I could be for them, my mother was always on my mind. I gave my children an extra dose of love, compassion, and interest because I remembered how much it hurt when my mother was cold, uncaring, and disinterested.

An exercise I like to suggest to survivors of sexual abuse is to write down a list of behaviors that were modeled for you by your abusers, which you are still hurt or angry about. Now take an honest look at those behaviors and find the ways in which you display the opposite behaviors. For example, if your parents were cold, unloving, and absent from your life, are you caring, loving, and present in your child's life today? Have you become a person you can be proud of because you behave differently than the people who hurt you? I am grateful that my mother was the person she was, because she showed me the kind of person I did not want to become.

As I indicated earlier, if you want to confront your abuser because you are hoping to get an apology or some admission of guilt, it might be a good idea to wait. Going into a confrontation with these expectations is a recipe for more hurt and disappointment. If you do decide that confronting your abuser is the right thing, I encourage you to work with a therapist or support network and take the time to role-play some likely scenarios in advance. Be sure you are prepared for all the things that could happen in such a confrontation, such as the perpetrator denying that the abuse ever happened, or even blaming you for it. That could send you into a spiral of shame that could last for months. Take care of yourself, first and foremost. You don't need to confront your abuser in order to find peace of mind.

When it came to confronting my mother in person, my therapist, Deborah, after reading my mother's letter and talking with her on the phone, advised me *not* to meet with her in person. Even if Deborah were part of that meeting, she said, it could potentially cause more harm than good, since my mother could not take any responsibility for the abuse she allowed to happen and actively participated in.

Although I have not met with my mother in person since 2008, and have not wanted to since she wrote me that toxic letter in 2010, I have come to a balance in my relationship with her. Although it takes two people to find reconciliation, I have discovered that it only takes one person to find peace.

CONFRONTING THE PERPETRATOR

In many ways, it was easier for me to deal with my feelings about Jack than it has been to wrap my head around how I feel about my mother. I may never find reconciliation with her. She may never even understand that she hurt me. But I have found my own balance with the pain she caused me—by choosing to see her as a damaged person who, like fire, burns anything that gets too close.

As I've said, hurt people *hurt* people. And much like Jack, my mother was only repeating hurtful behavior that had been modeled to her. Being aware of this makes her actions less painful for me, because I know that her abuse of me wasn't about me. My understanding that the story I had been telling myself for thirty-plus years was not the whole truth has allowed me to move freely up the Emotional Scale—something I would never have been able to do if I were still clinging to the old story of my childhood.

Being in Your Life Is a Privilege, Not a Right

The interesting thing about my journey with my mother is that eventually I had to make a decision: Was I going to continue to stay in contact with her and allow her to continue depressing me by sending me into a downward spiral of shame that could last for months, or was I going to accept the fact that she was *never* going to change—in which case, I would forgive her and move on with my life?

Society teaches us that "family is family," and that we should "honor our mother and father" and "forgive and forget." For those of us who have been sexually abused—or abused in any way, for that matter—that moral ideal can be a recipe for retraumatization. We are responsible for our own happiness, so if someone else is toxic to our happiness, we not only have the right but the responsibility to limit their engagement with us. This means that we can even make the choice to exclude them entirely from our lives.

Like most boys, when I was seven years old, I built a fort and hammered a sign on the door that read, "No Girls Allowed." While I have changed my mind about girls, I have realized that I was smarter and more confident at seven than I was at forty-seven. It has taken a few decades, but I have finally regained that sense of personal empowerment that allows *me* to choose who I want in my life. I have rehammered a mental sign into my recovery world, amended to read: "Only person(s) who bring me joy and happiness allowed." And that includes my own mother.

With the help of my therapist, my A.A. sponsor, and my wife, I have been able to gain some perspective and clarity about my mother, which has helped me to be more peaceful and happy. However, I have also learned that my newfound stability is fragile and needs protection. After I received that traumatic letter from my mother, it became clear to me that I wasn't ready for consistent contact with her. I could deal with brief communications with her, especially from a distance, but having her physically present in my life was just too much. When I violated my inner knowing because society said that I "should" call my mother, I found myself sliding all the way down to the bottom of the Emotional Scale in a matter of minutes.

Thus, I have made the decision that I will not allow anyone in my life who makes me feel less than whole and healthy. I would not allow my pastor, wife, or best friend to shame me, so I will not allow my mother to do it, either. However, I had to struggle for months with that decision. Religious and conventional wisdom says that if you forgive someone, you should feel fine about having him or her in your life. But that just isn't true for me. I am grateful that my mother gave me life, put food on the table, and provided a roof over my head. I am also grateful that she taught me a lot about the person I want to be—and the person I *don't* want to be. But my recovery is more important to me than kowtowing to society's mandate that I "should" let toxic people into my world just because they share some of my DNA.

The choice I made not to have my mother participate in my life is simply a healthy boundary I have set for myself. I don't need to apologize to anyone or seek validation from any source for the choice to remove a toxic presence from my life. Forgiveness does not mean that I have to let my mother in my life. I have the right to make my world a positive, loving place, where only people who are kind and supportive to me have the *privilege* of being invited. I don't owe anything to anyone who would jeopardize my happiness and peace of mind. It has been my experience that only people who are truly unhealthy themselves will try to make me feel bad about taking care of myself.

Confronting Jack

A big part of my recovery has been about moving out of shame and depression toward passion and joy. I had to pass through the different levels as I learned how to move up the Emotional Scale. Rage is better than depression, but it isn't as good as love or joy. We are not meant to live in rage, and we certainly don't want to stop ourselves on our journey by holding on too tightly to the anger that helped us to move out of shame. We need to find a way to keep moving up the scale.

Going all the way back to my teenage years, I imagined the day of reckoning that I would eventually have with Jack. I pictured a thousand revenge scenarios, but in every one of them I exposed him for the sick individual he was, and made him hurt.

Then, in January 2014, I came across Jack's page on Facebook. At first, my stomach turned and I felt the familiar sickening mix of rage and shame start to churn inside me. But I knew that I had a choice. As a man with almost a decade of recovery behind me, I had more tools at my disposal than I ever had before. I could *choose* now to take the familiar downward spiral journey back into darkness, or I could put some of my newfound skills to the test. It is always easier to slide down than it is to climb up, but I knew that if I didn't use my new skills this time, next time would be harder, and the time after that, harder still.

Just as I had become addicted to alcohol, I had become deeply entrenched in my negative thought patterns. In fact, it had been those negative thoughts that had led me to drink and drug in the first place. But when I came across Jack's Facebook page, I forced myself to remember that his abuse of me had not been personal—that Jack was a man who was chased by his own demons, and there was nothing wrong with me.

So I closed my eyes and thought about the people who loved me: my wife, my children, my sponsor, and my therapist. I looked at myself through their eyes instead of through Jack's. And it worked! It helped me to make my way through the landmines of my own thoughts and come out the other side. There are still times that I don't quite make it out of the minefield, but they are fewer and fewer.

Two days after I saw Jack's picture on Facebook, he died. At the sexual abuse/healing group I attended the following week, I talked about his death and how, when I read the posts from his Facebook friends, I discovered that he was still admired today. People were talking about him in the same way they talked about him when he was abusing me. "Jack is such a nice and caring man," someone wrote. "He did so much for me." It literally made my stomach turn.

One of the men in my group, "Ben," asked me if I had posted a response to all the positive comments about Jack. Proudly, I was able to respond, "No!" Ben had been sober for more than four decades, but he was still encouraging me to let everyone among Jack's family and friends know how evil he really was. On the other hand, I was grateful that I no longer felt tied to Jack in my thoughts. It was not my job to expose Jack's dark side to anyone—especially now, when he was dead and couldn't hurt anybody else.

The only thing that exposing the truth would have done was cause undue pain for innocent people, including me. I can't express how good it felt to be able to walk away. Since then, I have spoken with several survivors of sexual abuse who *did* carry out their revenge fantasies—and, without exception, it only made their pain harder to bear. Revenge may provide a brief relief, but, as with drugs and alcohol, everything is worse the next day.

Doing the work to climb up the Emotional Scale is hard work, but it makes everything better because it provides a *permanent* solution. Once you learn how to move yourself up the scale, you truly put the power to make yourself feel better back where it belongs—in your own hands and mind.

Chapter 11:
Blame and Shame

The search for a scapegoat is the easiest of all hunting expeditions.

—Dwight D. Eisenhower[71]

To blame others is to condemn them or accuse them of being at fault. When we have been hurt, often our first instinct is to assign blame to others. But the truth is that it feels lousy to blame other people, even if they are truly deserving of serious condemnation. Just as there is a difference between toxic and healthy shame, so there is a difference between toxic and healthy blame.

Toxic Blame and Toxic Shame

Toxic blame occurs when you either take on too much responsibility for unwanted outcomes, or you assign too much responsibility to others for those outcomes. Taking on too much blame leads to low self-esteem and depression.

Toxic blame also usually leads you to see yourself as a victim. When you feel responsible for everything, even events totally out of your control, it is easy to feel all alone in the world, with no one helping you. Or if they do, they don't help enough. When you feel overwhelmed and disempowered, the human reflex is to look for someone to save you. When they don't— often because they can't, sometimes because they won't, and sometimes because they are healthy enough to know how to say no when they mean no—you feel unloved, let down, and victimized. You start creating lists of everything you've ever done for them, and then feel justified when you condemn them for being selfish, ungrateful users. That is not to say that some people aren't selfish, ungrateful users. There are all types of people

[71]*Quotes About Blame*, retrieved from http://www.goodreads.com/quotes/tag/blame/.

in the world. But if most people around you seem like manipulators and users, the chances are pretty good that you're in a victim loop.

I'm a practical guy. When my construction company was hired to install stone veneer on a house, I didn't sit my men down and talk for hours about the client's interior decorating choices. Similarly, when it comes to my own chronic victim consciousness, I don't waste time hashing out the finer points of other people's character defects.

I'm interested in *me*, in *my* happiness, strengths, and weaknesses. Since I began to understand that my happiness (or depression) is in my own hands, I've become almost intolerant of wasting time on anything that doesn't go right to the source. And I've found that the source of manipulative friends is *me*.

Specifically, I notice that I start seeing users in my life when I slide back into the old habit of toxic blame. When I feel out of control, I can still fool myself into thinking that I have the power to control other people, and to "make" things happen the way I want. For example, if I am taking a biology class and miss a lab day, and my lab partner is late in sending me notes about the class, I may start to panic, and that can turn into toxic blame if I don't keep an eye on myself. I can start thinking things like, *I shouldn't have missed class*; or *I can't depend on other people*; or *I didn't need to go to the doctor's appointment that day..., I should have "sucked it up" and gone to class*; or *If only other people were more reliable, it wouldn't be so hard for me to take care of myself*; or *I have to do everything myself*.

I might work myself up into sending a sharply worded email to my lab partner, trying to shame him into dropping whatever he is doing, so he can immediately fix my problem. At that point, I'm "shoulding" all over myself, and all over my lab partner. In other words, I'm manipulating other people. I'm worked up and miserable. I'm angry and nowhere near a resourceful state of mind.

If I hadn't slipped into the toxic blame bath, I could have stayed in a resourceful frame of mind, realizing that there were many other ways I could have gotten what I wanted. For example, I could have emailed the professor, asking to do the lab myself; or called another classmate; or looked up the lab online and read about it; or asked for an extension; and so on. If I did choose to send an email to my lab partner, asking for his notes, that wouldn't be shaming and aggressive. It would be upfront, honest, direct, and kind. I wouldn't feel that I had to depend on him for my well-being, and therefore I wouldn't need to resort to desperate tactics of manipulation. I could just ask for what I wanted, clearly and kindly, knowing that I had other options available.

Many men in my life come up to me to complain about this very topic. They have piles of justifications for how other people really are to blame for their problems. When I tell them to focus on their own responsibilities, they say, "But, Randy, you don't understand. I really didn't have any other options. It really wasn't my fault."

It's telling that when individuals are in toxic blame, they are determined to protect their story about who is or is not at fault, even at the cost of their own happiness and peace of mind. In recovery groups, I often hear the insightful question, "Do you want to be right, or do you want to be happy?" The implication is that you can't be happy if you're stuck in blaming others for your own misery. Some people, however, are so entrenched in their victim story that they confuse their self-righteousness with happiness. But that is a false, empty victory based on denial. In all likelihood, it's been a long, long time since they have experienced true blissful joy.

Also, please remember that we are talking about *toxic* blame here. There is also *healthy* blame, which we will get to shortly. Toxic blame creates victim consciousness, which in turn creates victim stories about any and all unwanted circumstances in our lives. Pretty soon we can get stuck in a chronic victim loop.

If a habit of indulging in toxic blame has led us to a chronic victim consciousness, no matter what happens, it's never our fault. We become unable to take any responsibility at all. It's very common for children who have been abused to adopt the victim mentality. Chronic blaming and victim consciousness are not the same as assigning appropriate responsibility.

When we assign appropriate responsibility, we are looking at a situation objectively, analyzing it, and creating an accurate response. But assigning a blanket of blame to others in order to avoid our own responsibilities is not only inaccurate, it is harmful to ourselves.

Byron Katie has a great summation of this principle. "If you walk into a yard and a dog bites you," she writes, "the first time the *dog* bit you. But if you walk into that yard with the dog again, and the dog bites you a second time, that time *you* bit you and used the dog to do it."[72]

This is an ultimately empowering truth that can be initially hard to

---

[72] Byron Katie, *A response to "I hate my husband…,"* 2007, retrieved from http://www.byronkatie.com/2007/10/a-response-to-i-hate-my-husban/ (emphasis added).

accept. To be clear, children who are stuck in situations in which there is chronic abuse are *not* abusing themselves. This applies to us only as adults who now have the power to choose the situations in which we participate.

Slipping into toxic blaming patterns and then getting stuck in victim consciousness can become so familiar that it feels normal. The idea that *you* bite yourself can feel mean, even cruel. But it is one of the kindest things I have ever learned. Before my recovery, I was the king of victim consciousness. Everything was always somebody else's fault. I was always looking for weaknesses in other people, so when life didn't go my way, I could add those weaknesses to my stack of reasons that it wasn't my fault. I felt that taking responsibility for anything, however minor, would crush me. By admitting that I was wrong, by apologizing, I would be confirming my belief that I was fundamentally wrong and bad.

Toxic blame and toxic shame go hand in hand. When children are abused, they often turn to toxic shame in order to feel that they have some control over their situation. *If I'm being abused because I'm bad*, they think, *then if I were better, the abuse will stop.* In a child's way of thinking, that makes sense. But it can become a habit, buried so deeply in our minds that we are no longer aware of it.

A good indication of whether or not you are engaging in toxic shame is how easy or difficult it is for you to apologize. If, when you feel bad about something you said or did, you have a hard time saying "I'm sorry," it's very likely that you've got a big old pile of toxic shame buried inside you. It is only difficult to say "I'm sorry" if you feel that, by doing so, you're admitting that you are a bad person. Survivors of sexual abuse who live with toxic shame have a hard time differentiating between what they *do* and who they *are*. The truth is that you can be a good person who made a mistake or did something "wrong." Mistakes, poor choices, and bad behavior do not make you an immoral person. But survivors often live in a world in which they are terrified of being "bad." That can become almost a superstition, imbued with magical thinking. They might think, for example, *If I am bad, then bad things will happen.* That can lead to a pattern of toxic perfectionism, whereby the individual believes that if he can only be perfect all the time at everything he does, bad things will *never* happen.

The trouble with that perfectionism is that it can never work 100% of the time. Some individuals will be stuck for their whole lives in toxic shame, without even knowing it. But other individuals will transition from toxic shame to toxic blame, so that everything is the fault of *others*. That swings the individual from one unhealthy extreme to another.

There are many problems with chronic victim consciousness. Probably, the most important of these problems is that, even though blaming others may make us feel better temporarily, chronic blaming of others robs us of our personal power, causing us to stay as helpless as we were as children

No Longer Running from Anything

I had so much toxic shame woven into the fiber of my being that the toxic blame automatically boiled to the surface whenever my integrity as a man was threatened. I started seeing Deborah in 2005 because of the affair I had had the previous year. Naturally, when I first started seeing Deborah, everything about the affair, in my eyes, was Cathy's fault. She was not intimate enough with me, she did not give me enough attention, she did not... whatever. When I look back at the year before the affair, I would not have loved a person like me. In fact, I did *not* love myself.

Deborah helped me to see that while Cathy definitely played her part in the affair, it happened because of my toxic shame—which, unbeknownst to me, had taken over my life. I entered the affair because I couldn't understand how Cathy could love a flawed and tainted person like me. Contrary to all the evidence, I just *knew* that Cathy was going to have an affair and leave me. So, because I didn't want to feel the pain of another loved one leaving me, I left her for another woman—which I thought would fix all my problems. Toxic shame had consumed me, and because of it I was destroying every relationship in my life.

Over the course of my first year with Deborah, she and I worked on snippets of issues stemming from my abuse. During that period, we mostly worked on issues related to the affair. Also, I was still drinking and drugging—more than I let on to Deborah—and until I could resolve those addictions, I couldn't do the really deep work.

Toward the end of that year, at Deborah's urging, I entered the Betty Ford Center to face those addictions head-on. But I was still burdened by a tremendous amount of anger and rage that I had been told all my life I had no right to have. My healing was taken to the next level when both my addiction counselor, Melissa, and my spiritual counselor, Greg, told me that not only was it alright to be angry at God and Jack, but I had an absolute right to be angry at what had happened to me.

Every time I talked in group about my abuse, I would end by

laughing—until one night, Melissa asked me why. What had happened to me, she said, was no laughing matter. But I was totally unaware that I had been laughing. It was a built-in defense mechanism that I had developed somewhere along the way. In other words, I had walls up that I didn't even know about. However, the safer and more validated I felt, the more I talked; and the more I talked, the faster those walls came down.

Eventually, I stopped laughing and started crying. All my toxic shame had kept me from showing my emotions for thirty-plus years. The emotions around my father's death that I had been told to get over, the ruthless physical beatings I had endured from Jack, and all my emotions of feeling worthless and less than a man came pouring out of me. In one group session, in fact, I sobbed for twenty minutes. And when I left the room, I literally sat down somewhere outside and sobbed for twenty more.

Greg came out and sat down next to me, not saying a word. He just put a comforting hand on my shoulder and let all my caged emotions pour out of me. For the first time in my life, I was actually allowing my emotions to run through me without trying to dam them up or numb them down with drugs, alcohol, or work. I cried until I had no more tears. Those feelings had been inside me for decades, and although the tears hurt, the relief felt great. From that point on, I wasn't faking my way through life anymore. I wasn't running from anything. I wasn't desperate to hide my shame from others.

Finally, all my feelings had been validated, not only by my addiction counselor, but, more importantly, by my spiritual counselor. However, there was still much more for me to do. The whole time I was in treatment at the Betty Ford Center on an outpatient basis, I continued to work with Deborah, and still see her to this day. Once again, recovery is a marathon, not a sprint, which means that I will be working on my recovery for my entire life.

You Cannot Do It Alone

I am and always will be a victim of sexual abuse. However, today I no longer live as a victim; rather, I live as a courageous healing and thriving survivor. It took a lot of work with my sponsors in A.A. and CoDA (Co-dependents Anonymous), as well as with Deborah, to get me to this point. But once I realized that it was safe to ask for help from people who were sane, kind, and caring, my life turned around, and I've been asking ever since.

BLAME AND SHAME

This is a journey that I strongly recommend you not travel alone. It can be especially hard for men to reach out for help, because we've been conditioned to falsely believe that a "real man" doesn't need anyone else. But that's a lie—a lie I tried to live for thirty-plus years, and all I ever got for it was an empty bottle and a raging hangover. When I started reaching out, letting people in, not pretending that I had it all together, that's when the real healing began. The people I let in, besides Deborah, Greg, and Melissa, were Roy and Way Spiritual Dave.

Roy, my CoDA sponsor, was (and is) a compassionate and loving gentleman, perhaps twenty years my senior, who used to put his hand on my shoulder every time he saw me, and say, "Randy, you're enough and I love you." Then he would give me a hug. Roy loved me when I could not love myself. He validated my whole existence as a man.

Way Spiritual Dave, my A.A. sponsor, was always there to help me through my shame attacks. In fact, he walked into the rooms of A.A. carrying his own bag of shame, so he could relate to me and walk me through feelings that were similar to his.

By being rigorously honest with my sponsors in doing and sharing my step work with them, I enabled them to slowly show me how I was not to blame for any of my abuse. How could I have been? I was only a child. And, as I became a teenager, I was only doing what I needed to do to survive.

But as much as my sponsors helped me, Deborah brought about my biggest breakthrough. Many people, especially men, resist the idea of going to a therapist, since that's not seen as manly in our society. But that belief *must* change. Everyone needs someone to talk to, someone who can be fully trusted, and, in the case of trauma victims, someone who can help them through the rough times. If you don't already have such a person in your life, I strongly suggest that you find a qualified and experienced therapist who knows how to work with men who have been sexually abused. That will make your journey much less painful.

Deborah helped me to walk through the tremendous amount of anger and rage that I had been harboring for the past thirty-plus years. Because my mother and Jack had told me that I was not allowed to be angry—in fact, that I had no *right* to be angry—I turned my anger inward. Believing that I was at fault, I blamed myself for all my misfortunes. However, after many intensive one-on-one sessions with Deborah, who constantly reminded me that I was *not* to blame, my thoughts of self-condemnation have all but disappeared.

Today, I have accurately placed the blame for my abuse on my mother and Jack. Holding on to the feeling that it must have been my fault, holding on to all that pent-up anger and rage, only worked against me—trapping me in the role of victim, which forced me to swim in a river of toxic blame and shame. As a result, I destroyed my friendships and other relationships along the way. Living as a victim and holding on to the blame for my own abuse and the shame of it robbed me for decades of all my power. My abusers, on the other hand, although they had been out of my life for years, had all the power, controlling my every thought. I let the words they fed me as a teenager have power over me as an adult.

Healthy Anger

When used properly, anger is a healthy and acceptable emotion. For example, author Karla McLaren tells us that "healthy anger acts as the honorable sentry or boundary-holder of the psyche, but most information about anger focuses on the unhealthy expressive states of rage and fury, or the repressive states of resentment, apathy, and depression."[73]

Because I was told by my abusers that I had no right to be angry, I repressed my anger, which led to me being extremely resentful and depressed. On the other hand, when my anger reached a boiling point, I expressed it with rageful fury toward the ones I loved the most. It is that very anger that turned into toxic shame, which then turned into toxic blame. As my drinking intensified, and I fell deeper into my victim role, when I was triggered I would erupt like a volcano that had been sleeping for thousands of years, and all that hatred and anger that had been building up inside me would cascade down onto my wife, children, and friends like hot lava. That type of explosive anger is probably the only acceptable emotion that men can show in public.

Because I was told that I had no right to be angry, I came to believe that something was wrong with *me*. Therefore, half of my pent-up anger was directed toward myself. *I* was to blame for the abuse and everything that went wrong in my life. However, once my anger was validated by my therapist and my counselors, I was able to start expressing my anger in healthy ways that helped me to put the blame back on the shoulders of those who had harmed me: my mother and Jack.

On the other hand, I had to take responsibility for all the years that I

---

[73]Karla McLaren, *The Language of Emotions* (Boulder, CO: Sounds True, 2010), p. 4.

continued to abuse myself. After all, Jack had stopped abusing me when I was eighteen. The dog had quit biting me thirty-plus years ago, but, as Byron Katie notes, since then I had been biting myself and using the dog to do it.

In the case of my sexual abuse at Jack's hands, *he* did it. The responsibility for his actions lies with *him*. I, on the other hand, have no responsibility for what he did. Jack made his own choices. I am not capable of making choices for anyone in the world but myself. So Jack's choices were not my fault. But to this day, my mother believes that I need to take responsibility for my part of what happened to me as a kid. She believes that I am responsible for Jack abusing me, and is still trying to get me to agree that I deserved to be abused and punished. She wants me to admit my faults and to absolve her of any responsibility for her actions. The best interpretation I can make of her attitude is that she is blaming me for Jack's physical and psychological abuse, while totally ignoring his sexual abuse.

In any case, my mother's faults and limitations are not my responsibility. Nor is her guilty conscience. However, my own faults and limitations *are* my responsibility. Although it burned like acid when I looked back at the times that I did or said things that I wasn't proud of, admitting my part is what I needed to do for myself. Although the abuse created my extreme acting out—the drinking and drugging—there came a point when blaming others was counterproductive and toxic.

Do I still get angry with my mother and Jack about what happened to me? Absolutely I do. There are times that I feel I was cheated out of a lot of things in life because of them, so I allow myself to get angry, to process the feelings with my wife, sponsors, or therapist, and then let the anger go. There is a distinct difference between living an angry life and being angry. Let us not forget that anger is a perfectly good and healthy emotion. It is what we do with it and how we handle it that determines if it is healthy or unhealthy.

The Victim Mentality

What we do *after* the abuse has stopped is another matter. How we react to it after the fact has everything to do with *us*, for we are responsible for our own actions. Most perpetrators were abused themselves at some point in their lives. While that may explain their later behavior, it does not excuse the fact that they carried the cycle forward by abusing another person. In the same way, if survivors become addicts, abuse alcohol, or get in a car wreck, they are responsible for those actions.

I started drinking and drugging because of my abuse, even though I knew those behaviors were wrong. To take away the shame and pain I was feeling on a daily basis, I needed something to make me feel better, for I was no longer finding relief by playing my guitar, participating in sports, or believing in God. I needed something else, and I needed it *now*. For years, I thought I had found it in alcohol and drugs.

Using my childhood abuse as a reason to continue drinking and drugging became an unhealthy way to duck responsibility for my actions as an adult. Alcohol and drugs kept me stuck in the victim mentality, which prevented me from getting better.

Although I was sexually abused by Jack for five years, from age twelve to seventeen, I was physically, emotionally, and spiritually abused by either Jack or my mother from age four to twenty. During the five worst years, I was sexually abused dozens of times, physically abused countless times, and emotionally and spiritually abused every day. Nevertheless, the sixteen or seventeen years of childhood abuse from others add up to less than half of the thirty-plus years that I abused *myself* as an adult with alcohol, drugs, and toxic blame and shame. Those choices were mine, not my mother's or Jack's.

Jack stopped hurting me the day I left the house. But I hurt myself for decades afterward, using memories of him to do it. Every time I told my victim story, it only got longer and more detailed, which only did more harm to *me*. In a way, I abused myself worse than my mother and Jack ever did, and for that I owed and owe myself amends.

I first started to make amends to myself when Deborah invited me to write in a journal. It took me a while, but eventually I apologized to my inner child for abandoning him and forgave myself for all the harm I had inflicted on myself over the years. Then I released myself from any and all responsibility for the abuses inflicted on me by my mother and Jack. Lastly, I promised that whenever I caught myself starting to slide back into the memories that lead to rage and depression, I would immediately try to focus instead on all the things that make me happy, grateful, and joyful. Deliberately wallowing in the memories of a painful past had not served me well, and in fact almost killed me.

I am in charge of my own happiness, so I owe it to myself to catch myself in the early stages of the kind of negative thinking that will send me back down the rabbit hole of guilt and shame. However, things work a little differently with emotional triggers, which can come in many forms—as smells, tastes, sounds, or touches. Trauma survivors are highly likely to have triggers that start a cascade of negative memories and emotions. While the survivors are not responsible for the appearance of those triggers, they *are* responsible for their responses to them.

My own responsibility kicks in at the moment I realize that I've been triggered. At that point, I have choices. I can decide to milk the memory in order to feed my pain and despair. Or I can take care of myself by pursuing one or more healthy behaviors, which can include: journaling, taking a walk, meditating, calling a friend, or even just inhaling deeply and reminding myself that I am in a safe place today, surrounded by people who love me and want to help me.

I now understand where my responsibility for myself starts and ends. I generally don't take on too much responsibility for others, but when I do, a feeling of anger and disempowerment in my gut lets me know that I may be engaging in some kind of toxic blame.

Placing the appropriate responsibility back on my abusers takes the power away from them and returns it to me. Placing appropriate responsibility on myself also empowers me—to love myself, not to listen to those negative voices of the past; to say *no* when I mean *no*, and *yes* when I mean *yes*; and to step out and take risks, because the only way I can truly fail is not to try at all. Finally, if I can believe that I can accomplish anything I want in my life, I can live as a thriving survivor rather than as a victim.

Is "Why Did It Happen?" Really the Question to Ask?

Most survivors spend a lot of time wondering: *Why me? Why did the abuse happen? Why are people so messed up? Why didn't anyone believe me?* We think that if only we could get an answer to these questions, we would feel better. The reality is that we probably will never know the answer to these questions. However, as noted earlier, one answer that I have come to understand is that hurt people *hurt* people. It's a simple truth, but I didn't find it very satisfying, at least not at first. Knowing this doesn't make everything magically better, but it does help to bring wisdom, compassion, and maturity to painful memories. Once we have survived the abuse, allowing wisdom to sweeten the bitterness can only help us to heal.

Holding on to rage, determined to hate our abusers, and getting everyone to agree that those abusers were the worst persons on Earth just repeatedly retraumatizes us. Being abused as a child is not a "Get Out of Jail Free" card for every wrong action we have ever taken, but it is a reason to treat our past behavior with compassion.

I chose to start taking responsibility for my own actions when I moved out of my parents' house. At eighteen, I thought I was ready to be a man. What I didn't understand at the time was that being a man does not mean simply providing financially for a family or being emotionally strong. Being a man is about taking responsibility for my actions. Being a man is about letting go of the story that my mother is a horrible person who should have protected me from my stepfather. All that may be true, but it is childish to hold on to it, for it only allowed the bitterness and rage to consume me, to the point that I turned to drink and drugs to numb the pain. Now that the abuse is over, stepping up and being a man means learning to be a good person, while protecting my family and myself. My mother was a hurt person, who hurt people because she didn't have anything other than hurt to give them.

Today, rather than spending time condemning others for my childhood abuse, I honor myself for having survived it. As it turns out, "Why did it happen?" was not the question I really needed to ask. What I really needed to know was, "How can I heal? How can I be happy?" Once I started asking the right questions, the right answers began to show up.

The Courage to Get Real

After I told Cathy about my abuse, she didn't walk away from me in horror, as I had feared, but instead became absolutely dedicated to our relationship. In fact, she went so far in wanting to help me that she became codependent in our relationship. Nevertheless, her deep and profound love for me carried me through my highs and lows for several years. But no matter how much others may love you, they cannot fix you; it is *your* responsibility to do your own healing work to fix yourself. Cathy's love for me was amazing. However, because I was not working on the root causes of my problems, her love was not enough, and eventually my newfound self-esteem started to fail again.

Because I put all my reliance on Cathy, not on God or myself, I was unstable. Although anchoring my reliance on a loved one was unfair to her, it was also very human. When I told Cathy about the sexual abuse, and she still loved me, it became very easy for me to depend on her love and approval, instead of working on developing self-love and self-approval. Even small arguments with Cathy could totally devastate me.

Once again, I started drinking and drugging on a regular basis to deal with both the old shame from the abuse and the new shame of feeling like a failure as a husband. My life slowly started to slip into the chaos of addiction. In fact, it took more than two decades of pain for me to finally find the courage to face my fears and confront my past on my own.

It was only when I built a true foundation of recovery for *myself* with my own sweat and tears that I started to find the happiness I had looked for in my wife and at the bottom of a bottle. Although you may have people in your life who love you, it is not their responsibility to make you happy. It is not even possible for another person to truly give you the stable happiness you need. No one can do your work for you. But that's great news! Because, once you learn how to make yourself happy, content, and peaceful, no one can ever take that away from you. People might shake you up here and there, but once you practice soothing yourself, bringing yourself back to your center, and regaining your happiness *on your own*, you will walk through the world with a confidence and sense of joy that most people will never know.

Healing from your childhood wounds, your alcohol or drug addiction, and your codependency issues requires you to become rigorously honest with *yourself*. Many people think of honesty as something they have with another person. But this kind of honesty is 100% internal. You *must* become rigorously honest with *yourself*. And one of the first things you must be honest about is your own egotism. A.A.'s *Big Book* puts the matter like this:

> Selfishness—self-centeredness! That, we think, is the root of our troubles. Driven by a hundred forms of fear, self-delusion, self-seeking, and self-pity, we step on the toes of our fellows, and they retaliate. Sometimes they hurt us, seemingly without provocation, but we invariably find that at some time in the past we have made decisions based on self which later placed us in a position to be hurt.[74]

There are a lot of self-help books and workshops out there, but I believe that the primary tools that are essential for every survivor of sexual abuse

[74] Alcoholics Anonymous, *The Big Book*, 4th ed., p. 62.

are the Twelve Steps of Alcoholics Anonymous—or rather, the specific modifications of those steps for victims of sexual abuse:

> 1. We admit that we were powerless over the abuse and the effects of the abuse, which have since made our lives unmanageable.
>
> 2. We have come to believe that a loving higher power, greater than ourselves, can restore hope, healing, and sanity.
>
> 3. We have made a decision to turn our will and our lives over to the care of God, as we understand God.
>
> 4. We make a searching and fearless inventory of ourselves, the abuse, and its effects on our lives, and renounce the lie that the abuse was our fault.
>
> 5. We admit to God, ourselves, and another human being the exact nature of our wrongs and our strengths.
>
> 6. We are entirely ready to have God help us remove all the debilitating consequences of the abuse.
>
> 7. We humbly ask God to remove all the unhealthy and self-defeating consequences stemming from the abuse.
>
> 8. We make a list of all persons we may have harmed, including ourselves, and are willing to make amends to them all.
>
> 9. We make direct amends to such people wherever possible, except when to do so would injure ourselves, them, or others.
>
> 10. We continue to take personal inventory as new memories and issues surface. We continue to renounce our shame and guilt, but when we are wrong, we promptly admit it.

11. We seek through prayer and meditation to improve our conscious contact with ourselves and God, asking only for knowledge of His will for us and the power and courage to carry that out.

12. Having had a spiritual awakening as a result of these steps, we try to carry this message to other survivors and practice these principles in all our affairs.[75]

The key to change is doing the work, which requires rigorous, unflinching honesty. For those of us who truly complete the steps, life changes exponentially.

For male survivors of sexual abuse who attend A.A. meetings and are working on A.A.'s Twelve Steps, I should caution you that it is highly likely that your sponsor will *not* be able to help you with issues related to that particular abuse. Any good sponsor will tell you as much. A.A. isn't set up for sexual abuse recovery, and therefore I strongly suggest that, if at all possible, you find an experienced therapist who has been specifically trained to help patients heal from sexual traumas.

At my very first A.A. meeting, I trotted out my well-practiced story about my difficult childhood, without going into any details, but having the victim part down pat. To be clear, this was the story that I had developed over the years to justify my behavior, both to myself and others. As I said earlier, only you know the difference between the stories you tell that are true and necessary and will help you to heal, and those that you have ready for occasions on which you want to elicit specific responses from others.

To my surprise, on this occasion my story failed to elicit the response I wanted and was used to getting. Instead of pitying me and accepting my excuses, an old-timer whom everyone called "Crusty Rusty" said something that changed my life right then and there. "If you're drinking because of him, her, it, or anything else," he said, "you'll never quit drinking." In essence, he was telling me that I would never quit drinking so long as I thought of myself as a victim. That is the moment I decided I would do whatever it took to stay sober, for I recognized that I had been acting as the victim of abuse that had stopped thirty-plus years earlier.

---

[75]The wordings for these twelve steps are the author's adaptations of handouts he has been given at various recovery meetings.

Step Four

We make a searching and fearless inventory of ourselves, the abuse, and its effects on our lives, and renounce the lie that the abuse was our fault.

While all twelve steps require rigorous honesty, it is at Step Four that the rubber meets the road. Step Four will lead you into a freedom unlike any other you have ever experienced before. This is the point at which you can begin to see how so many of your problems were self-created through behaviors that may have served you well as a child, but have failed you as an adult.

As difficult as Step Four may seem, it is actually very simple. People just tend to complicate things when they are frightened by the prospect of facing something new. Doing this work will help you to discover how you have been self-centered, and how your resentments have fueled your anger, hatred, and prejudices. You will uncover the areas of conceit and greed that have been causing harm to yourself and others. You will see how your lust and indifference have interfered with your relationships with your spouse, partner, loved ones, family, friends, and co-workers.

Step Four will also help you to see how you have been hiding behind your phoniness (self-pride, lying, arrogant dishonesty, and false façade) as well as your fear. It is a nerve-wracking and daunting task. However, if you are willing, it is actually quite simple. It's a little like jumping into cold water. The initial shock may take your breath away, but pretty soon you've forgotten how cold it is, and you're happily swimming around, perfectly comfortable in water that you were initially afraid to dive into.

Your story is in your head. It is your story, and only you know your truths. So this is where the rigorous honesty starts. No more lying to yourself, no more denial, nothing but truth. No one else can do this for you.

You begin simply by sitting down in a comfortable quiet spot with no distractions: just you, your thoughts, paper (possibly a whole pad), pencil, and your Higher Power from Step Three. (These steps are numbered for a reason!) Take your paper and divide it into four columns. At the top of the first column, put the words *I'm Resentful At*. In this column, you will then write down the name of every person and institution, past or present, that you are or have been resentful toward.

Next, at the top of the second column, write *The Cause*. What caused the resentment toward that person or place?

At the top of the third column, write *Affects My*, and then describe how the action of the other person or institution affects your self-esteem, sexual relationships, security, personal relationships, pride, and so on.

Lastly, in the fourth column, write *My Part in It*. We have a part in everything that happens to us, with the *exception* of being abused.

You do not have to do all this in one day. It's a big task, and very important to your healing process. Take your time and be thorough. It is very likely that you will do Step Four more than once. I've done it at least four times. Below are two brief examples, one in which I did *not* have a part in my resentment, and one in which I did:

I'M RESENTFUL AT	THE CAUSE	AFFECTS MY	MY PART IN IT
my mother	She instigated and allowed the physical and emotional beatings I received from Jack.	Self-esteem, pride, sexual relations, self-respect, security	None

I'M RESENTFUL AT	THE CAUSE	AFFECTS MY	MY PART IN IT
Jimmy	He treated me like a true friend when we were alone, but snubbed me when we were with others.	Self-esteem, pride, self-respect, security, relations with others	I allowed it to happen by continuing to put myself in a position to be harmed, although I knew what the outcome would be.

Remember, this is your life, your story, and the only one who will be cheated if you are not rigorously honest is *you*.

A simple tip: If you become confused about writing something down, put it on paper anyway, just as it came to your mind. Don't "self-edit." You will only be cheating yourself out of your own healing.

Step Five

We admit to God, ourselves, and another human being the exact nature of our wrongs and our strengths.

Up to now, we have been holding on to our secrets because we believe that they are so vile and unforgivable that if anyone ever found out about them, we would be cast out of society, hated, and reviled. Many of us have held on to fear and shame for decades. The only way to discover if it is possible to be loved despite admitting to the wrongs we have done in the past is to own up to them to other people and find out. In all the years I have been in recovery, after all the stories I have heard from others in recovery, I have never heard a single soul say that he or she regretted this step.

In fact, the opposite is true: this step will set you free if you let it. You have lived in fear, perhaps for decades, that if people knew who you really are, they would hate you the way you hate yourself. I cannot explain the feeling that came over me when I found out just how wrong I was about this. The only one who hated me was *me*. Seeing the love and compassion and respect in the eyes of my sponsor, Way Spiritual Dave, after I shared my Fourth Step with him was when I began to learn how to love myself.

More often than not, skipping this step will result in relapse. As *The Big Book* tells us, "If we skip this vital step, we may not overcome our addiction."[76] I have seen many a man fight this step, so afraid of what others might think of him that he would rather drink again and keep replaying the old patterns that keep him living in a life of misery, addiction, and pain.

It is easy to sit down alone with yourself and God and put your Step Four down on paper. The *Twelve Steps and Twelve Traditions* put it this way:

> Somehow, being alone with God doesn't seem as embarrassing as facing up to another person. Until we

---
[76] Alcoholics Anonymous, *The Big Book*, 4th ed., p. 72.

actually sit down and talk aloud about what we have so long hidden, our willingness to clean house is still largely theoretical. When we are honest with another person, it confirms that we have been honest with ourselves and with God.[77]

When I sat down with Way Spiritual Dave, a man I fully trusted, and did my Fifth Step—yes, I was nervous and scared. Was he going to make fun of me and embarrass me? Was he going to tell everyone my secrets? Was he going to think I was dirty, tainted, and evil? My trust had been shattered so many times in the past, and now I was supposed to bare my soul to a newfound and presumably trustworthy friend. Once Dave found out who I really was, would he hate me the way I hated myself?

As I sat with Dave and slowly started revealing my life to him, I was met with compassion, understanding, laughter (not *at* me, only *with* me), and genuine love. I discovered some amazing things that day. First of all, I found out that some of the times that I had thought I was to blame for something, I actually *wasn't*. At other times, when I believed I was *not* to blame for something, I *was*. But the most transformative lesson I learned that day was that things that I had believed only *I* had experienced had actually been experienced by others as well—even by people whom I respected, like Dave.

As I shared my feelings with Dave, he occasionally shared some of his experiences with me in order to help ease my mind. Things that I had thought I could never be forgiven for, I discovered were forgivable. Admitting the truth to Dave allowed me to have my story reinterpreted, so that I could now see parts of it that I had not been able to see before. That freed me from the bondage of my past secrets.

As I left Dave's house after completing Step Five, I felt a huge sense of relief, as if the weight of the world had been lifted from my shoulders, and this was the first day of a new, wonderful, happy life. I had more to learn and more to unlearn, and there were still seven more steps in front of me and a lifetime of healing, but I felt that I had a place in the world and didn't feel ashamed anymore.

---

[77]Alcoholics Anonymous, *Twelve Steps and Twelve Traditions* (New York: Alcoholics Anonymous Worldwide Services, 1953), pp. 59–60.

Chapter 12: Forgiveness

The truth is, unless you let go, unless you forgive yourself, unless you forgive the situation, unless you realize that the situation is over, you cannot move forward.

— Steve Maraboli[78]

"Randy, you have to forgive, forget, and move on!"

I have heard variations of those words over and over, not only since my childhood, but even after I entered recovery. I heard them from my mother, from spiritual people, from well-meaning friends, and from misguided therapists. I heard them on TV shows and in movies, and read them in books and magazines.

Every time, I cringed and shouted back in anger and frustration, either in my head or out loud, "You have no idea what they did to me! You would be angry and hateful, too, if what happened to me happened to you!"

Countless times, if Cathy tried to make me feel better when I was in a cycle of anger, shame, or depression, I would shout at her, "Don't say a damn thing to me until you have walked in my shoes!" To my way of thinking back then, anyone who approached me with the idea of "forgiving, forgetting, and moving on" deserved to have his head torn right off his shoulders. I never believed it would be possible to forgive Jack and my mother. I thought that forgiving them meant letting them off the hook, admitting that what they did was okay and that I probably even deserved what they did to me. I thought that forgiveness meant that *I* was the bad one all along. I thought that forgiveness was intended to make *them* feel better.

The reality is that forgiveness is the last key to total freedom and

---

[78]Steve Maraboli, *Unapologetically You: Reflections of Life and the Human Experience*, 2015, retrieved from http://www.goodreads.com/author/show/4491185.Steve_Maraboli/.

happiness. Forgiveness is about *me*. It is an entirely selfish act, which often can make the difference between survival and recovery.

I still remember the day that I felt the first sense of what forgiveness could mean for me. I was walking out of my therapist's office, feeling physically lighter, as if decades of anger and resentment had been a literal weight on my shoulders, sinking me deeper into the ground.

But wait, Randy! you might be thinking. *You have no idea. My abuse was different....*

We *all* have different stories. No two survivors have had the same experience. I may not know exactly what happened to you, but I probably know how you are feeling, not only from my own experience, but from working with thousands of survivors over the years. The metaphorical knives that wounded us in the past may have come in different sizes and shapes, but the wounds they left behind are remarkably similar.

Forgiveness is a process. You might start by forgiving someone verbally, but saying the words is not enough. Too often, we say the words because we think they are what other people want to hear from us. Or we believe the words express the "right" or "spiritual" thing to do. Verbal forgiveness can be a step in the right direction, but it's not *true* forgiveness. It won't free you from the pain you carry inside.

If you do the work it takes to truly forgive, you must do it because it will make you whole and happy, not because it's the "right" thing to do. For me, the final step to finding true peace was through the fierce grace of forgiveness—the alternative to living in a state that I call "unforgiveness."

What Is Unforgiveness?

Unforgiveness is a combination of delayed negative emotions toward a transgressor—for example, anger, bitterness, fear, hatred, hostility, and resentment. So long as I kept my heels dug in and was unwilling to forgive Jack and my mother, I was filled with negativity. But it was hard for me to understand why I still felt that way after all the intense work I had done on myself. I just wasn't willing to forgive. How could holding on to my unforgiveness be blocking me from happiness?

The physical effects of unforgiveness are similar to the physical effects of stress. They can include: anxiety, decreased immune function, fatigue, headaches, intense negativity, irritability, muscle tension, out-of-control emotions, and stomachaches.

Aside from the physical symptoms, unforgiveness kept me locked in a mental prison for decades. The abuse I suffered at my caregivers' hands stopped when I moved out of the house at eighteen. However, rage and pain kept both Jack and my mother present in my mind. Over and over, I relived the sexual abuse and the beatings from Jack, remembering how worthless I felt when my mother watched the beatings—or worse yet, instigated them. No matter how successful I became in the world, I couldn't stop the internal voices from my past.

There is a saying that I both love and hate: "Don't let your past circumstances define you." As a recovered survivor of sexual abuse, I am now onboard with this philosophy, but I have seen people doing more harm than good trying to help a survivor with this kind of advice.

For a survivor stuck in the prison of his past, this notion is hard to comprehend. Our past *has* defined us. Our past is the reason we are who we are today, and we simply cannot just turn a switch in our brain and be different. That takes time. But so long as we are unforgiving, we stay stuck in the prison of our past. So long as we allow our perpetrators to steal our freedom, we struggle to become our authentic selves. Forgiveness is the key to true freedom, wholeness, and happiness.

What Forgiveness Is Not

For decades, I was confused about what forgiveness really is, who it is for, and what I had to do once I forgave someone. However, once I began my recovery, it became clear to me what forgiveness is *not*. Josh Howerton, a pastor in Spring Hill, Tennessee, has stated my thoughts succinctly (with my comments following in parentheses):

1. Forgiveness is not approving or diminishing the abuse or sin. *(The sinfulness of the abuse never changes.)*

2. Forgiveness is not enabling the abuse or the sin. *(Forgiveness actually defuses the power of the sin.)*

3. Forgiveness is not denying a wrongdoing. *(It can never be denied that you were abused and hurt.)*

4. Forgiveness is not waiting for an apology. *(You forgive the abuser, whether or not he or she ever apologizes.)*

5. Forgiveness is not forgetting. *(You will never forget.)*

6. Forgiveness is not ceasing to feel the pain. *(It's okay for it to hurt, but you just don't stay stuck in the pain.)*

7. Forgiveness is not a onetime event. *(Sometimes you need to forgive on a regular basis.)*

8. Forgiveness is not neglecting justice. *(You can forgive and still pursue justice.)*

9. Forgiveness is not trusting. *(You need to be exceedingly careful about whom you trust.)*

10. Forgiveness does not mean reconciliation. *(You are not required to allow your abuser back in your life to have a relationship with him or her.)*[79]

True forgiveness requires self-examination and the willingness to be wrong. You don't want to mistake sanctimonious false forgiveness for the real thing. Sanctimonious forgiveness appears when you *seem* to be forgiving another person, but are only actually establishing your superiority. That is a common misunderstanding of the expression *Be the bigger person*. It only hurts you in the long run to pump up your ego by "forgiving" others because you are "bigger" than them. Don't do that to yourself.

Really being the bigger person requires you to have the strength to look inside *yourself* and find ways that you have wronged others. Being the bigger person means realizing that everyone makes mistakes, and your behavior is not the same as who you are. You can love a person and hate his behavior. True forgiveness requires you not to confuse the two issues. It means looking at another person and understanding that everyone does the best he can, but sometimes life gets the better of him. It means extending the same compassion to others that you give yourself. That can be exceedingly difficult if you haven't learned how to first forgive *yourself*.

If you find the idea of forgiveness especially hard to swallow, it is most likely because you are struggling with self-forgiveness. That is natural for survivors of sexual abuse. Because many of us picked up a warped idea of how our behavior affects our world, we hold ourselves to impossible

---

[79]Josh Howerton, *10 Things Forgiveness Is Not*, 2012, retrieved from http://www.bridgesh.com/.2012/01/sermon-note-10-things-forgiveness-is-not/.

standards. Our magical thinking during a childhood riddled with abuse makes us believe that if we were only "better," then we could stop the abuse from happening. As we have discussed in previous chapters, this makes a child's world less frightening in the short run because it gives him a sense of having some control over his life. But in the long run, as we carry this false belief into adulthood, it can wreak havoc in our lives.

You were not responsible for your abuse. You did not cause it. You were powerless to stop it. Self-forgiveness for survivors has to go all the way back to the false beliefs of childhood. There was virtually nothing you could have done to stop the abuser from abusing you. Accepting that fact is the first step in self-forgiveness. Without it you will continue to measure yourself against an impossible standard, believing that bad things that happen to you now are your fault.

You have to learn how to stop hating yourself before you can try to quell the rage you have for others. Self-forgiveness is a process. You can't just say, "I forgive myself for everything." Those are empty words. Self-forgiveness means making lists of the things that you are angry with yourself about, and examining them in a healthy way. (See Step 4 of A.A.'s Twelve Steps.) Ask yourself, "What was my part in this? What was out of my control? What am I responsible for, and is there someone to whom I need to make amends? What did I feel that I needed and wasn't getting? What can I do differently next time?"

I discovered that there is nothing esoteric or contemplative about self-forgiveness. It is one of the most active parts of my recovery, requiring real-world action. Every day, I make living amends and strengthen my self-forgiveness. The truth is that we have all been perpetrators of harm to others at some time or other. Hurt people *hurt* people, so we have all been hurt at some point and then lashed out from that place. But we are *not* our behavior. Learning to separate the person from the action can be difficult, but it has to start from inside each of us.

Through recovery, I have learned that although I have done things I bitterly regret—things I once thought were unforgivable—those actions don't have to define who I am. I can change. I am not my past behavior. Forgiveness is an act of grace through understanding that I did the things I did because of what I believed at the time.

As I grow and learn how to be more conscious of what I believe—how to have more self-awareness, become less reactive, and be more introspective—my beliefs change. As my beliefs change, my behavior changes. But underneath everything, I have always been the same unique individual: a boy who dreamed of being a firefighter, who loved to surf, and who loved to build things. The essential components of selfhood are constant. Finding my own innocence in the reactions I have had out of pain or fear was essential to my self-forgiveness.

Finding the innocence in others may be a little more difficult, but involves the same process. But let me be clear. Forgiveness does *not* mean letting the abuser back into your life. Finding true compassion is necessary for real forgiveness, but it doesn't have to turn you into a mindless, accepting simpleton. You will still be capable of discernment. My mother is innocent in the same way I am. She did what she did because she believed her thoughts, just as I did what I did because I believed my thoughts. The trouble is, she *continues* to believe those thoughts, so she is still toxic to me. Although I forgive her because I understand on the most fundamental level why she did what she did, that does not mean I have to invite her back into my life.

Degrees of Forgiveness

What I am about to say may surprise you: True forgiveness is about realizing that the mechanism for all human behavior is the same, and that we are all equally guilty and equally innocent. Aside from accidents, of course, like tripping over a crack in the sidewalk, human beings act because they believe what they think. The people I tend to like—people in recovery, truly spiritual people—are the ones who actively question what they think, and who work to be kind instead of right.

But, Randy, you might be thinking, *what I've done isn't nearly as bad as what other people have done to me.*

That may be true. There *are* different levels of offenses. Nevertheless, the mechanism is always the same. We believe our thoughts, and based on what we believe, we act.

Now, you may think that your abuser was a manifestation of pure evil, and therefore impossible to forgive. However, that actually makes your job easier. Holding on to anger or hatred against someone who is so mentally ill that he or she is literally insane would be like ruining your own life because you can't let go of what a tornado did to you.

You can be right, or you can be happy. For many years, I wasted a great deal of energy justifying my rage. I made lists of the transgressions that Jack and my mother committed against me, and had all the proof that what they did was unforgivable. But that just ruined my own life. I had proof that I was right, but I was a drunk, cheating on my wife, and constantly feeling less than.

I know survivors who maintain their anger against their perpetrator because they feel that they will sink into despair without it. Some of us have carried blind rage for so long that we don't know who we would be without it. It can be scary to consider letting go of something that feels so formative and familiar. But remember, you can climb up the Emotional Scale. Letting go of rage doesn't mean that you will fall into despair.

It isn't necessary to rank the degrees of offenses in order to forgive them. Whether the offender is your best friend saying something that upsets you, or your partner cheating on you, or your abuser hurting you, the mechanism behind all human action is identical: We believe what we believe, and we act out of those beliefs.

Your best friend may have believed that her being in a rush made it necessary to cut you off in the middle of your story. In other words, she believed something, and that caused her to act out. Your partner may have believed that he or she could only be happy with someone else, and so left you for that other person. Again, it was the belief that caused the action.

At some point, all of us have believed in something that we found out later was not true. Then we regret what we did, because we realize it was based on a false belief. What is different between healthy people and unhealthy people is that the latter *still* justify what they did—because they can *never* be wrong. But recovery demands more from us. We don't get to waste time justifying past behavior, because we know that just keeps us sick and miserable. Instead, we choose to question our beliefs, acquire new, more accurate information, and create better beliefs.

On the day that I truly started to forgive Jack and my mother, Deborah, my therapist, explained to me in detail how perpetrators think. She also described the normal process that boys go through when they are discovering and developing their sexuality. Jack crossed a line that he should not have crossed, she said. But then, reminding me that hurt people *hurt* people, she stated that Jack had probably been abused himself as a boy. Thus, his abuse of me had nothing to do with sex. Rather, it was all about power—specifically, wanting someone else to share his pain with him.

That made me wonder what life was like for Jack when he was growing up. I also tried to imagine what it was like for him, when he was abusing me, to live with the pain of his past and the guilt he felt for what he was doing to me. I also wondered what it was like for him to climb back into bed with my mother after sexually abusing me. What did Jack believe that made him think it would be okay to do what he did to me?

Asking these questions is not the same as feeling sorry for Jack—although, in a way, I do feel sorry for him. But I don't feel sorry for him in a "holier-than-thou" way. I don't pity him. I feel compassion for him because I now understand that I have abused other people myself. Not sexually. I've never sexually abused a child or anyone else. But, for many years, I believed that I was justified driving drunk and risking the lives of everyone unfortunate enough to be on the road with me. I risked other people's lives for my own convenience because of what I believed at the time.

If you are religious, you recognize that all faiths—Christianity, Buddhism, Islam, Hinduism, Judaism—teach this type of compassion. This is what the Buddha did, what Christ did. Forgiveness has nothing to do with condoning abusive behavior. Forgiveness is about compassion.

What Forgiveness Means
Forgiveness means that we accept our pain.

Acceptance does not mean approval. I have found that there is a tendency in people who have trouble with forgiving, myself included, to maintain a shaking-a-fist-at-the-sky approach to recovery. I would rail against the world: "It shouldn't have happened! It's not right! It's not fair!" But all that did was keep me stuck feeling lousy. Remember, on the Emotional Scale, there are levels of bad feelings. Anger, which is what I felt when I was "shoulding" all over the place, beat the pants off despair. Holding on to despair only kept me from moving any higher up the Emotional Scale.

My mother and Jack hurt me deeply, scarring me physically, emotionally, and spiritually, and I wallowed in that pain for more than thirty years. But once I started my recovery, I came to a place of acceptance in order to move forward. What they did to me was absolutely wrong, but how long was *I* going to let it ruin my life? In order to grow and move forward, I had to accept the fact that the abuse happened, and understand that obsessing on "shoulds" was only hurting me. It helped to remember that acceptance does not mean approval, and so did thinking about natural disasters. It doesn't make any sense to spend time debating whether or not a hurricane should or should not have happened. What makes sense is to get in there and clean up the mess it left behind.

Forgiveness means that we accept responsibility for how our pain has impacted others.

For many years, my abuse defined me. I was a victim, and I milked it for all it was worth. I didn't always realize that I was using my pain to justify my behavior toward others, but sometimes I definitely did realize it. I manipulated women, including my wife, into feeling sorry for me and making excuses for me. I also manipulated friends and business associates into indulging my temper and irritability.

My favorite line was: "Until you have walked in my shoes, don't say a thing to me about my behavior." Much of the pain that I inflicted on my world was a direct result of what I believed about myself because of the abuse. Understanding that did not excuse my irresponsible behavior, but it did help to make me more compassionate toward myself.

I learned that, in order to challenge those old beliefs and to do the real work in recovery to create positive change, I had to begin to tell a different story about myself. *Forgive* became an active verb in my life. Wanting to improve my self-esteem, I worked on doing things that made me feel truly good about myself. I looked into my past and found quiet ways to make amends to others and myself on a daily basis. For example, since I had risked the lives of other people while I was driving drunk, today I am a very safe, courteous driver. I forgive myself daily.

Forgiveness means letting go of our "right" to punish another person.

This one is big. I was carrying around so much rage, hate, anger, and fear inside myself that I was just a bomb looking for an excuse to go off. I wanted to be the cool nice guy, but I felt like a fraud. I was loving on the outside, but I immediately wanted revenge when anyone crossed me. I didn't want justice. I wanted revenge. But I never fought anyone physically, because I was afraid that if I did, I might kill him.

Instead, I developed a vicious tongue and was a master at character assassination. If you upset me, by the time I was done with you, you had to reach up to hit bottom. In fact, I learned that verbal assault tactic from Jack. Like him, anytime I felt threatened, I humiliated others. I felt justified in unleashing that kind of assault on other people because, after all, in my mind, they deserved it. Forgiveness means that we can no longer justify our bad behavior based on other people's bad behavior.

That truth was especially hard to accept when it came to Jack. For thirty-plus years, I had plotted his murder on a daily basis. Since he lived in the high desert of Southern California, I pictured myself sitting behind rocks in the mountains above his home with a high-powered rifle. As he walked out on his porch, I would take him out with a headshot. Thankfully, although I believed that I would be fully justified and it would make me feel better, I also knew that it would hurt my family, and it would mean that Jack had won, for I would not only be trapped in the emotional prison of dealing with his abuse, but I would be locked away in a literal prison for the rest of my life.

Fortunately, my "Reasons Not to Murder Jack" won out, so I didn't do it. At least, not physically. I did assassinate his character every chance I got, and I was less than kind in how I spoke about my mother as well.

When we are consumed with rage, the feeling of letting it out, "releasing steam," is a huge relief. Because it feels so good to yell and scream when rage blows us up like a balloon, it can be really scary to let go of our justification for acting out.

Thankfully, for me, one of the best side effects of forgiveness has been to acquire a new sense of control over my emotions. Now, when I feel that I am acting out of anger or fear, I can go to the source for relief. But that source is not Jack, it's *me*. I have to address the thoughts in my own head that are causing me such pain.

The fact is that ranting and raving did release some emotional steam for a while, but I always felt worse afterward. As I said, I have spoken to survivors of sexual abuse who have taken actual revenge on their perpetrators, and they have all told me the same thing. It made them feel better for a moment, but then it just made everything worse. On the other hand, I have never had anyone tell me that sitting down and working on painful, limiting beliefs has made things worse for them. It makes things better—permanently.

Forgiveness helps us to gain a visceral understanding about not taking things personally. People's actions or words toward me, which can be painful, have less to do with me than with their own insecurities and inability to process their emotions. Whether they are standing me up for a meeting or sexually abusing me, it isn't personal, and it isn't my fault. Now, with a clear mind, untainted by rage and frustration, I can see that and get on with becoming the person I want to be and make myself happy.

The Power of Prayer

In addition to working on your own beliefs, you can find guidance and comfort from prayer. I know that prayer has helped me. When I started in recovery, I wasn't ready for any spiritual mumbo-jumbo about the "power of prayer," but as I became more desperate to heal, I was willing to try anything. Looking back on it now, I can see that those early prayers broke up the constant stream of negative thoughts in my head and gave me positive ones in their place. That helped to train my mind out of its pattern of negativity and to become more comfortable with positive thoughts.

Here is a powerful prayer exercise from *A.A.'s Big Book:*

> If you have a resentment you want to be free of, if you will pray for the person or the thing that you resent, you will be free. If you will ask in prayer for everything you want for yourself to be given to them, you will be free. Ask for their health, their prosperity, their happiness, and you will be free. Even when you don't really want it for them and your prayers are only words, and you don't mean it, go ahead and do it anyway. Do it every day for two weeks, and you will find you have come to mean it and to want it for them, and you will realize that where you used to feel bitterness and resentment and hatred, you now feel compassionate understanding and love.[80]

I remember getting on my knees the first time to pray for Jack, and telling God I didn't mean a word I was saying. But as I kept praying, over time my resentment and anger slowly dissipated, and I eventually found a place of peace. I challenge you to try this for two weeks and watch how the peace begins to wash over you and how free you become as a result of a simple prayer.

Retaking Control of Your Life

For years, I replayed in my mind the scenes from my childhood, reheard the terrible things my mother and Jack said to me, and refelt the pain and fear. But every time I did that, I was handing them control over my life. In effect, it was like giving my mother and Jack the keys to my car and then sitting in the back seat. I let them control what I thought, how I felt, and what I did.

So long as I held on to my resentment and anger toward my mother

---

[80] Alcoholics Anonymous, *The Big Book*, 4th ed. (New York: Alcoholics Anonymous Worldwide Services, 2001), p. 552.

and Jack, they owned me. The broken tapes of my childhood continued to play, locking me into the role of victim and sabotaging my every move to become whole. But once I forgave Jack and my mother, I was able to start changing the tapes that I had been playing for the past thirty-plus years and start the part of my healing journey that led me to true wholeness and peace.

Forgiveness is for *you*, not the perpetrator. However, you may be thinking, *Randy, you don't understand. You just don't get it. How can I forgive someone who did the things this person did to me?*

I *do* get it. At one time, I felt the same way. I was convinced that I was never going to forgive Jack and my mother. But then, I came to a place where I realized that by not forgiving them, by refusing to understand the difference between people and their behavior, I was not only making it impossible to forgive them, but I was keeping myself locked in the back seat of that car, cruising through the worst memories of my life *forever*.

If you are at least *willing* to let the process begin, the rest will fall into place as you do the work. It probably won't happen overnight—but, then again, it just might. What do you have to lose? You can remain in the grips of your perpetrator's torment, or you can choose to forgive and move toward peace and serenity. It's your call.

Forgiveness vs. Reconciliation

Forgiveness is for you, *not* the perpetrator. I know I've said this several times, but it's not an editing mistake. I'm repeating it because this is the biggest misconception I have found around the idea of forgiveness. It is actually a selfish act, for *your* benefit only.

People often confuse forgiveness with reconciliation, as if they were the same thing. They aren't. Reconciliation is the final step in the forgiveness process, but it is the "cherry on top"—an extra bonus when it occurs.

The space for reconciliation opens up when two people admit the nature of their wrongs to each other and ask for forgiveness, or at least for an opportunity to make amends. Reconciliation is wonderful when it happens, but forgiveness is too important to your peace of mind for it to be dependent on whether or not your perpetrators are able to admit how they wronged you. I have never heard of perpetrators going to their victims and asking for forgiveness. In most cases, they blame their victims, or flat out deny that any abuse ever took place.

FORGIVENESS

To this day, my mother simultaneously denies that I was abused, while stating that I was the cause of that very abuse. One of the reasons I don't recommend confronting your perpetrators is that it is unlikely that they will be healthy enough to walk the recovery path with you. On the other hand, it is unfair for your recovery to be held back by their issues. Their illness has already stolen enough of your happiness. It's time you take it back. It takes two people to reconcile, but only one to forgive.

One night in church, a guest pastor, Papa Brock, was preaching about forgiveness. I remember it as if he were singling me out. "Hear me and understand me," he said. "Forgiveness does not mean that the person you forgive will ever be allowed in your life again. Forgiveness does not mean that you will ever have a relationship with that person again. That person hurt you, and hurt you deeply." What a relief it was to hear those words. I had been struggling with that issue for years, but the struggle came to an end that night.

Redefining Forgiveness

I found that I had to redefine forgiveness for myself, because the self-righteous fake variety didn't work for me. Neither did the idea that forgiveness was something I had to do to be a good person. It is a universal spiritual principle, and the best of all faiths emphasize it as an act of loving kindness, compassion, equanimity, and sympathetic joy, welcoming the good fortune of others. Genuine forgiveness incorporates many subtle flavors of a bigger concept. It means wiping the slate clean, cancelling debt, and pardoning abusive behavior. It also implies the cessation of resentment as a result of a real or perceived offense, disagreement, or mistake. It means giving up my right to hurt you for hurting me. Whether you are a Christian, Buddhist, Hindu, or Native American, the principle is the same: in order to be forgiven, you must forgive.

Hopefully, you're thinking, *Okay, Randy, I'm convinced. I'm tired of holding on to all this resentment and allowing my perpetrator to live "rent free" in my head. How do I start this forgiveness process?*

Start by forgiving yourself. It is difficult, if not impossible, to forgive others before you forgive yourself. Self-forgiveness is often especially difficult for survivors of sexual abuse, who tend to be pretty hard on themselves. You have to realize the inaccuracy of the child-logic that made you believe that if only you were better, bad things wouldn't happen to you.

Take a look at the behaviors that you have not forgiven yourself for and see what your responsibility was. Don't inflate or minimize the part you played. Look at it objectively and with compassion. Then look deeper and see if you can find what you believed when you did what you did. Given the thoughts you had at the time, weren't you doing the best you could? While not condoning whatever acts you regret, see what you would have done better if you could have. That is your innocence. Forgive yourself for not knowing a better way at the time. You were only doing what you had been taught back then. Commit to learning better ways in the future so that you don't repeat the past.

Make living amends. Self-forgiveness is an active daily practice. See if you can find ways to make living amends for the behaviors you are most angry at yourself about. Don't tell anyone about your living amends. That is between you and God. If you hurt an animal, how can you make amends today? Donate time or money to a shelter? Take the spider outside instead of killing it? Little actions are just as good as big ones.

Once you see the innocence in yourself, work to see the innocence in others. Don't start with the most difficult person to forgive. Start gently, perhaps with someone who cut you off in traffic. Instead of reacting with immediate anger and judgment, see if you can remember a time that *you* cut someone off in traffic. Perhaps it was an accident, or maybe you were eager to get somewhere quickly, or you may have been feeling so powerless that day that cutting someone else off was the only way to feel that you mattered in the universe. Whatever your situation was, start looking for ways to empathize with the impulses that lead you to "bad" behavior. We are all human, and we all react to stress and negative beliefs.

We all have very similar negative beliefs: *I'm not good enough. He or she doesn't love me. I always mess things up. I'm scared of the future. I'm ashamed of the past. I'm not smart enough. I'm ugly. I'm a bad person.* These negative beliefs cause us to act out to try to make ourselves feel better. Start to notice how you act from these negative thoughts, and see how your behavior is not the same as who you are as a person.

Deliberately cultivate feelings of love and appreciation for people whose behavior you don't like. Again, start with baby steps. See what you can love about your co-worker who always steals your food from the refrigerator. Look for ways that behavior does not define a person. Start to work your way up toward people who have really hurt you. Without condoning their behavior, see if you can find empathy for the pain that hurt them so much that they feel they have to hurt others in order to feel better.

FORGIVENESS

Focus on the present. For many years, I focused on my past, the very part of my life I couldn't change. Eventually, I realized that the past was over, and the only place the abuse was still occurring was in my own head. If you are living mostly in the past, ask yourself this one simple question, "How's it working for me?"

Shifting your mental focus from past pain to the present moment takes practice. Start by bringing your focus back to what you are doing right now. Find the joy in life in the here and now—sitting with your favorite pet, walking in the garden or on the beach, or playing a musical instrument. Know that your past will always be a part of you, and you will inevitably think about it. But whenever you do, just gently bring yourself back to this moment.

Make space for peace to enter your life. As you focus on the present, concentrate on your breathing. Imagine that each breath going out is the pain of the past being released from your body and mind; and each breath coming in is peace, entering you and filling you up. Release the pain of the past, and let peace enter your life. Then go forward, thinking no longer of the past, but only of peace in the present.

Cultivate compassion. See if you can go beyond empathy and actually wish for happiness for the people who have hurt you. Again, you are not doing this for *them*. They won't feel it; you will. As you allow love to grow in your heart, overtaking anger and hatred, you will find greater happiness and peace.

I know how hard even the *thought* of forgiveness can be, but I am hopeful that this book has made it easier for you to start the process. If you are a Christian, you know that countless scriptures impress upon you the importance of forgiveness. It is part of the Christian faith to activate the grace of forgiveness. In Buddhism, the practice of forgiveness prevents harmful thoughts from wreaking havoc on your mental well-being. Buddhism recognizes that feelings of hatred and ill will leave a lasting effect on your mind and heart. Therefore, Buddhism encourages the cultivation of thoughts that leave a wholesome effect. Many Native American traditions tell us to "walk the path of light without holding contempt for anything or anyone."

Whether you are a Christian, Buddhist, or Native American, or hold any other faith, or none at all, your path to an abundantly free and happy life is to forgive those who have harmed you, no matter what their offense was. Until you forgive, you are still hostage to your abusers. When you do forgive, you set yourself free.

Chapter 13:
Finding Your Authentic Self

Owning our story can be hard, but not nearly as difficult as spending our lives running from it. Embracing our vulnerabilities is risky, but not nearly as dangerous as giving up on love and belonging and joy—the experiences that make us the most vulnerable. Only when we are brave enough to explore the darkness will we discover the infinite power of our light.

—Brené Brown[81]

We get a lot of payoff in our society for being inauthentic. We grew up learning how to pretend to be what we thought other people wanted us to be. We are taught that we receive love and approval from others based on how well we conform to what they want from us. The price tag for that kind of approval is far too high. We give up our own sense of self-worth when we change who we are in order to get someone else's approval.

You might be thinking, *Naw, Randy, that's not me. I'm not that guy. I'm not a fake.*

I didn't think I was that guy, either. But as I delved deeper and deeper into personal growth, I realized that I was inauthentic most of the time.

When I started being more authentic, I became happier. I've seen that happen over and over again with other people. The degree of happiness you have in your life is linked directly to how authentic you are. If you're unhappy, you're not being true to yourself.

Being inauthentic includes any behaviors that cause you to hold up an ego-mask. Everybody has several of these. But understanding the difference between being authentic and inauthentic can be tricky. If you are like most people, you are mostly authentic most of the time. The inauthentic part comes from exaggerating certain aspects of your

---

[81] Brené Brown, *The Gifts of Imperfection: Let Go of Who You Think You're Supposed to Be and Embrace Who You Are* (Center City, MN: Hazelden, 2010), p. 6.

personality and minimizing others.

I missed out on a lot of happiness because I truly believed that I was a straight-shooting, even brutally honest, what-you-see-is-what-you-get kind of guy. But I was kidding myself. That personality was actually inauthentic. I wasn't brutally honest. I said "yes" to people when I wanted to say "no." I put myself last and everyone else first so that they would like me. I pasted on a happy face when I was sad, insecure, or vulnerable.

Although I didn't realize it at the time, being inauthentic was costing me my happiness and self-respect. No matter how hard I tried, I was wrong if I did and wrong if I didn't. No matter what I did, it was never enough. I never felt good enough, and I never felt loved.

I spent a lot of time trying to manipulate the people around me into giving me what I wanted from them, and that meant that I spent a lot of time being angry, resentful, and lonely. It wasn't until I was in my fifties that I came to understand that all I needed to do to be happy was to be true to myself, and stop trying to be someone that other people would think was lovable.

A lot of the trouble for men in particular (and especially for male survivors of sexual abuse) comes from feeling that they have to measure up to gender norms. I couldn't admit to being scared, vulnerable, or sad, because that wasn't manly. I had built up a façade of being manly since the abuse started when I was twelve. Inauthenticity can be obvious, or it can be subtle, but either way it costs us our self-worth and happiness.

Some survivors feel that they need to overcompensate for their abuse by being overly macho. In my own case, my hunting trips and my four-wheel-drive truck were partially authentic, since I genuinely love hunting and trucks, but they were also part of my façade. I consciously built up an image of "Randy, the Man's Man," based on what I thought my friends, clients, and employees thought was masculine. Notice how convoluted this gets: I was more invested in what I thought other people thought about me than I was in finding out what I thought about myself.

The problem with being inauthentic is that you spend all of your time crafting your masks. You labor over them, adding things that you think will make people like you, and hiding things that you think will make people dislike you. You spend a lifetime working on those masks. You put them on so many times that they can come to feel that they are really you. But deep down, you know that the façades that you are presenting to the outside world aren't who you really are.

Survivors Speaks Out

S: I was thirty years old when I realized that my favorite color was red. Prior to that, my favorite color was whatever your favorite color was. Whatever someone else's favorite color was, was mine too. I had a need as a child to be able to assess my abuser's mood, and I guess I just never stopped doing that.

S: I had no idea I was being fake. Blending in was a knee-jerk instinct. I took on the personality of other people even when I didn't need to. I didn't even know I was doing it. I learned to be a chameleon when I was a child, and I eventually lost the ability to know who I really was.[82]

Author Janet Woititz says that one of the classic signs of adult children of alcoholics is that they lie when it is just as easy to tell the truth.[83] In a similar vein, survivors of sexual abuse can be inauthentic when it's just as easy to be real. We have been so invested in protecting ourselves by anticipating the moods and needs of others that we probably don't even know when we aren't being real.

When I was invested in my masks, I would make fun of men who seemed less masculine than me. That's not really who I am. I was just afraid that if I was kind to them, my friends would think less of me. I know it sounds silly. Believe me, it's hard for me to be this vulnerable with you right now, but recovery is about being radically honest. And it's important for survivors to see authenticity in another survivor.

Approval masks are responsible for a great deal of pain in our lives. We don't see it that way at first. I truly believed that my masks were the only things that kept me safe in the world. I was a winner and thought people liked me for that quality, so I did everything I could to shore up that image. I became even more aggressive, more competitive, and went over the top on collecting manly toys. I had to have the latest, greatest, most expensive toys, and they had to be better than everyone else's.

The sense of urgency I had about winning, about having the best toys, and about being the most masculine dude around the campfire created tension and anxiety, not joy and happiness. I was afraid that if I weren't the best, people wouldn't like me. And beneath that fear was another, deeper

---

[82]David Lisak, "The Psychological Impact of Sexual Abuse: Content Analysis of Interviews with Male Survivors," *Journal of Traumatic Stress*, 7: 4 (1994), 544–545.

[83]Janet Woititz, *Adult Children of Alcoholics* (Deerfield Beach, FL, Health Communications, 1983), p. xxvi.

one: if they saw who I *really* was, they would see that I was dirty, broken, and less than because I still felt ashamed about what had happened to me as a child.

What I eventually discovered was that people didn't like me *because* I was macho and competitive and successful; they liked me *despite* those qualities. I couldn't see it, but the masks I had created were actually pretty obnoxious. They became my armor, and wearing them was the only way I knew to get love and approval. The most painful thing about those masks was that, deep down, I *knew* that the person I was revealing to the world wasn't really me. So when people love us, we believe they actually love the mask, not the person behind the mask. In fact, our masks keep us from experiencing real love. The wider the gap between the person we pretend to be and the person we really are, the less we are able to feel love from anyone.

This is part of the reason our partners and family members mean so much to us. Over time, in a good relationship, we will eventually let other people in and show them who we really are, a little at a time. We admit our fears and own up to what we think are our flaws. After they see us at our best and our worst, and they *still* love us, we start to trust that love because we realize that they see more of who we really are, and they still love us.

But some survivors are too afraid to drop their masks and let anyone else in. Some of them can go through life never truly feeling loved for who they are, because they never let anyone see their true self. They know that other people say they love the person they are pretending to be, but at the same time, they know the others don't really know the person behind the masks. Then they wonder why they are depressed, isolated, have trust issues, and feel alone.

Being authentic is tough. It's easier in the short run to conform. We see celebrities and characters in films and on TV who tell us who we are *supposed* to be. In America, given our diversity and commitment to individuality, there is a wider range of social archetypes than, say, in Sweden, where the population and the culture are more homogeneous. But even here in America, there are a limited number of ways that we define ourselves.

This definition of self begins when we are children. Society teaches us that we're smart or athletic, sensitive or strong, a mama's boy or a bully. Then, in high school, we branch out a little. We can be a jock, a preppy, a punk, or a nerd, to name a few archetypes. And as we move into the working world, we get defined by our careers. White-collar workers are different from blue-collar workers. Entrepreneurs are like *this*, doctors are like *that*, and engineers are like some third thing.

It's easier to conform to the normative standards of a group you want to be identified with than it is to go inside yourself and follow the beat of your own heart. It's tough to go up against norms, even in America.

For example, if a woman wants to work in construction, she's going to take some heat from men *and* women because they think of that as masculine labor. But what if she's just a heterosexual woman who happens to love to build things?

What about a man who wants to be a nurse? Or a jock who loves to sing in the choir? It can even be hard for a child to go into a different profession than the one his parents want for him. We don't allow a lot of leeway in our archetypes, and it can take an almost unbelievable amount of personal strength and mental discipline to buck the "rules"—qualities that are not exactly in abundant supply for children who are being sexually abused.

It is a lot easier to suppress a part of ourselves in order to conform than it is to buck society and follow the dictates of our hearts. If you have done this, don't beat yourself up about it. We all do it. Survivors of sexual abuse tend to do it almost pathologically, and we pay a heavy price for it.

It is a human trait to want to fit in and be accepted. This urge is so strong that being shunned or ostracized by one's social group has been considered one of the most severe forms of punishment by human societies throughout history. Socrates actually chose poison over having to leave Athens forever.

Even most nonconformists conform to the norms of some group. Punk rockers, for example, rebel against society at large, but conform to the dictates of a smaller subgroup. Hippies have their own rules for acceptance. And so on. But truly following one's unique authentic self is a moment-to-moment experiment in courage and self-awareness. It's difficult, but the rewards are extraordinary.

It's difficult because, in many ways, it goes against our genetic programming. We all need to be accepted by others. That's human nature, and I was certainly no exception. From a very early age, I tried to fit in with other kids and be accepted by them. What I didn't understand until recently is that I didn't have to conform to be accepted. Ironically, the more authentic I am, the more acceptance I find from all the people I encounter.

When I was a child, like most of us, I didn't have any role models who showed me how to find my authentic self. Quite the opposite: conformity was celebrated, and true individuality, when it deviated from American social norms, was punished. We were coming out of the 1950s and *Father Knows Best*, when Sunday was for church, and dinner was served at 6:00. My mother and Jack worked much harder at preserving the image of the perfect American Family than they did on finding authentic happiness.

Eventually, the combination of my emotional scars from being sexually abused and my intense desire to be accepted by my peers led me to drugs and alcohol. I knew very well that abusing drugs and alcohol was illegal, morally wrong, and a form of unkindness to myself. I even knew that drinking and drugging was self-destructive. But I didn't care, because it made me feel better. Or so I thought.

I believe that most people have an inner moral compass, which points them toward ethical behavior. When we are unkind to others, or even to ourselves, we feel the consequences of that unkindness in our spirit, whether we want to admit it or not. When I spent my days being mean and hateful to others or myself, I always felt horrible afterward.

Today, when I am kind and compassionate to myself and others, I feel peaceful and content. It's simple. Being a good person is a spiritual and universal principle that we must uphold at all costs. We don't need to be told to be kind, because deep within each and every one of us, our spirits will tell us when we are being unkind to ourselves or others.

I didn't have many friends in high school, because by the time I turned fourteen, I was convinced that my shame was visible, and everyone could see that I was dirty and broken. Certain that I would be rejected by other kids, I kept away from most of them, and fell in with the fringe kids—the loners and stoners. Kids who are hurting the most seem to be the ones who turn to drugs and alcohol to find some kind of peace. Given my social circle, I was exposed to a lot of drugs and alcohol from a very young age.

I didn't fit in with the "normal" kids, whom I perceived as being naturally self-confident. Even as a very young boy, I felt different and lacked self-confidence. I could even sense the difference between the insecurity I was feeling and what I saw other people calling typical childhood insecurity.

The pain of carrying a secret about sexual abuse leaves a wound that festers. On top of that, there were all the "normal" teenage problems to add to my burdens. In fact, given my insecurity because of the sexual abuse and the shame that went with it, a "normal" problem like asking a girl to a dance became so distorted in my mind that it felt like having to lift a thousand-pound weight. So I didn't fit in with the "normal" kids.

Originally, I didn't fit in with the outcast kids, either, back when I was drinking and drugging. But eventually I came to a point in my life where all I wanted was to be accepted, to be completely a part of any group. I was tired of feeling lonely and judged by everyone. Plus, those kids told me that booze and drugs would make me feel better and take away my worries. The right words were said at the right time, and my drinking and drugging days were off and running. I traded my morals, values, and ethics—in fact, my authentic self—to be accepted.

The minute I began using mind-altering substances, I was no longer my authentic self, no longer the person that God had created me to be. For the next thirty-plus years, I was a chameleon, becoming whoever I needed to be and doing whatever I needed to do to fit in.

The only real way out of emotional pain is to go through it. Going around it never works. For many years, I was able to pretend that "I was fine, thank you very much," but I spent decades of my life going around in vicious circles of shame, self-loathing, escapism, and victimhood. I didn't know what I truly wanted. I wasn't capable of following my bliss, because all I thought about was my next drink or my next high. That kind of thinking will mess with your inner GPS.

Since becoming sober and starting to walk through the pain instead of wasting time looking for ways to detour around it, I have discovered that being authentic is harder than it once seemed. I used to think that being authentic was about telling the truth, even being brutally honest, or not being a slave to social trends or fashions. I've come to learn that it involves so much more.

Don Miguel Ruiz's book *The Four Agreements*, specifically the chapter entitled "The Domestication and the Dream of the Planet," has been indispensible in my search for my own authenticity.[84] According to Ruiz, our dreams are formed by the rules of our parents and society:

> We are born with the capacity to learn to dream, and the humans who live before us teach us how to dream the way society dreams. The outside dream has so many rules that when a new human is born, we hook the child's attention

---

[84]Don Miguel Ruiz, *The Four Agreements: A Practical Guide to Personal Freedom* (San Rafael, CA: Amber-Allen, 2012).

and introduce these rules into his or her mind. The outside dream uses Mom and Dad, the schools, and religion to teach us how to dream.[85]

I was born into this world without getting to choose who my parents would be. I was given a name without a choice. I was told which church and which God I was to believe in without a choice. I was told which schools I would go to, which college I would attend, and which career I would pursue.

The dreams of society and my parents' dreams were already forming their idea of me even before I was born. According to Ruiz, our grandparents raised our parents according to society's dreams during our grandparents' generation. Our parents then raised us according to the dreams of their generation, and so on. The laws, rules, beliefs, and social events of our society combine to form an aggregate social dream, which is then passed on from generation to generation. The dreams may change a little over the decades, but the idea that success is equivalent to the degree to which we conform to the social dream remains the same.

One of the ways this affects survivors of sexual abuse in particular is that our overarching social dream is only now just beginning to deal with male childhood sexual abuse. For many of us, this means that in addition to the burden of the abuse itself, we have had to hide our secret because it deviates from the "normal" social dream.

Children seek the approval of their parents, siblings, and friends, all of whom are subject to the dream of the society as a whole. For most people, that dream continues on unquestioned into adulthood. I certainly allowed society's dream to guide my choices and behavior for nearly four decades. I learned what was wrong and what was right according to the social dream. Everything I believed in was within the context of that dream. What we consider beautiful and what we consider ugly, or what we think of as acceptable or unacceptable are all based on the particular flavor of the dream to which our family unit subscribes.

For the most part, children simply agree with the dream of their parents without asking any questions. As we fall deeper and deeper into the trance of the social dream, it becomes ever more difficult to become authentic. We learn not to think for ourselves, but to accept the "truths" that are passed on from generation to generation. As a child, I didn't even know I had a choice. I accepted the "truths" Jack and my mother passed on to me,

[85]Ruiz, *The Four Agreements,* p. 2.

even down to the smallest details.

They had their own variation of their social dream. Jack was a "work hard, play hard" blue-collar American Dreamer. My mother dreamed herself as a TV sitcom housewife.

Because dreams can also be nightmares, the pressure to conform to the overarching dream of the era has pushed many families down a rabbit hole of dysfunction—my own family certainly included. To varying degrees, all of us are victims of victims. Being inauthentic isn't personal, it's a human condition. Creating façades is not just an individual coping skill. On an individual level, it's true that we all have masks. But on the family level, we have the image of the perfect family. And as a society, we have the American Dream. It's human to conform.

Personalities, aptitudes, and desires are warped to fit this vast social construct. On the one hand, a shared dream holds a society together, but when it is too rigid, it becomes destructive and suffocating. In my family, everything had to look perfect on the outside: how we were perceived by the neighbors was far more important than authenticity or even happiness. Finding my authentic self wasn't even on the playing field of my family's dreams.

As a child, I agreed with the dreams of my family and society because I didn't know I had an alternative. When I began to see the discrepancies between the abuse at home and the image that Jack and my mother worked so hard to project to the community, I started to rebel. Jack and my mother were the perfect Christians at church and steeped in sin at home.

The image of the perfect family was so different from what I experienced on a daily basis that I quickly grew disillusioned and stopped conforming blindly to the social dream. Although I eventually woke up to the problems within the dream, I didn't know what to do about them. All I knew was that I didn't fit in anywhere. I tried drinking and drugging. I developed the perfect macho persona. But thirty-plus years later, I was still miserable.

Children from happier homes tend to believe that happiness can be a part of conforming to society's dream, so they tend to conform to it. But children who don't fit into their family of origin tend to rebel. Whether we are from a happy or unhappy home, we all learn at a very early age that to be accepted and approved, we must conform to the dreams and rules of our parents and society. In many ways, we are indoctrinated from birth into a culture of people-pleasing.

As a society, we have a very short tolerance for authentic self-expression. Crying is acceptable for the first year or two of our lives. After that, tears and anger are met with disapproval and the withholding of love until we return to a more agreeable behavior—agreeable to our parents, that is.

Most of us can remember being scolded for not wanting to talk to a stranger, or to hug or kiss a disliked relative. Most of us remember our parents telling us to "give Auntie Marge a kiss goodbye," combined with a look that promised unpleasant consequences if the kiss weren't given. It's incredibly telling that, even in healthy families, toddlers are taught that they aren't even allowed to decide who they do and do not want to touch.

When saying no would embarrass someone else, usually an adult, we are taught to say yes. We learn to preempt the embarrassment of others by guessing which behaviors we can present, and which behaviors would be the most pleasing and least offensive. In this way, we turn into social chameleons until we forget who we originally were.

When a child turning cartwheels just for the joy of it receives attention and approval for those cartwheels, he begins to perform them in order to receive that approval. But cartwheels only get so much approval. Eventually, the trick becomes old, and the adults become less exuberant, but the child has forgotten that originally he was happy just doing the cartwheels. In these little ways, trick by trick, we become dependent on the approval of other people for our happiness. The fact is that our happiness actually lies in our own hands, but since we started getting approval for our cartwheels, we have forgotten how to find it by ourselves.

It is our job in life not to just get by. We owe it to ourselves to thrive and live joyful, prosperous, loving lives, once again performing cartwheels just because they bring us joy. I have heard countless stories of men who have become lawyers or doctors only because that's what their parents wanted. Since then, they have come to hate their careers and resent their parents for pushing them to pursue work in a field in which they had little genuine interest. When the desire to be accepted is combined with something as innocent as parents' well-intentioned goals for their child, the pressure on that child can become unbearable, especially if the parents' dreams run counter to what the child's authentic self is trying to tell him.

Because acceptance is so important to human beings, meeting social norms and parents' expectations can feel good. For many people, that feeling is sufficient to sustain them throughout a lifetime. They may not have lived their own dream, but they were happy enough pursuing someone else's. For other people, though, the pleasure that comes from satisfying their parents is not enough. When the yoke of pulling a metaphorical wagon made up of someone else's dreams gets too heavy, that can lead to resentment and despair.

For survivors of sexual abuse, this issue can be especially relevant. One of the most common effects of childhood sexual abuse is the loss of a strong sense of self. This often manifests as co-dependence and an almost overwhelming need to people-please. When this desire is driven by unhealed emotional wounds, we can never be pleasing enough to enough people to get enough approval. We dash frantically from person to person, performing trick after trick, desperate to fill up a cup of approval. In fact, we are so desperately chasing after approval that we never stop to notice that there's a gaping hole in the bottom of our cup. The pleasure we get from pleasing others drains out almost as fast as it comes in, and resentment rushes in to fill the void. If we get too caught up in this cycle, we can temporarily lose the ability to recognize our own desires. We know less of what we want for ourselves than we know of what others want for us.

An Expert Speaks Out:
Allen Berger, Ph.D.,
On Understanding the True Self[86]

We are each born with a true self, which is like an acorn. The DNA of the acorn has all the programming necessary to grow into an oak tree. Yes, it will be like other oak trees, but it will also be unique. According to Dr. Karen Horney, one of the unheralded geniuses in psychology, "You need not, and in fact cannot, teach an acorn to grow into an oak tree, but when given a chance, its intrinsic potentialities will develop."[87] Just like the acorn that is genetically programmed to become a unique oak tree, we are programmed to become our true self.[88]

Given the proper set of circumstances, we will develop the unique forces of our real or true self. We will develop the ability to experience the depth of our own feelings, thoughts, wishes, desires, and needs. We will develop

---

[86] Dr. Berger wrote this essay specifically for this chapter.

[87] Karen Horney, *Neurosis and Human Growth: The Struggle Toward Self-Realization* (New York: W. W. Norton, 1950), p. 17.

[88] Horney, *Neurosis and Human Growth*; Abraham Maslow, *Toward a Psychology of Being* (New York: Van Nostrand, 1962).

the faculty to express ourselves and spontaneously and respectfully relate to others. We will learn to equally honor our need for togetherness and our need to be ourselves. We will come to realize our own set of values and purpose in life. We will be able to tap our own resources to satisfy our needs and to regulate ourselves by soothing our pain or disappointment. We will develop a solid yet flexible self.

An acorn cannot reach its true potential unless it grows in a nurturing environment and climate, which have to provide certain critical elements. There needs to be an adequate amount of sunlight and water. The soil needs to contain certain nutrients.

If these nutrient conditions are adequately met, then the acorn will eventually become what it is destined to be: a beautiful oak tree with a set of unique qualities and characteristics. However, the developing acorn cannot be exposed to harsh conditions until it is well-rooted and has matured to a certain point.

The conditions for successful human development are highly similar. Like the acorn, we have basic needs that must be satisfied for us to thrive. We need shelter, food, and water. We need a secure and warm attachment that will provide us with love and nurturing. We need to be seen and celebrated. We need intellectual and spiritual stimulation. We need encouragement and empathy. We need to be protected from traumas or abuse.

We also need a certain amount of healthy friction with the wishes and wills of others. We need to have expectations placed upon us, but these expectations can't be beyond our reach. If these conditions are adequately met, we will develop an inner security and an inner freedom that enable us to be responsible to our own feelings and express ourselves according to who we really are. We will be able to support ourselves and stand up for ourselves. We will grow along spiritual lines. Unfortunately, this rarely happens.

What Goes Wrong?

Through a variety of adverse influences, we do not grow according to our individual possibilities. Our development can be easily distorted by a host of factors, such as our desire to please, our need to belong or to be loved and accepted, incorrect learning, bad habits, anxiety, the dynamics of our family, traumas, and cultural traditions and rules.

We need to belong to ensure our existence. We need love and acceptance to thrive emotionally and spiritually. So we are hardwired and motivated to seek it. The fear that we don't belong, that we aren't worthy of love or acceptance, creates a "basic anxiety" that permeates our psyche. This anxiety drives us to look for a solution that will ensure love and acceptance. Our anxiety makes us feel out of control, so we decide that we need to take control of our lives and control how others feel about us.

We head out on a quest to ensure love and acceptance by controlling our environment. What we don't realize is that this makes us dependent on our environment for our self-esteem. We lose control of our lives by trying to take control. What a mess!

Horney calls this path the "search for glory."[89] We search for a way of being that will create security, make us feel that we belong, and ensure love and acceptance. Our solution shapes our personality, our beliefs, and our behavior. Here's what happens.

To solve the problem created by our basic anxiety, we develop a way of being that is based on an idealized image of who we should be. Dr. Alexander Lowen made this observation: "Desperation creates illusions; illusions create more desperation."[90] We believe this idealized self will give us inner security. But this is not our true self. It is a false self or a fabricated self, which means that we will never attain inner security. Our emotional well-being will be dependent on how well our false self is accepted or performs.

In order for our idealized self to crystallize into the false self, we must shape our personality accordingly. This is accomplished through our pride system, which rewards and punishes us to ensure that we develop according to its idealized specifications or laws. We feel good and proud of ourselves when we act, behave, think, or feel the way we believe we should (reward). We despise ourselves or even hate ourselves when we don't (punishment).

The laws and specifications of the pride system amount to a collection of "shoulds." These become a tyranny that exercises absolute control over our lives. We

---

[89] Horney, *Neurosis and Human Growth*.

[90] Alexander Lowen, *Bioenergetics: The Revolutionary Therapy That Uses the Language of the Body to Heal the Problems of the Mind* (New York: Penguin, 1975), p. 165.

are driven to be the way our idealized image demands, and we dare not question its authority. These idealized specifications are absolutes: they are shaped by the gender rules in our culture, and they are not negotiable.

This process creates pervasive "black-and-white" thinking. Our false self requires blind obedience. Therefore, we do not question its tenets or its authority. Rather, we perceive these ideals and feel them as the way we are supposed to be. We don't realize that we have internalized a set of ideals that may or may not fit with who we really are. But, you see, how we really feel is not that important. What *is* important is that we live up to this idealized image that we have chosen as our path to emotional security.

I used the following analogy to describe this process in *12 Smart Things to Do When the Booze and Drugs Are Gone*:

"Have you ever seen a beautiful bonsai tree? A bonsai artist works patiently over many years to constrain what should be a full-sized tree into perfect miniature. She constantly prunes the tree, wraps wires around its branches to shape them, deprives it of water, and trims its roots to fit a tiny pot. Such a tree becomes perfect to look at. And yet…and yet. It is not its true self. It is a tree made to conform to a vision of miniature perfection."[91]

This is what we have done to ourselves with our "shoulds." They are the wires we wrap around our true selves to shape us into our idealized image.

So we sell out our true selves during this process. We sell out big time. We lose ourselves in this process. We reject our true self in favor of a fabricated false self. We abandon and alienate ourselves from who we really are. We become estranged from our true self at a very deep level. Our anxiety leads us to believe that we aren't good enough the way we are, and therefore we must become something we aren't—to be okay. We develop a life based on phony aspirations and compulsions. What a tragedy! We reject ourselves for an ideal. So let's look at what this does to the development of our personality.

The Fragmented Self

We are born with a large number of possible

---

[91] Allen Berger, *12 Smart Things to Do When the Booze and Drugs Are Gone: Choosing Emotional Sobriety Through Self-Awareness and Right Action* (Center City, MN: Hazelden, 2013), p. 26.

characteristics and possible selves. We have the capacity to experience a wide range of emotions and mental states. We can cry or rage. We can be loving or hateful. We can be brilliant or quite stupid. We can be creative and flexible or fixed and rigid.

When these characteristics become woven or grouped into a cluster, they become selves. Each of us has our own population of these selves, which can manifest in many different ways. They can be loving and gentle or selfish and self-centered. They can be the A student or the class clown, the jock or the nerd. They can be the life of the party self or the shy self. Our selves can be sexy or puritanical. We can be patient or impatient, generous or stingy, vindictive or forgiving. We can be a brave self or a cowardly self, a risk taker or a conservative self. The list can go on and on and on. How can all these selves exist in the same person without driving him (or her) nuts? This is an important question that must be answered.

All these selves can live together if they can live in harmony rather than in conflict. Therefore, mental health is best understood as the coordination of all that we are. So a healthy person is one who has coordinated and found harmony among all of his possible characteristics and selves. We can say that a person who has achieved this mental and emotional state is truly at peace with himself.

Unfortunately, this rarely happens. Instead of integrating and coordinating all of these characteristics and selves into a whole, fully functioning person, we become fragmented and conflicted. Fragmentation happens early in life.

As I discussed, sometime in our youth we made a decision to shift the focus of our growth away from self-actualization toward actualizing a concept of who we *should* be. We redirected our growth away from becoming the self that we truly are to becoming an idealized self.

We believed that this new direction would give us the best chance to belong—to be loved and accepted. We imagined that this would guarantee our emotional security, that we would always feel that we belonged rather than feeling apart from or alone or isolated.

We paid and continue to pay a huge price for this shift in our growth force. As Dr. Horney noted, the development of the phony self is always at the expense of the true self. We lose ourselves to protect ourselves and to ensure our existence. What a paradox!

In order to actualize the concept of who we should be, we emphasize some personal characteristics or selves at the expense of others. Some selves are essential for organizing our personalities along the lines delineated by the concept of who we should be. Other selves or characteristics might be desirable but non-essential, and still other characteristics or selves will be disowned and rejected because they are unwelcome guests.

This means that the goal of recovery is to liberate the constructive forces of the real self, which will result in a more integrated, more appropriately organized personality that functions better under any conditions.

Good Selfishness

Society tells us that being selfish is bad. No matter the context, we should strive to be selfless and unconditionally giving. But it's just not true. By putting ourselves consistently last and donning the mantle of "Most Self-Reliant," we can get so good at hiding our own needs that eventually they hide from us.

When we blindly accept the social rules that tell us to fear selfishness and to strive for self-denial, we start to think that our needs are something to be repressed, never indulged. But this cultural taboo against selfishness needs to be turned into a more sustainable and accurate framework for emotional health. By choosing good selfishness, we can reconnect with our authentic needs and stop abandoning ourselves.

Good selfishness just means taking care of ourselves, instead of passive-aggressively denying our own needs and taking care of other people with the secret hope that they will later do the same for us. Good selfishness means saying yes when we truly mean yes, and saying no when we mean no. Good selfishness is about having healthy boundaries.

What we think of as selfishness is really self-care, and we are all allowed to take care of ourselves. But we survivors of sexual abuse in particular are used to giving up on ourselves. We are so used to sacrificing the most intimate things we have—the sanctity of our bodies, our physical safety, and our emotional needs—that we have become accustomed to sacrificing everything else, too.

But this is not to be confused with bad selfishness, which is *not* caring about other people. Bad selfishness is being rude, inconsiderate, intolerant, and only interested in our own agenda.

Our society tells us that it's selfish to say no when someone asks us for help. That's considered unloving. But that logic falls apart when we examine it instead of mindlessly accepting this part of society's dream.

If someone—even someone I love very much, like my wife, Cathy—asks me to do something, and I know in my heart that I don't want to, but I give her a dishonest yes, I have lied to her and set up a situation that can only lead to resentment. For example, Cathy might ask me to go shopping with her in the afternoon. But if I have reserved that afternoon for meditation and playing my guitar, and I have promised myself and my inner child that I will set that time aside as sacred, I have been dishonest with her and untrue to myself.

If inside of me there is a conflict and I know that my honest answer is no, but I still say yes, the whole time I am shopping I am going to be upset at myself, at Cathy, and the world. I'm going to resent her for asking, and I'm going to be angry with myself for saying yes. I might even start to believe that my needs are not as important as hers, and that accompanying her on shopping trips is more important than keeping a promise to myself.

If I give Cathy a dishonest yes, I am putting her desires over my own happiness and mental health. Then I automatically resent her, even if I love her very much. I start keeping score, making lists of all the favors she owes me. If she then refuses to give me help when I feel she's in my debt, all hell may break loose because, in my mind, I did all those things for her when I didn't want to, and now she won't even do *one thing* for me!

There are many, many problems with this scenario. First of all, none of it is honest and aboveboard. I lied to Cathy and said yes when I meant no. Then I created a hidden contract that said she owed me some kind of unnamed favor in the future.

It would be far better to make that contract visible by being up-front about my expectations and what I want in return. I could say, "I am going to say yes although I want to say no. But in return, when I ask for a favor that you don't want to give, I hope you will say yes. Do you agree to these terms?"

At least that's honest.

But an even better answer would just be an honest no. It doesn't have to be mean. I don't have to be a jerk to say no. I can just say, "Honey, I love you and I wish I could say yes and mean it, but my honest answer is no. Is there something else I can do for you instead?" In the case of the shopping trip, I could offer an alternative, such as going at a different time.

The idea is that just because someone asks me to do something doesn't mean that I have to say yes. This can be surprisingly difficult for survivors of sexual abuse to understand. Because of our childhood traumas, we can feel that we *have* to say yes, or something terrible may happen to us.

Developing self-care can liberate a great deal of stuck energy, which can otherwise manifest in repressed anger, depression, or resentment. It can also drastically improve the quality of our relationships. But, like most aspects of personal development, it takes hard work.

It may seem ridiculous to say that it's hard work to discover your own wants and needs and pursue them, but it is. You might be thinking, *Randy, that's just crazy talk. I've been going after what I want for my whole life.*

But have you really? Or have you been pursuing those things that you *think* you should want? Have you been seeking pleasures that distract you from deeper emotional pain? And has one of those pleasures been the immediate high that comes from getting someone's approval for saying yes, although you will pay for it later?

Let's face it. Other people's approval is the most addictive drug ever created. It feels wonderful when other people say things like, "Isn't he great, that Randy?! He's just always willing to help. He'd work himself to the bone for someone else." But that flash of good feeling wears off like the warmth from a hot bath. Pretty soon you're cold again, and you have to do even more to get people to approve of you.

Eventually, you are worn down to the bone, emotionally exhausted. Then, when you look around, expecting other people to wear themselves to the bone taking care of you, and they don't, that feels like a betrayal. Now you are angry, resentful, and lonely. You forget that you are capable of making yourself happy—that *inside* you there is a quiet voice that tells you what you want to do. It's the same voice that tells you if your answer to a question is an honest yes or no. But that small, quiet voice gets drowned out by other, louder voices that start a shouting match.

Those voices inside your head say things like: *No one is ever there for me. People never give as much as I do. Others take advantage of me over and over again.*

When I was drinking, I used to say to myself that I wanted to go out and have a beer with the guys after work. I told myself, *I deserve it because I work hard, and I'm a good provider. So, I should be able to kick back and enjoy myself a little.*

But if I had been truly honest with myself, I didn't really want a beer.

I wanted relief from those incessant voices in my head that drove me all day and all night. I wasn't fully aware of the conversations or the words that were going on in my head; I just felt dirty or less than. It was only when I started slowing down my mind that I could hear the self-destructive comments—words like: *You're worthless. You don't fit in. Everyone knows you're a fake.*

If you are experiencing these kinds of thought patterns, I suggest cognitive behavioral therapy for you or something similar to the work of Byron Katie to help unravel these painful beliefs. But whether you experience them as words or emotions, they can be merciless, leaving you feeling out of control and hopeless.

Good selfishness is about stopping the cycle of the approval addiction. It's about turning *inside* and finding authentic answers within yourself, paying attention to your authentic voice because it is the most important voice in the world.

I didn't need approval from others, I needed my own approval. I needed the feeling that I used to get when I was sixteen, and paddling furiously out to meet an incoming wave. The power of the ocean would lift my spirits to a place that surpassed mere happiness and flowed into bliss.

No one was watching, and it wouldn't have mattered if anyone were. All the joy came from within myself. I followed my authentic voice down to the beach, slipped into the water, and surfed for the sheer joy of it. Thirty-plus years later, I wanted to get back to a mental place like the one I had when I rode waves.

Finding your authentic self is the surest way to get back to self-fulfillment, pure joy, and true independence. If you are still worried about other people's feelings, think of it this way: When your happiness is your own business and no one else's, you will be far more effective at reaching out and helping others. Ironically, good selfishness serves not just you but everyone else in your life.

So the question is, how do you get there?

Following Your Bliss

Renowned scholar Joseph Campbell, who studied the mythologies of peoples across cultures, races, creeds, geographical borders, ages, and genders, found that the underlying message of all of them was to "follow your bliss."[92] Campbell's powerful conclusion has resonated throughout

---

[92]Joseph Campbell, *Pathways to Bliss: Mythology and Personal Transformation* (Novato, CA: New World Library, 2004), p. xxiv.

the world, reprinted on posters, bumper stickers, t-shirts, and coffee mugs in just about every language on the planet. But acting on that excellent advice is hard. Most of us are so conditioned to follow our pleasure, or our responsibilities, that we have nearly forgotten that our bliss is what we are truly meant to find.

Following your bliss is one sure path to being your authentic self. But if you are anything like me—or most other people, for that matter—your mind can be a fairly unfriendly antagonist. People are so conditioned by the voices of their parents, peers, and society at large that when they so much as have a spark of an idea of what their blissful path might be, it is crushed nearly before they can even recognize the quiet whisper of their authentic self.

I remember the first time I felt crushed in that way. Since the age of ten, I had dreamed of becoming a fireman, like my dad. In the late 1970s and early 1980s, that was fairly easy to do. You had to pass a civil service exam, go through fire academy studies, and complete the physical fitness requirements.

So, when I was eighteen, I started talking to a few firefighters I knew, and, on their advice, drove around to six or seven different departments in Orange County, filling out applications. A month later, I received a letter from the county, stating that I had a test date. Immediately, I could feel the excitement bubbling up deep inside me. It surpassed happiness. It was as if I had caught an awesome wave. In fact, I was so excited that I couldn't stand still.

In my overwhelming flood of joy, I ran to tell my mother and Jack the great news. I wish I had known then what I know now. As a kid, I not only wanted to be a firefighter, but I also wanted their approval. I hadn't yet learned that seeking validation from others about following my own bliss could often kill that inner voice.

I don't think that most other people are actively trying to hurt us, or even to discourage us from reaching for what truly brings us deep joy. Some people just want to spare us the pain of possible disappointment, worrying that we might be venturing beyond what they perceive as our capabilities. Then they try to guide us back to a "sure thing," in order to prevent us from failing and being crushed. Or our dreams might trigger their fears.

Other people may not be so charitable. Having given up on their own dreams and bliss, they resent the joy they see in us when we start to venture toward ours, so they try to quash it.

Still others may have an idea about who and what we should be, and they will do anything and everything to manipulate us into following *their* path for us.

But trying to figure out whether or not someone is actually being actively hateful, or just trying to help in a misguided way is ultimately a waste of time. I have found that giving people the benefit of the doubt reduces the anger and hatred that I have inside myself. I have more inner peace when I assume that other people are coming toward me from a good place rather than assuming that they are out to get me.

For a long time, I wanted to blame Jack and my mother for everything I didn't like about my life. I wanted to believe that they were evil, hateful people who lived to hurt me every chance they got. But maturity in the recovery process involved coming to understand that they were just broken themselves. Perhaps some of the time they intended to be hurtful, but for the most part, they were just being themselves, and I was the person who was unfortunately in their path.

Looking back, my mother and stepfather's responses to my joy at receiving my letter from the fire department were totally predictable. That understanding makes the memory hurt less today. But back then, I was devastated.

When I ran into the house, flushed with excitement, filled with that sense of purpose and joy that Joseph Campbell would have said was proof positive that I was on the track to my personal bliss, my mother and Jack told me that the test would be much too hard for me, and I would never pass it. From their words, the message I internalized was, "Who are you kidding? You're no hero. You're just not good enough."

They had struck a lethal blow, for I allowed my little fire of joy to be utterly extinguished in that one minute. They continued on, however, for quite some time in the same vein, as though they wanted to cover all possible bases—to salt the charred fields, as it were. The test, they said, would be all about firefighting knowledge that I just didn't have and wouldn't be able to learn without proper and expensive schooling. I'd never pass.

Besides, I reasoned, I had been working in construction for the last three years and was making good money, and I got to be outdoors as I wanted. So, what was I complaining about?

After that, my construction career continued for some forty years.

For twenty-one of those years, I owned a highly successful masonry construction company. But to this day, every time I pass a fire station or see a firetruck, my gut clenches with despair and regret.

On that summer afternoon in 1975, I not only abandoned my dreams, but I gave up believing in my internal voice. I gave up living my life as I wanted to, in favor of the much less rewarding feeling that comes from getting temporary approval from other people.

One of my personal frustrations in the self-help department is that well-meaning people tend to toss around a lot of really great-sounding advice and then walk away without providing any instructions for how to begin. For a long time, I felt that way about Joseph Campbell's "follow your bliss." But when I finally read his work, I realized that Campbell actually does tell his readers exactly how to find their bliss.

When you get right down to it, following your bliss, when you haven't been taught to even know what "bliss" is, is darn hard. In America, we are taught to go after what we "want," but if you are a careful listener, you will hear that you are only supposed to want a few things: success, money, status, and a family.

But here's the catch: you can't find bliss in *any* of those things. You can find happiness in some of them, some of the time—but not bliss. Bliss can only be found through coming to know yourself, then figuring out how to love yourself, and then listening to yourself and following the inner instructions that come.

Happiness can feel like bliss, only less intense, more fleeting, and not as solid. We can even find temporary happiness in getting love and approval from other people. But when we depend on love and approval from other people in order to *be* happy, we spend our lives people-pleasing and missing out completely on the really good stuff, the bliss.

The thing about bliss is that it's usually very quiet. It's not fireworks and trumpets. It's a feeling that starts with a gentle, almost imperceptible peace. Usually, it gets stamped out the moment it appears. Americans—men in particular—are not encouraged to be peaceful. We are encouraged to be productive, so we tend to mistake peaceful for lazy, and the second we do that, we lose our bliss.

Because bliss builds on itself, it starts off as peace, and if we are very still and quiet and let it be, it grows bigger and bigger until it expands to include happiness, joy, ecstasy, and tranquility. But you can't go looking for the loudest point; you've got to start with the quiet peace.

But—so long as I got to keep my wife and kids and grandkids—I'd trade it all in a heartbeat for a second chance at that firefighter's test. I wish I could have those last four decades back, so that I could spend it being true to myself. I am learning to do that today, but I am struggling with it the way a baby struggles to walk. I fall down a lot. Sometimes I cry. Sometimes I stumble along the way. But even groping around the edges of living an authentic life for a single day beats the pants off living for someone else's approval for a lifetime.

The road to recovery is the road back to your true authentic self. That road brings you happiness because, at some point, it stops being about healing from pain and starts being about finding your joy. Healing from pain isn't the final step in the process. We don't want to survive just to find a way to make it through every day. We deserve to thrive—to wake up in peace and go to bed filled with gratitude, spending the minutes in-between in pure joy.

It's not that life is supposed to be easy. It's a challenge—even for those among us who never experienced abuse or trauma in childhood. But the challenge is not in how to avoid pain, or how to keep out in front of it. The challenge is in how to surf the waves, knowing that whatever comes next, the strength inside you is more than equal to the task.

You learn to be okay with falling down from time to time, because you know that making mistakes doesn't define your character. And you know that you have everything you need to get up and start over, incorporating new lessons into your personal toolbox.

The man that you dream of being, the man who you know you are inside, is the man recovery will reveal to you. Learning to love yourself, to listen to your heart and to follow the voice that leads you to joy, is the reward of recovery.

There is a wonderful life out there. Survivors are already closer to it than most people because there comes a point when the coping tools of the regular world will not cut it for our pain. That is great news. When the coping skills fail, it's time to start looking for a deeper way to live a happy life.

I'm not saying it's easy. I'm saying it's worth it.

You're worth it, and you can do it.

Relevant Websites

Go to: *www.1in6.org* for additional resources, a list of professionals, and notices of upcoming events.

Go to: *www.abphd.com* for information about Dr. Allen Berger's services and to purchase his books.

Go to: *www.CedarColorado.org* for the Gender Matters, Men Matter Conference.

Go to: *www.courageoushealers.org* for more information about Randy's foundation and to leave a comment about his book.

Go to: *www.creativechangeconferences.com* for information on the annual "It Happens to Boys" Conferences.

Go to: *www.dangriffin.com* for more information about Dan Griffin's services, The Man Rules, and to purcahse his books.

Go to: *www.drmichunter.com* for more information about Mic Hunter's services and blog and to purchase his books.

Go to: *www.goodmenproject.com/author/dangriffin* to become a part of the Good Men Project and to get a glimpse of what enlightened masculinity might look like in the twenty-first century.

Go to: *www.ithappenstoboys.org* for more information on signs of sexual abuse and to talk to someone if you have been sexually abused.

Go to: *www.johnbradshaw.com* for more information about John Bradshaw's services and to purchase his books.

Go to: *www.johnleebooks.com* for more information about John Lee's services and to purchase his books.

Go to: *www.malesurvivor.org* for additional resources, a list of professionals, and notices of upcoming events.

Go to: *www.thehealingman.wordpress.com* to follow Randy's blog.

References

Alcoholics Anonymous, *The Big Book*, 4th ed. New York: Alcoholics Anonymous Worldwide Services, 2001.

Balaban, Anne. *Common Sense Is Uncommon: Helping You Live Up to Your Potential*. Bloomington, IN: iUniverse, 2011.

Berger, Allen. *12 Smart Things to Do When the Booze and Drugs Are Gone: Choosing Emotional Sobriety Through Self-Awareness and Right Action*. Center City, MN: Hazelden, 2013.

Blue, Ken. *Healing Spiritual Abuse: How to Break Free from Bad Church Experiences*. Downers Grove, IL: InterVarsity Press, 1993. Retrieved from http://dallascult.com/?page_id=559/.

Bradshaw, John. *Homecoming: Reclaiming and Healing Your Inner Child*. New York: Bantam, 1990.

Brown, Brené. *The Gifts of Imperfection: Let Go of Who You Think You're Supposed to Be and Embrace Who You Are*. Center City, MN: Hazelden, 2010.

Campbell, Joseph. *Pathways to Bliss: Mythology and Personal Transformation*. Novato, CA: New World Library, 2004.

Campbell, Joseph, and Moyers, Bill. *The Power of Myth*. 1988. Retrieved from http://billmoyers.com/spotlight/download-joseph-campbell-and-the-power-of-myth-audio/.

Changing Works. *Coping Mechanisms*. 2015. Retrieved from http://changingminds.org/explanations/behaviors/coping/coping.htm/.

Crutcher, Chris. *King of the Mild Frontier: An Ill-Advised Autobiography*. New York: HarperCollins, 2003. Retrieved from http://www.goodreads.com/quotes/968221-as-a-child-abuse-and-neglect-therapist-i-do-battle/.

Delaplane, David, & Delaplane, Anne. *Victims of Child Abuse, Domestic Violence, Elder Abuse, Rape, Robbery, Assault, and Violent Death: A Manual for Clergy and Congregations*. Special Edition for Military Chaplains, 4th edition. Rockville: MD: National Criminal Justice Reference Service, 2001.

Diamond, Stephen. *Essential Secrets of Psychotherapy: The Inner Child*. 2008. Retrieved from https://www.psychologytoday.

com/blog/evil-deeds/200806/essential-secrets-psychotherapy-the-inner-child/.

Donnelly, Denise A., and Kenyon, Stacy. "'Honey, We Don't Do Men': Gender Stereotypes and the Provision of Services to Sexually Assaulted Males." *Journal of Interpersonal Violence*, 11: 3 (1996).

Griffin, Dan. *A Man's Way Through Relationships: Learning to Love and Be Loved*. Las Vegas: Central Recovery Press, 2014.

Harmon, Katherine. "Addicted to Fat: Overeating May Alter the Brain as Much as Hard Drugs." *Scientific American*, 2010. Retrieved from https://www.scientificamerican.com/article/addicted-to-fat-eating/.

Heatherton, Jacquie. "The Idealization of Women: Its Role in the Minimization of Child Sexual Abuse by Females." *Journal of Child Abuse and Neglect*, 23: 2 (1999).

Herman, Judith Lewis. *Father-Daughter Incest*. Cambridge: Harvard University Press, 1981.

Herman, Judith Lewis. *Trauma and Recovery: The Aftermath of Violence—From Domestic Abuse to Political Terror*. New York: Basic Books, 1992.

Hicks, Esther, & Hicks, Jerry. *Ask and It Is Given: Learning to Manifest Your Desires*. Carlsbad, CA: Hay House, 2004.

Horney, Karen. *Neurosis and Human Growth: The Struggle Toward Self-Realization*. New York: W. W. Norton, 1950.

Howerton, Josh. *10 Things Forgiveness Is Not*. 2012. Retrieved from http://www.bridgesh.com/2012/01/sermon-note-10-things-forgiveness-is-not/.

Hyena, Hank. *Semen Warriors of New Guinea*. 1999. Retrieved from http://www.islandmix.com/backchat/f6/semen-warriors-new-guinea-80304/.

Jenny, Carole, Roesler, Thomas A., & Poyer, Kimberley L. "Are Children at Risk for Sexual Abuse by Homosexuals?" *Pediatrics*, 94: 1 (1994).

Johnson, David, & VanVonderen, Jeff. *The Subtle Power of Spiritual Abuse: Recognizing and Escaping Spiritual Manipulation and False Spiritual Authority Within the Church*. Bloomington, MN: Bethany House, 1991.

REFERENCES

Katehakis, Alexandra. *Mirror of Intimacy: Daily Reflections on Emotional and Erotic Intelligence*. Los Angeles: Center for Healthy Sex, 2014.

Katie, Byron. *I Need Your Love—Is That True?* New York: Three Rivers Press, 2005.

Katie, Byron. *A Response to "I hate my husband…,"* 2007. Retrieved from http://www.byronkatie.com/2007/10/a-response-to-i-hate-my-husban/.

Katie, Byron. *Who Would You Be Without Your Story?* Carlsbad, CA: Hay House, 2008.

Kids Safe Foundation. *A Child Who Keeps Secrets: An Easy Target for a Predator!* Retrieved from http://www.kidsafefoundation.org/a-child-who-keeps-secrets-%E2%80%A6-an-easy-target-for-a-predator/.

Lee, John. *The Anger Solution: The Proven Method for Achieving Calm and Developing Healthy, Long-lasting Relationships*. Philadelphia: Da Capo Press, 2009.

Lee, John. *Breaking the Mother-Son Dynamic: Resetting the Parents of a Man's Life and Loves*. Deerfield, FL: HCI Books, 2015.

Lisak, David. "The Psychological Impact of Sexual Abuse: Content Analysis of Interviews with Male Survivors." *Journal of Traumatic Stress*, 7: 4 (1994), 525–548.

Lisak, David, Hopper, Jim, & Song, Pat. "Factors in the Cycle of Violence: Gender Rigidity and Emotional Constriction." *Journal of Traumatic Stress*, 9 (1996): 721–743.

Lowen, Alexander. *Bioenergetics: The Revolutionary Therapy That Uses the Language of the Body to Heal the Problems of the Mind*. New York: Penguin, 1975.

McGreevey, Sue. "Meditation's Positive Residual Effects: Imaging Finds Different Forms of Meditation May Affect Brain Structure." *Harvard Gazette*. 2012. Retrieved from http://news.harvard.edu/gazette/story/2012/11/meditations-positive-residual-effects/.

McLaren, Karla. *The Language of Emotions*. Boulder, CO: Sounds True, 2010.

Manning, Brennan. *Abba's Child: The Cry of the Heart for Intimate Belonging*. Colorado Springs, CO: NavPress, 2002.

Maraboli, Steve. *Unapologetically You: Reflections of Life and the Human Experience*. 2015. Retrieved from http://www.goodreads.com/author/show/4491185.Steve_Maraboli/.

Maslow, Abraham. *Toward a Psychology of Being*. New York: Van Nostrand, 1962.

Matsakis, Aphrodite T. *I Can't Get Over It: A Handbook for Trauma Survivors*, 2nd ed. Oakland, CA: New Harbinger, 1996.

National Child Traumatic Stress Network (NCTSN). *Understanding Child Traumatic Stress*. 2015. Retrieved from http://www.nctsn.org/resources/audiences/parents-caregivers/understanding-child-traumatic-stress/.

National Institute of Alcohol and Alcoholism. *NIH Publication No. 03–5340*. June 2012. Retrieved from http://pubs.niaaa.nih.gov/publications/FamilyHistory/famhist.htm/.

Office on Violence Against Women, U.S. Department of Justice. *Sexual Assault*. 2015. Retrieved from http://www.justice.gov/ovw/sexual-assault/.

Rape, Abuse, and Incest National Network (RAINN). *Who Are the Victims?* 2009. Retrieved from https://rainn.org/get-information/statistics/sexual-assault-victims/.

Rich, David. *How to Be an Adult in Faith and Spirituality*. Mahwah, NJ: Paulist Press, 2011. Retrieved from https://books.google.com/books?id=22Wp65TgCPsC&pg=PT102&lpg=PT102&dq=When+this+ultimate+crisis+comes.../.

Robbins, Tom. *Still Life with Woodpecker*. New York: Bantam Books. 1980.

Rogers, Fred. *Quotes*. Retrieved from http://www.goodreads.com/author/quotes/32106.Fred_Rogers/.

Ruiz, Don Miguel. *The Four Agreements: A Practical Guide to Personal Freedom*. San Rafael, CA: Amber-Allen, 2012.

Scarce, Michael. *Male on Male Rape: The Hidden Toll of Stigma and Shame*. Cambridge: Perseus Publishing, 1997.

Sexual Assault Response Services of Southern Maine. *Sexual Assault and Rape Statistics, Laws, and Reports*. Retrieved from http://www.sarsonline.org/resources-stats/reports-laws-statics.

South Eastern CASA (Centre Against Sexual Assault). *Trauma Responses in Children*. September 3, 2012. Retrieved from http://www.secasa.com.au/pages/trauma-responses-in-children/.

REFERENCES

Weiten, Wayne, Lloyd, Margaret A., Dunn, Dana S., & Yost Hammer, Elizabeth. *Psychology Applied to Modern Life: Adjustment in the 21st Century*, 11th ed. Belmont, CA: Wadsworth, 2012.

Werdell, Phil. *Science of Food Addiction*. Retrieved from http://foodaddiction.com/wp-content/uploads/acorn_brochure.pdf/.

Williamson, Marianne "Only Light Can Cast Out Darkness." In Deepak Chopra, Debbie Ford, and Marianne Williamson, *The Shadow Effect: Illuminating the Hidden Power of Your True Self*. New York: HarperCollins, 2010. Retrieved from http://www.theshadoweffect.com/custom/book.php/.

Woititz, Janet. *Adult Children of Alcoholics*. Deerfield Beach, FL: Health Communications, 1983.

YWCA of Greater Flint [Michigan]. *Sexually Abused Child Trauma Response by Age Group*. March 30, 2011. Retrieved from https://volunteermanual.wordpress.com/2011/03/30/sexually-abused-child-trauma-response-by-age-group/.

www.ingramcontent.com/pod-product-compliance
Lightning Source LLC
Chambersburg PA
CBHW030435300426
44112CB00009B/1018